W9-CTO-349

Smileys and Emoticons to Use in Email, Chats, and More

Smileys—also called emoticons—are a great way to express emotions in email, chats, and instant messages. Here's a bunch of them to use whenever the occasion warrants:

:-)	The original smiley; shows humor or happiness
:-}	A smiley with an embarrassed smile; you're embarrassed
:-(	A frown; shows sadness
;-)	A wink; shows a joke or flirting
:=)	A smiley with a big nose
:'-(	A smiley crying; shows sadness
:-D	A big smile; you're happy
:-o	A surprised smiley; you're shocked or surprised
=:-O	A frightened smiley
:-|	A bored smiley; you're bored
:-x	You're giving someone a kiss
:-)8	A smiley with a bow tie
8-)	A smiley with glasses
:-()	A big-mouthed smiley
=:-)	A smiley with a punk haircut
:-b	A smiley sticking out his tongue
$-)	You just won the lottery

Abbreviations and Cybershorthand for Email and Chats

In addition to emoticons, many people use abbreviations and cybershort-hand phrases in their email and chats. Here are the common ones:

ASAP	As soon as possible	IM	Instant message
<bg>	Big grin	IMHO	In my humble opinion
BRB	Be right back	IMO	In my opinion
BTW	By the way	L8R	Later
B4N	Bye for now	LOL	Laughing out loud
CUL	See you later	ROF	Rolling on the floor
FAQ	Frequently asked question	ROFL	Rolling on the floor, laughing
F2F	Face to face	S/AC	Sex, age check (asking for gender and age)
FWIW	For what it's worth		
FYI	For your information	THX	Thanks
<g>	Grin	WFM	Works for me
GAL	Get a life	WU	What's up?
IC	I see		

Best Sites for Cool Ways to Communicate Online

There are all kinds of great sites where you can communicate in cool ways online. Check these out and you won't go wrong.

Free Greeting Cards

http://www.americangreetings.com
http://www.bluemountainarts.com
http://www.e-cards.com

http://www.hallmark.com
http://www.usagreetings.com

Free Email

http://www.bigfoot.com
http://www.excite.com and click
Free Voicemail/Email
http://www.zdnetonebox.com and go to the mail area

http://www.hotmail.com
http://www.yahoo.com and click
Yahoo! mail

Free Faxing

http://www.efax.com
http://www.faxwave.com

http://www.fax4free.com

Free All-in-One and Voice Mail Sites

http://www.getmessage.com
http://www.jfax.com
http://www.mytalk.com
http://www.onebox.com

http://www.shoutmail.com
http://www.telebot.com
http://www.rockettalk.com
http://www.zdnetonebox.com

Best Sites for Getting Free Web Pages

http://www.geocities.com
http://www.angelfire.com
http://www.tripod.com

http://www.xoom.com
http://www.fortunecity.com
http://www.theglobe.com

Great Places to Chat

http://www.yahoo.com
http://www.excite.com
http://www.lycos.com

http://www.thepalace.com
http://www.talkcity.com

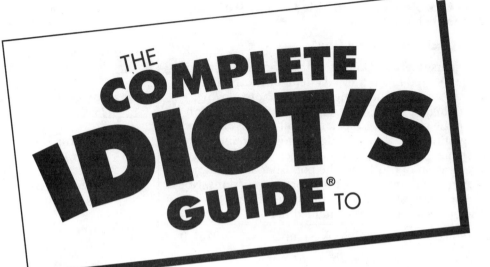

THE COMPLETE IDIOT'S GUIDE® TO

Cool Ways to Communicate Online

by Preston Gralla

A Division of Macmillan USA
201 W. 103rd Street, Indianapolis, IN 46290

The Complete Idiot's Guide to Cool Ways to Communicate Online

Copyright © 2000 by Que®

International Standard Book Number: 0-7897-2255-0

Library of Congress Catalog Card Number: 99-65789

Printed in the United States of America

First Printing: March 2000

02   01   00   4   3   2   1

Trademarks

Warning and Disclaimer

Publisher
Greg Wiegand

Acquisitions Editor
Stephanie J. McComb

Development Editor
Gregory Harris

Managing Editor
Thomas F. Hayes

Project Editor
Casey Kenley

Copy Editor
Sossity Smith

Indexer
Deborah Hittel

Proofreader
Jeanne Clark

Technical Editor
Chris Faust

Illustrator
Judd Winick

Team Coordinator
Sharry Gregory

Media Developer
Jay Payne

Interior Designer
Nathan Clement

Cover Designer
Michael Freeland

Copy Writer
Eric Bogert

Production
Jeannette McKay

Contents at a Glance

Contents

About the Author

Preston Gralla is the author of 14 books, including the best-selling *How the Internet Works,* as well as *The Complete Idiot's Guide to Online Shopping* and *How to Expand and Upgrade PCs*. He has written widely about computer technology and the Internet for many newspapers and magazines, including *USA Today,* the *Los Angeles Times, PC Magazine, Boston Magazine, and PC/Computing,* and is the online shopping columnist for *Access* magazine. He is a frequent guest on television and radio discussing computers and the Internet, and has appeared on the *CBS Early Show*, CNN, MSNBC, as well as on dozens of other national and local shows. He is executive editor of ZDNet Downloads at www.zddownloads.com and has won many awards for writing and editing, including an award for Best Article in a Computer Magazine from the Computer Press Association. He lives in Cambridge, Massachusetts, with his wife, two children, and a rabbit named Polichinelle. He also writes the free *Gralla's Internet Insider* email newsletter. To subscribe to it for free, send email to preston@gralla.com with the words SUBSCRIBE NETINSIDER on the subject line.

Dedication

Dedicated to talkers, jabberers, yackers, yentas, and communicators everywhere. If a tree falls in the forest and nobody talks about it, does it exist? Not as far as the communicators of this world are concerned.

Acknowledgments

Thanks have to go to many people for helping with this book. Once again, thanks to Stephanie McComb for trusting me with this book. And thanks to Development Editor Nick Goetz, Project Editor Casey Kenley, Copy Editor Sossity Smith, and Chris Faust for reviewing the book to make sure it is technically accurate.

Thanks go to my agent Stuart Krichevsky. And, of course, thanks as always to my wife, Lydia, and children, Mia and Gabe.

Tell Us What You Think!

As the reader of this book, *you* are our most important critic and commentator. We value your opinion and want to know what we're doing right, what we could do better, what areas you'd like to see us publish in, and any other words of wisdom you're willing to pass our way.

As a Publisher for Que, I welcome your comments. You can fax, email, or write me directly to let me know what you did or didn't like about this book—as well as what we can do to make our books stronger.

Please note that I cannot help you with technical problems related to the topic of this book, and that due to the high volume of mail I receive, I might not be able to reply to every message.

When you write, please be sure to include this book's title and author as well as your name and phone or fax number. I will carefully review your comments and share them with the author and editors who worked on the book.

Fax: 317-581-4666

Email: consumer@mcp.com

Mail: Greg Wiegand
          Que
          201 West 103rd Street
          Indianapolis, IN 46290 USA

Introduction

The best thing about your computer and the Internet might be the new twist it adds to the very thing that makes us all human: communicating with others. The Internet lets you communicate with friends and family, with people around the world, and with people you otherwise never would have gotten to know.

All that, of course, might be a little bit old hat to you by now. But a slew of Internet technologies lets you communicate in amazing new ways never before possible. With the right hardware, software, and a little bit of know-how, you'll be able to get in touch with people in all kinds of great, cool ways.

That's what you'll find out in this book: all the cool new ways you can use the Internet to communicate with others. Whether you're just getting started on the Internet, or whether you're a long-time cyberpro used to email and beyond, you'll find amazing things in this book—you'll find out how to use your computer to do remarkable things, such as how to

➤ Turn your computer into a videophone and talk and see people all over the world.

➤ Videoconference on the cheap, whether for your home, small business, or larger office.

➤ Turn the Internet into your private telephone system, and make calls for free to anyone else in the world who has a PC.

➤ Make long-distance calls from your PC to any telephone in the world and be charged only pennies a minute.

➤ Buy and install Netcams, digital cameras, scanners, and other hardware you'll need to communicate in cool ways.

➤ Make email do all kinds of fancy tricks, such as sending and receiving video-mail, and dressing it up with fancy fonts, colors, and pictures.

➤ Get a slew of free communications service on the Web, including free voice mail, faxing, and email.

➤ Use the most popular chat and instant messenger programs, and learn insider tips on how to get the most out of them.

➤ Create Web pages for free and use them to communicate in neat new ways.

➤ Put a Webcam on your Web page.

➤ Group-surf and chat at the same time.

And there's more as well. The CD in the back of this book is jam-packed with software that you can use for doing all this and more. So come on into the book. You'll find yourself communicating with others in ways you never thought possible.

How to Use This Book

I've organized this book into seven parts. They'll teach you everything you need to know about cool ways to communicate online, starting with how to set up the hardware, and moving on to advice on how to do it all.

In Part 1, "Let's Get Cool! Amazing Ways You Can Communicate Online," you'll get the basic background of all the neat new ways you can communicate over the Internet. You'll learn about all the new ways to communicate, learn how they work, and find out what kind of hardware and software you'll need in order to use them.

Part 2, "How to Set Up Cool Hardware for Communicating Online," gives you the rundown on what hardware you need to buy for communicating online in cool new ways, and how to go about buying it. You'll learn all about Netcams, digital cameras, scanners, sound cards, microphones, and more.

In Part 3, "Cool Ways to Communicate with Email," you'll learn all kinds of fancy email tricks, and you'll see how you can use email in all kinds of new ways. You'll learn how to send and receive voice mail and video mail, how to use colors, pictures, and special fonts in your email, how to send email greeting cards, and a lot more. And as a bonus, there's an entire section devoted to email-related free services you can get—things like getting a free fax number, free voice mail, and more.

Part 4, "Can We Talk? Using the Internet as Your Telephone," covers all the remarkable ways you can use the Internet to talk directly to others as if you were talking on a telephone. You'll see how you can talk directly PC-to-PC with people all around the world—and not pay a penny while doing it, even if they're on the other side of the planet. You'll find out how you can make a phone call to telephones from your PC, and pay only pennies per minute, even if you're calling people overseas. I'll show you how to install and use the software, do troubleshooting, and have fun in the bargain.

In Part 5, "The Eyes Have It: Doing Video Over the Internet," I'll show you how you can turn your PC into a videophone, and how to make videophone calls and do videoconferencing over the Internet. I'll show you what software to get and how to use it, and offer troubleshooting advice. You'll learn the proper etiquette for video calls, and find out how to use chat programs as a way to find video partners.

In Part 6, "Using a Personal Web Page to Communicate with the World," you'll learn how to build your own Web page to communicate with other people. You'll find out how to get free Web pages, be shown quick-and-easy ways to build Web pages, and be shown the kinds of contact information to put on your Web page to make it easier to communicate with others. And also you'll learn how to put a Webcam on your Web site so you can broadcast from your living room to the world.

In the last section of the book, Part 7, "But Wait, There's More. Other Cool Ways to Communicate Online," you'll learn how to use chat and instant messaging programs, including the most popular one, ICQ—and you'll find all kinds of insider tips and secrets on how to get the most out of them. And I'll show you more as well, things such as how to create your own free email newsletter, how to do group surfing of the Web while you chat, how to mark up Web pages with graffiti, and other cool stuff.

You'll also find a glossary, entitled "Speak Like a Geek: The Complete Archives," that defines computer and technical terms that you might be confused about. And in the appendixes you'll find details about the programs on the CD in the back of the book. And you'll find a list of the best sites to go to on the Internet for more information on cool ways to communicate online.

Extras

To help you communicate in cool ways this book also gives you extra secrets, inside tips, and bits of information that will help. You'll find them in these boxes:

Cool Tips

This Cool Tips box offers tips, advice, and extra information for helping you choose the perfect PC.

Walkie the Talkie

Our friend Walkie the Talkie box defines computer terms for you.

Mayday

This Mayday box tells you about things to watch out for when buying a PC.

You'll also notice that special type is used throughout the book. Italic is used for new terms; monospaced type is used for Web addresses and for anything you're supposed to type; and anything you choose, click, or select will be bold.

About the Author

Preston Gralla is the author of 14 books, including the best-selling *How the Internet Works,* as well as *The Complete Idiot's Guide to Online Shopping* and *How to Expand and Upgrade PCs*. He has written widely about computer technology and the Internet for many newspapers and magazines, including *USA Today,* the *Los Angeles Times, PC Magazine, Boston Magazine, and PC/Computing,* and is the online shopping columnist for *Access* magazine. He is a frequent guest on television and radio, discussing computers and the Internet, and has appeared on the *CBS Early Show*, CNN, MSNBC, as well as on dozens of other national and local shows. He is executive editor of ZDNet Downloads at www.zddownloads.com and has won many awards for writing and editing, including an award for Best Article in a Computer Magazine from the Computer Press Association. He lives in Cambridge, Massachusetts, with his wife, two children, and a rabbit named Polichinelle. He also writes the free *Gralla's Internet Insider* email newsletter. To subscribe to it for free, send email to preston@gralla.com with the words SUBSCRIBE NETINSIDER on the subject line.

Acknowledgments

Thanks have to go to many people for helping with this book. Once again, thanks to Stephanie McComb for trusting me with this book. And thanks to Development Editor Gregory Harris, Project Editor Casey Kenley, Copy Editor Sossity Smith, and Chris Faust for reviewing the book to make sure it is technically accurate.

Thanks go to my agent, Stuart Krichevsky. And, of course, thanks as always to my wife, Lydia, and children, Mia and Gabe.

Dedication

Dedicated to talkers, jabberers, yackers, yentas, and communicators everywhere. If a tree falls in the forest and nobody talks about it, does it exist? Not as far as the communicators of this world are concerned.

Part 1

Let's Get Cool! Amazing Ways You Can Communicate Online

You're a cool kind of cat. You wear dark shades indoors, you listen to early Miles Davis records (and only refer to him as Miles), you wear a black beret even in the heat of summer, you sport a nifty little goatee (or if you're a woman, you wear black leotards), and you play the bongo drums. And you don't say goodbye to people—instead you murmur Ciao, baby.

Okay, maybe you don't say Ciao, baby. And maybe early Beatnik isn't your idea of cool. But when it comes to keeping in touch with others online, you definitely are looking for cool ways to communicate.

Well, you've come to the right place. In this section of the book, you'll learn about all the cool ways you can communicate online—from making Jetson-like videophone calls to using your PC as your private global telephone system (and making calls all over the world for free), to instant messaging and beyond. So come on along. And bring your bongo drums with you—just put them near your PC's microphone and you'll learn how to broadcast your playing to your friends everywhere.

Chapter 1

All the Cool Ways You Can Communicate Online

In This Chapter

➤ All the amazing ways that email can be made to do fancy tricks

➤ Looking at how you can turn the Internet into your private telephone system

➤ The ways you can use video to communicate with others online

➤ How you can use your own personal Web page to communicate with others

➤ The many different kinds of free communications services you can get online, such as free faxing and voice mail

➤ A whole lot of other cool ways to communicate over the Internet

---

Time to get cool—with communicating on the Internet, that is. Maybe you've done some communicating online already, by using things such as email. Perhaps you've done a bit of chatting or you've used "instant messenger" programs. Or maybe you're a flat-out beginner.

No matter what your experience with communicating online, as you read this book you're about to learn tons of neat new tricks and amazing ways you can communicate online. You'll learn how to use the Internet like it's your private telephone system, and talk to people across the world using a microphone and speakers—and you won't have to pay a penny. You'll learn that you can in essence turn your computer into a videophone, how you can create your own email newsletter for free, how you can send and receive video email, and all kinds of other tricks.

In this first chapter, we'll take a brief tour of all the cool ways you can communicate online, from using the Internet as your telephone system to email to videophones and beyond.

Using the Internet as Your Private Telephone System

For a lot of people, the computer has supplanted the telephone as the main way to communicate with friends and for business—mainly through email and chat. (Anyone with a teenager can vouch for this, in spades. It's no longer just the phone lines that they tie up—now it's the computer as well.)

But chat is becoming almost old hat, because you can now use the Internet as your private telephone system. You're no longer tied to merely typing on your keyboard— now you can use the computer to talk in real-time to people all over the world. To do that, you'll just need the right hardware, and the right software. The hardware—a sound card and a microphone—comes with just about any new computer. And you can get the software for free—including software on the CD in the back of this book.

So the price of yakking with friends and strangers just got a whole lot cheaper. Here are all the ways you'll be able to use the Internet as your private telephone system:

➤ With special telephone software, you can talk for free between your computer and any other computer anywhere in the world. To do this, both people will have to have the same kind of Internet telephone software installed. If you're using one kind of Internet telephone software, and your friend is using a different one, you won't be able to talk to one another.

Walkie the Talkie

What Do Full Duplex and Half Duplex Mean?

When using Internet telephone software, you'll probably come across the terms *full duplex* and *half duplex*. Full duplex means that both people can talk simultaneously—the voice data gets transmitted at the same time in both directions, just like a telephone. Half duplex means that only one person can talk at a time, like a walkie-talkie. Most modems you buy today allow for full-duplex communications, although some older modems might not. Your sound card and drivers need to be full duplex as well.

➤ With that same telephone software, you'll also be able to place calls from your computer to any telephone in the world, whether it is down the street, across the continent, or across the world. Note that these calls won't be for free. You'll have to pay for them. However, you'll usually pay much less for making phone calls this way, especially when calling internationally. Unfortunately, the voice quality usually isn't as good as a regular telephone. The faster the connection, the better quality the call. So if you make a call using a slow modem, expect garble and gabble.

➤ You can talk over your computer with others when you use chat and instant messenger programs such as Yahoo! Messenger. You run the chat software, just as you normally would, and when a buddy comes online, you invite them to a voice chat. Then you yak away, using your voices instead of your keyboard. It's free, no matter where you're located. .

To find out how to use the Internet as your own private telephone system, turn to Part 4, "Can We Talk? Using the Internet as Your Telephone."

Eye See: Using Video as a Way to Communicate Online

Remember all those cool sci-fi gadgets and gizmos we were supposed to be using right around now as the millennium hits? We were going to have personal mini-jets instead of cars. Dick Tracy wristwatches. Robot maids and valets. And videophones, of course.

Guess what? Maybe you can't yet check your Dick Tracy wristwatch as you zoom high above the city in your personal mini-jet with your robot valet as your driver, but it's easy to use a videophone. All you need to do is hop onto the Internet and spend a little time setting up hardware and software. You'll be able to talk to and see people all around the world—and often, you can do it with more than one person at a time.

To do that, you need two things: a special video camera attached to your computer (often called a Netcam) and videoconferencing software. The most popular videoconferencing software is NetMeeting, from software behemoth Microsoft, and Cu-SeeMe, from software little guy White Pine Software.

Walkie the Talkie

What's the Difference Between a Netcam and a Webcam?

The terms *Webcam* and *Netcam* are often used interchangeably, although there's really a difference between the two. A Netcam, in general, refers to a video camera attached to the Internet that enables you to participate in videoconferencing with other people. A Webcam, generally, is a video camera that has been attached to a Web site and shows live or nearly live pictures or video on that Web site that anyone can see. But you'll find that the two are often confused, and so the terms are generally used interchangeably.

There are a number of different ways to use videoconferencing software. In general, you can

➤ **Connect directly with someone when you know his or her Internet address or email address** When you connect this way, you and someone else know each other's contact information, and you make contact directly to that one person. You don't need to go to any other Internet sites or servers.

➤ **Go to a Web site or videoconferencing directory and find people who want to videoconference** When you videoconference this way, you look for a partner at one of the directories.

➤ **Use a chat program such as ICQ to find other people to videoconference with** A program like ICQ lets you know immediately when friends and acquaintances are online. And when it tells you that they're online, it also will enable you to participate immediately in a videoconference with them.

There's a lot of other cool stuff you can do when you use video as a way of communicating online. To check it all out, turn to Part 5, "The Eyes Have It: Doing Video Over the Internet."

Tell It to the World: How to Use Web Pages to Communicate

The Web isn't just a place for you to get news, stocks, and sports information, spend too many of your hard-earned dollars on online shopping, or in general, muck around while surfing from site to site. It's also a way that you can become your own broadcaster. At little or no cost, you can tell the world about yourself, about your ideas, and it's a great way to make contact with others.

You won't even have to be a programmer or Web geek to do it—so don't worry, you can leave your pocket protectors, beanie hats, and oversized black glasses behind (unless you like those things that is—but then, that's the great thing about the Web; it's a great place for even the fashion impaired.)

There's a whole lot of ways that you can use the Web to communicate with others. Here are the most common:

➤ **You can create free Web pages with the help of your Internet service provider (ISP) or America Online**   After you have your own Web page, you can use it as a way to let others know about yourself—and to get in touch with people who share your interests.

➤ **You can create free Web pages at Internet sites such as www.geocites.com**   There are many places on the Internet that will let you create Web pages for free. One of the great things about these sites is that they're deliberately built as a way for people to communicate with others, so they're a great way to get in touch with other people. These pages are so easy to set up that you can literally create one by simply filling in a pre-set template, as you can see in Figure 1.1, from the GeoCities site.

Figure 1.1

Anyone can build a home page by simply filling in a form, as you can see on this free home-page building site at www.geocities.com.

➤ **You can hook up a Webcam to your site and broadcast your life to the world**   Are you an exhibitionist? Do you want people to get a live view of your frog collection? Do you want people around the world to be able to see the view outside your window. (Right now, all I see outside mine is fog, smoke, and a gauzy-looking skyline of Boston.) You can do all that by setting up a Webcam, a live video camera that broadcasts directly to your Web site.

To find out about all this and more, turn to Part 6, "Using a Personal Web Page to Communicate with the World."

All the Cool Freebies You Can Ever Imagine

Here's what I think is one of the world's greatest riddles. How is it that billions of dollars are being made by Internet companies, with countless millionaires being made overnight—and yet many of those companies are making their money by giving things away for free?

Got me. I never did well in economics.

But the truth is, the Internet today is a cheapskate's paradise. And many of the freebies given away enable you to communicate with others. Here's a sample of what you'll find:

➤ **Free faxing services**   You can get your own personal fax number for free—and whenever someone sends you a fax, it'll be delivered straight to your email inbox. You also can send faxes for free as well, without having to pay for the cost of a phone call. Pictured here in Figure 1.2 is the site www.fax4free.com, which lets you send faxes for free.

Figure 1.2

Free, free, free! Among the many cool free ways to communicate online is www.fax4free, which lets you send faxes for free.

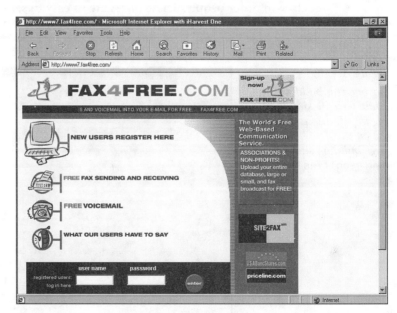

➤ **Free email**   Dozens of sites will give you a free email account. You pay nothing, and get and send all your email for free.

➤ **Voice mail**   Want your own voice mail and answering machine? No problem. Those crazy Web guys and gals, looking for ways to make oodles of money, let you have your own free phone number and voice mail service where anyone can leave you a voice mail. The voice mail is delivered to your email box, where you can read it. Or you can even call up and have the message read to you by a robot voice. So how do the Web guys and gals make oodles of money doing this? Who cares! The point is, you can have yet another cool way to communicate, and you don't have to spend a cent.

Other Cool Ways to Communicate Online

There's even more cool ways to communicate online, as you'll see throughout the book. Here's the rundown:

Cool Tips

Get Free Faxing, Email, and Voice Mail—All in One Place

How's this for the ultimate cool, free way to communicate: Free faxing, email, and voice mail? Yes, it exists. Just head to www.onebox.com and sign up—it's all there at no cost to you.

➤ **You can chat with instant messenger programs, and with cool programs like ICQ**   Friends, family, strangers, who knows, maybe even aliens...you'll meet and talk with all kinds of people with instant messenger and chat programs. And these programs increasingly include things like news and stock reports in them as well. I'll show you how to use them all.

➤ **You can set up your own personal email broadcast—for free**   Have you ever wanted your own personal newspaper or newsletter? If so, the Internet is a great way to publish, and for free. I'll show you how you can send out email broadcasts far and wide. (Or far and narrow, if that's your intended audience.)

➤ **You can do group surfing mark up Web pages with graffiti**   Yes, strange but true. You and a group of people can surf together from site to site, commenting on the pages you visit. And you can even deface...excuse me, mark up...Web pages so that others can see your comments.

I'll show you all these cool things and more in Part 7, "But Wait, There's More. Other Cool Ways to Communicate Online."

Email's Not Dull Anymore—Making It Jump Through Hoops

Email. Yawn! So what else is new? Sure, it's a quick-and-easy way to keep in touch with others, but let's face it, on the coolness chart, email rates just below spending a Sunday afternoon mowing your lawn and just above watching milk boil. (You say you like mowing your lawn? Then come over to my house, please...it could use a cut. As for boiling milk, you can do that at your house.)

Well, I've got a surprise for you. Believe it or not, there are a ton of fancy things you can do with email; things beyond just sending and receiving plain, ordinary text. Send and receive homemade videos and pictures, using all kinds of coding so that you can stuff email with colors and fonts and other neat things, such as voice mail messages...all kinds of things. What kinds of things, you ask? Read on—that's what I'll tell you about in the rest of this section.

Using Smileys and Signatures in Your Email

Just sending out email with your name in it is kind of dull. At the end of your message, you'll usually just put your name, hanging out there plain and lonely.

But maybe you're the kind of person who wants more personalized email. Maybe you like to express yourself not just in the text of your message, but in your signature as well. Maybe you're a John Hancock sort of guy or gal who likes his signature to be noticed, to be big and bold.

Whether you like your signature to be big and bold, small and timid, or anything in between or beyond, you can add a specialized signature to your email messages. The signature isn't a signature like you're used to signing in ink. Instead, it's text that's added automatically at the bottom of your email. It can be something simple, like your name, email address, affiliation, and similar contact information, formatted with text characters, and spacing. Figure 1.3 is an example of what I mean.

Figure 1.3

Here's an example of an email signature.

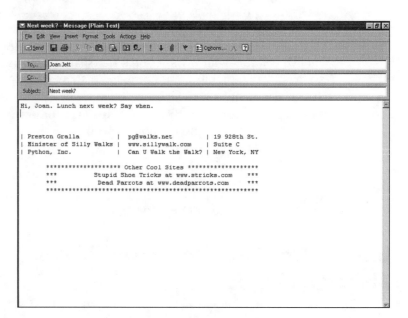

And it can get a lot fancier than that. You can create pictures using spaces and characters, and become a Picasso of the keyboard, with your work of art at the bottom of every email you send out.

You also can express yourself with *smileys,* those little faces and other pictures that you have to look sideways to see, and that you can create with characters you find on your keyboard, like these: :] :) ;) and many others. Smileys also are called *emoticons.* That's because smileys are generally used to express emotions of some kind—happiness, sadness, boredom, and existential angst. (Okay, maybe existential angst is pushing it a bit.) And so they're sometimes called "emoticons"—a cross between "emotion" and "icons."

Using Fonts, Colors, and HTML in Your Email

There's a lot more you can do with your email than add signatures and smileys. You also can add fonts, colors, and special HTML coding to your email as well. In essence, anything you see on a Web page you can send (and receive) in your email. In fact, you can send and receive entire Web pages by email.

To do all this, you'll need an email program that supports HTML. Most these days, including Outlook, can do that. In Figure 1.4 you can see an example of Outlook reading an HTML email newsletter.

To learn about all the neat ways to communicate with email, turn to Part 3, "Cool Ways to Communicate with Email."

Cool Tips

You Can Use Different Signatures for Different Emails

After you start using signatures, you might not want to stop. You can set up multiple signatures in your email program, and choose among them when sending email. For information about how to do it, turn to Chapter 7, "Tons of Fancy Email Tricks."

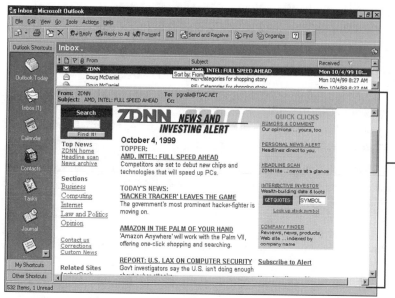

Figure 1.4

Here's an example of an email newsletter you can read if you have the right email software, such as Outlook.

The email message appears here

Sending Video and Audio Messages with Email

But wait! as they say on late-night TV, there's more! You can send and receive home-made video with email, and can send and receive voice mail as well. To do that, you'll need the right hardware to record video and voice, and you'll need the right software, to send and receive it and play it back. For information on how to do it all, turn to Chapter 8, "Tons of Fancy Multimedia Email Tricks."

Other Cool Email Stuff

Yes, there's even more cool stuff you can do with email. You can use your email inbox as your universal message center, for example, and in one spot can get all your faxes, voice mail, and email. And I'll show you ways that you can use email to broadcast the same message simultaneously to many people using many different communications methods, including voice, fax, email, and paging—and you can do all this for free. For the lowdown, turn to Chapter 10, "Getting and Using Free Email, Voice Mail, Faxes, and Other Services."

The Least You Need to Know

➤ You can personalize your email by adding a "signature" with contact information, a quote, and even pictures to the bottom of every email you send out.

➤ There are ways that you can use fonts, colors, pictures, and special HTML commands in your email—but the people you send the email to will have to have an email program that reads HTML.

➤ You can talk to others over the Internet with a microphone and speakers, as if you were talking to them over a telephone—and you can also make calls to regular telephones as well.

➤ To videoconference with others over the Internet, you'll need special software, such as Microsoft's NetMeeting or CU-SeeMe from White Pine Software.

➤ You can use free Web pages given to your by your Internet service provider (ISP) or a site like GeoCities at www.geocities.com to communicate with others.

➤ Many sites such as OneBox at www.onebox.com will give you free communications services such as free faxing, voice mail, and email.

16

Chapter 2

What You'll Need to Communicate

In This Chapter

➤ A rundown on the hardware you'll need for communicating over the Internet

➤ A look at the kinds of software you'll need for communicating in neat ways online

➤ What kind of high-speed Internet connections you can get for communicating online

You want to get cool. You want to have your own videophone, you want to turn the Internet into your personal telephone system, and you want to do all kinds of other neat stuff using your computer and the Internet.

Good for you. I hope to see you there. But before you go, there are a few things you'll need. You'll have to get the right hardware, the right software, and the right Internet connection. How to know all that? Easy. Read on, and you'll get an introduction to everything you need to know.

What Kind of Hardware You'll Need

You want to broadcast your face and voice to the world with an Internet video camera—or at least talk with friends and family using your computer as a videophone. Or you want to use your computer as a telephone, spanning the globe, making long-distance calls to other people on their computers for free. Or maybe you want to send pictures, recordings, or videos of yourself via email. For whatever reason, you want to communicate in cool ways over the Internet.

Here's the prototypical good news/bad news scenario for all this. Good news: It's easy to do. Bad news: You'll probably have to buy some hardware to do all that. For transmitting video, you'll need some kind of Netcam. For talking over your computer, you should get a microphone, even if you already have one built into your computer. And to send pictures, you need some way to get pictures into your computer.

Walkie the Talkie

Do You Like to Watch?

Even if you don't have a video camera, you can still participate in videoconferencing—but you'll only be able to watch, listen, and talk. Without a video camera attached to your PC, you can't transmit your picture. But if you use videoconferencing software such as Microsoft NetMeeting or CU-SeeMe, you'll still be able to see and hear others who are videoconferencing.

Read on for a brief rundown on what you'll need. For more details on what to buy, how to buy, and how to set all these neat gizmos up, turn to Part 2, "How to Set Up Cool Hardware for Communicating Online."

Eye Get It: When You'll Need a Netcam

If you want to be able to send videos of yourself to others, or be able to participate in videoconferences, you're going to need a Netcam, sometimes called a Webcam.

Whatever you call them, these "cams" are small video digital cameras that you attach to your computer, and then point at you (smile!) so that others can see you live, or so that you can record yourself on a video, and then send that video to others.

Netcams are generally fairly inexpensive, usually costing less than $250, and can usually be found for about $100—good news for those of us whose pocketbooks aren't bulging with extra cash. They're cute little gizmos that sit unobtrusively somewhere around your PC. You can see one pictured in Figure 2.1.

There's a lot of decisions you'll have to make when it's time to buy a Netcam—you'll have to pore over things like image size, frames-per-second, and other kinds of specs. Don't worry about all that stuff now—I'll tell you everything you need to know about them in Chapter 4, "How to Choose a Web Video Camera."

Figure 2.1

Makeup, please! Here's a Netcam ready to record your every movement.

The Digital Difference—A Netcam Is Different from a Digital Video Camera

A Netcam is a small, inexpensive device you attach to your computer for Web-based videoconferencing and recording videos that you can send via email. Don't confuse a Netcam, though, with the much-more-expensive digital video camera (sometimes called DV cameras). DV cameras are full-blown video cameras that you use just as you do any other video camera, except that they record the videos in digital formats that you can use on a computer. You can carry them around, just as you can any regular video camera. And you also can attach them to your computer and use them for videoconferencing, and anything you can use a Netcam for. Their quality is much higher than Netcams. So why not buy a DV camera instead of a Netcam? In a word: money. DV cameras generally cost at least $1,000, and professional-level models run to $10,000 and more. So if your first name is Bill and your last name is Gates, you'll probably want to buy one. Otherwise, it's wise to stay with a far-less-expensive Netcam.

For now, what you need to know is that there are two general types of Netcams:

➤ **PCI Netcams** These are Netcams that require you to open your computer up, put in a special kind of device called an add-in card, and then attach the Netcam to the card. Don't worry, it's not as complicated as it sounds.

➤ **USB Netcams** These are Netcams that attach to your computer using what's called a USB (Universal Serial Bus) port.

Cool Tips

It's Easy to Install Add-in Cards

Pitch alert! If you want to know how to install add-in cards and other neat things in your computer, get a copy of my book *How to Expand and Upgrade PCs*. Okay, now back to our regularly scheduled book.

This is a kind of port that you'll find on all new and newer computers. The HomeConnect camera I showed you earlier in this chapter is a USB Netcam. USB Netcams are incredibly easy to set up. Just plug them in, follow some simple directions, and voilà—you're ready to broadcast to the world. There is a downside to them, though: Their quality isn't as good as PCI Netcams. So as the saying goes, you pays your money and you takes your chances. If you're lucky enough to have bought a computer recently, you may have gotten a computer with what's called USB 2.0 in it. If you do, it means you can get a superfast Netcam, and so the quality will be every bit as good as PCI Netcams.

Say Cheese! How About Digital Cameras?

We can't all be video stars all the time. There are times when you're communicating and you want a picture to say a thousand words for you (give or take a dozen or two). Maybe you want the world to see a picture of your new baby (Hey, Greg: Cecilia is a beauty!), or some event you've been to (Jerry: Great pics of Burning Man). You might want to send the pictures via email or post them on your Web site.

No matter what you want to do, an easy way to get pictures into your computer is to use a digital camera. When you use a digital camera, it records the picture on the camera's hard disk instead of on film. After you have the pictures on your camera's hard disk, you transfer them to your computer.

When it comes to buying a digital camera, there are specs and all kinds of tech stuff you should know. Fear not, I'm here to help, and I'll tell you everything you need to know about it in Chapter 6, "How to Set Up Scanners and Digital Cameras." So head to that chapter if you want a propeller-head's view of what to buy.

Cool Tips

**You Can Get Pictures from Your
Regular Camera into Your Computer**

You don't have to buy a digital camera if you want to get pictures from your regular camera into your computer. All you need to do, when you have your pictures developed, is tell the developer that you want your pictures on disk or delivered to you over the Internet. For a small extra fee, you'll be able to get pictures delivered that way. And if you're an America Online user, you can use the "You've Got Pictures" feature to get your pictures delivered straight to your America Online account.

No great surprise when it comes to digital cameras: the more money you spend, the better quality picture you'll get. You can get them for as little as $80 or so, or well over $1,000. For reasonable quality, though, expect to pay in the $200-or-above price range.

There are generally two ways that you'll get pictures from your camera into your PC. You'll either connect your camera to your PC via its serial port or its USB port. It's a better idea to get a USB camera instead of one that connects via a serial port. USB ports transfer data faster than do serial ports, and USB cameras are usually easier to set up than cameras that connect to your computer with a serial port. (You may also come across a kind of "card reader" that attaches to your computer and reads pictures from the camera's card directly. They're rare, though.)

Scanning for Scanners

Another simple way to get pictures into your computer is by using a scanner. A scanner takes any picture or drawing, converts it to a computer file, and then sends it to your computer.

Specs, specs, and more specs. There are all kinds of complicated things to keep in mind when buying a scanner. I'll clue you into all of it in Chapter 6.

But there are a few things to know now. Figure that you'll pay at least $100 for a reasonable scanner, and maybe more, if you want very good quality. But for most purposes, something in the $100 to $250 price range should do well for you.

As with digital cameras and Netcams, there are several different ways you can connect your scanner to your computer. Here are the two most common:

> ➤ **Via the parallel port**   You'll plug some scanners into your parallel port—the place where you plug in your printer. The problem with these kinds of scanners is that you might have to plug and unplug your scanner and printer when you want to switch between printing and scanning.

> ➤ **Via the USB port**   Here's the best way to go. Setup is a snap, and you don't have to worry about plugging and unplugging the scanner and printer when you want to use one or the other.

Walkie the Talkie

You Can Add USB Ports to a Computer that Doesn't Have Them

As you can probably tell by now, USB ports are often the best way to connect hardware such as digital cameras, Netcams, and scanners to your computer. But what if you have a computer with USB ports? Worry not. You can always buy a kit to add them. You'll need to have Windows 98 on your computer to install a kit. Figure on spending about $50 or a little more—but it'll be $50 well spent. For a list of kits for adding USB to your computer, go to www.allusb.com and click **Cards**.

The Sound Card, Speakers, and Microphone

If you're going to talk with others over the Internet, you'll need a sound card, speakers, and a microphone. The good news here is that most computers sold these days include all this equipment in some form or other.

You know the routine by now: We won't cover all the specs for all this hardware in this chapter. For specs on what to buy, turn to Chapter 3, "Setting Up Sound Hardware." But here's the basic rundown on what you need to know:

➤ Ideally, your sound card should be *full duplex*. That means that you and the person you're talking to can both talk at the same time. If your sound card can't handle full duplex, you'll have to take turns talking. I don't know how *your* friends are, but mine aren't that polite, so I suggest getting a full-duplex sound card. You may also be able to update an existing sound card to full duplex by merely updating the drivers. Visit the manufacturer's Web site for information.

➤ The quality of the speakers you'll use aren't that important if you'll only be using them for talking. Aside from using the speakers for talking to others, though, if you use them to listen to music, you'll need a higher quality speaker.

➤ A microphone will help sound quality when you're talking to others. A number of computers include built-in microphones, but using a plug-in microphone makes for better sound quality and can filter out some of the background noise. You also can buy a headset, which is a combination microphone and head-phones. They're great for making Internet telephone calls.

What Kind of Software You'll Need

You'll of course need more than just hardware if you want to do things like using your PC as a videophone or telephone. You'll need the right software as well.

If you get all the hardware you need to communicate in cool ways, you've probably spent a pretty penny (or an ugly one, for that matter). Well, I hope you're sitting down when you read what I have to say next, because it might shock you. Here goes: Much of the software you'll need will cost you...absolutely nothing. That's right. Free. As in zero. Nada. No dinero. Contrary to popular opinion, sometimes there is a free lunch. That's Internet economics at work again for you. Not all the software is free, of course, but still most of it is.

Here's the kind of software you'll use to communicate in cool ways online:

➤ **An email program that reads HTML**   This way, when you send and receive email, you can use and read fancy fonts, pictures, and other neat Web stuff. Free programs such as Outlook Express (which comes with Microsoft Internet Explorer) and Netscape Messenger (which comes with Netscape Communicator) read HTML. They'll also let you send and receive attachments to your email—and let you send and receive video mail and voice mail.

Walkie the Talkie

To Watch Video Mail and Listen to Email Voice Mail, You'll Need Multimedia Software

If you want to be able to watch videos that someone sends to you via email, or listen to a voice mail they send you, you'll need special multimedia software. The most popular ones are RealPlayer G2, available for free from www.realnetworks.com, and Windows Media Player, which might have come with your computer, and also is available for free from www.microsoft.com. If you're running Windows 98, go to www.windowsupdate.com.

➤ **PC telephone software**   Want to talk to other people using your computer? You can do it for free, with several kinds of PC telephone software. They'll have to have the same kind of telephone software installed as you do. Pictured in Figure 2.2 is the popular MediaRing Talk 99 PC telephone software. MediaRing and similar software is...yes, you guessed it...free.

➤ **Chat and messenger software**   Want to chat? Then you'll want instant messenger kinds of programs such as America Online Instant Messenger, Yahoo! Messenger, and Microsoft's MSN Messenger. Take a wild guess—how much do you think they cost? Correct. They're free.

➤ **Videoconferencing software**   You're in Des Moines, Iowa. You have a friend in Shanghai. You want to have a videoconference using your computer. No problem. Just get some videoconferencing software. One of the most popular ones, Microsoft NetMeeting, is, naturally, free. To use another popular one, Cu-SeeMe, you'll have to fork out some dough.

Figure 2.2

With MediaRing Talk 99, you can talk for free to other people anywhere in the world—as long as they have MediRing also installed.

Cool Tips

You Can Download Most Free Software from the Internet

As you can tell from this chapter, there's a whole lot of free software you can get that helps you communicate online. Much of the software you can download for free from an Internet download site. A good one to check out is ZDNet Downloads at www.zddownloads.com.

➤ **Other kinds of software**   There are a lot of other miscellaneous kinds of software you'll need, depending on which cool ways you want to communicate. If you want to send video mail, you'll need some kind of software that will let you record videos, such as PictureWorks Live. Often, this software will come for free along with whatever Netcam you buy. Software for recording voice clips is built into Windows. And if you plan to send pictures to others, and want to dress them up before sending, you'll need some kind of graphics software. Graphics software will come with the scanner or digital camera that you buy. And a good piece of graphics software is Paint Shop Pro, which you can try out for free before deciding whether you want to buy it.

The Need for Speed: What Kind of Internet Connection You'll Need

Gralla's First Rule of Internet Communications: Faster is better.

It's really that simple. The faster your connection, the better you'll be able to communicate using things such as Netcams, Internet telephones, and sending and receiving video mail and voice mail. Why is that, you ask? Is it because you can talk faster when your connection is faster? Nice theory, but no, that's not the reason. Here's why you want as fast a connection as possible if you're looking to communicate in cool ways on the Internet:

➤ **The sound quality will be much better on Internet telephone calls** When you have a slow connection, the sound will be garbled and fuzzy, kind of like a scratchy old "78" vinyl record. (Never heard of vinyl records, especially 78s, sonny? Ask your grandparents or your parents about them. Your mother should know.)

➤ **The video will be much crisper and clearer when doing videoconferencing** Videoconference over a slow connection, and the images are often blurry and ill defined. And there also might be a noticeable lag between the time you see someone's mouth move, and when you hear the sound actually coming out of their mouths—think of it as the Grade B Japanese movie effect or the Power Rangers effect.

➤ **Video mail and voice mail will be sent and received much more quickly** Videos and voice files tend to be quite large, often taking up several megabytes or more. If you have a slow connection, it will take a long time for those files to be sent and received via email.

Walkie the Talkie

A Need for Speed

High-speed Internet connections are often called "broadband" connections. And if you want to really sound geeky-cool and on the cutting edge, call a high-speed connection a "fat pipe."

Walkie
the Talkie

A 56K Modem Doesn't Really Send at 56K

Here's a conundrum: A 56K modem doesn't really send data at 56K. Instead, it sends data at a slower rate of 33.6K—yet another reason why a 56K modem isn't really high-speed. A 56Kk modem can receive data at about 56K, which is where it gets its name.

What Kinds of Fast Internet Connections Are There?

If you heed my First Rule of Internet Communications, you know that you need a fast connection. There are many different kinds of them. Here's what you need to know about each:

➤ **56K modem**   A 56K modem isn't really a fast Internet connection, but considering that today's 56K modems are in the range of 180 to 190 times faster than the first modems invented, they're kind of fast. If the only way you can get onto the Internet is with a modem, make sure that it's a 56K modem. Older 28,800 modems are really too slow for most of the cool ways you can communicate online. With 56K modems, voice quality won't be the best, video quality won't be superb, and files will take a while to get back and forth. But still, it's a start. 56K modems aren't fast enough to be considered "broadband."

➤ **Cable modem**   A cable modem is fast—*really* fast. It can zoom by at 1.5 megabits a second, which is many times the speed of a 56K modem. When you use a cable modem, everything goes faster, you get great sound and video quality, and files get sent and received super-quick—or as they say here in my Cambridge, Massachusetts, hometown: "wicked fast." Using a cable modem doesn't interfere at all with your use of TV—you can use both at the same time. (Although, don't you think you watch too much TV already? Do you really need to see a *Gilligan's Island* rerun for the fifth time?) Figure on paying about $40 or so a month for a cable modem. That might sound steep, but keep in mind that when you have a cable modem, you won't need a second phone line for your computer, so it comes out to about the same price as a normal Internet connection and second phone line. I connect to the Internet using a cable modem. And it can vouch for it—it really *is* wicked fast. To get onto the Internet via a cable modem, check with your local cable company. By the way, cable modems in different parts of the country might go at different speeds, so check with your cable company before signing up.

A Cable Modem Isn't Really a Modem

The cable "modem" you use to get onto the Internet really isn't a modem at all—it's a different kind of technology. To use a cable modem, you have to attach a network card to your computer, in essence the same kind of card that people in corporations use when they're connected to their business's computer network. The cable "modem" connects that network card to the same cable in your house that delivers cable TV signals.

➤ **DSL connection**   The newest high-speed way to get onto the Internet is with a *DSL* (Digital Subscriber Line) connection. This requires a special DSL modem. Not all areas of the country have DSL service yet—check with your phone company. As of now, DSL service tends to be more expensive than cable modem service. And while in theory, it can offer an even higher-speed connection than most cable modems, the pricing on high-speed DSL is so outrageously high that unless your last name is Rockefeller, or you've just received several hundred thousand stock options, it's beyond your reach.

➤ **Other high-speed connections**   There are a variety of other high-speed ways to get onto the Internet. At work, if your computer is on a local area network, you probably have a fast Internet connection called a T-1 connection. And in some places, at home you can get a high-speed connection called an ISDN connection. I don't recommend ISDN connections. Setup can be a nightmare, it's not as fast as DSL and cable modem connections, and it's all-around a flaky way to get online. So why bother?

The Least You Need to Know

➤ For participating in videoconferences and using your computer as a video-phone, you'll need a Netcam. They're usually available for under $150, and often much less.

➤ Digital cameras and scanners are good ways to get pictures into your computer so that you can send the photos to others, or post them on your personal Web site.

➤ If you use a plug-in microphone instead of your computer's built-in microphone when making Net phone calls, the sound quality will be much better. If your computer doesn't have a built-in microphone, you'll have to buy one and plug it into your sound card.

➤ Much of the software you'll need for communicating online is free—you can get it at an Internet download site such as ZDNet Downloads at www.zddownloads.com.

➤ For videoconferencing, using the Internet as your telephone, and sending and receiving video mail and voice mail, you should have a high-speed "broadband" connection, such as a cable modem or DSL connection.

Part 2

How to Set Up Cool Hardware for Communicating Online

Hardware. Can't live with it, can't live without it.

If you're going to communicate in cool new ways, you need cool new hardware. Cool things like Netcams, microphones, scanners, and digital cameras.

Of course, while using all that hardware is cool, setting it up might not be. What if you're the kind of person who quakes in his boots and breaks out in a cold sweat every time you even think of adding anything to your PC?

Have no fear, I am here. I'll teach you how to choose the right hardware for communicating in cool ways, and then I'll show you how to install it all and set it up. I'll even give you tips on things like how to make sure the lighting is right in whatever room you use your Netcam. Lights, camera, action!

Chapter 3

Setting Up Sound Hardware

In This Chapter

➤ How to make sure you have the right sound card for communicating online

➤ How to install a new sound card if you need one

➤ What you can do if there's a problem with your sound card

➤ Why you need a microphone

➤ Making sure that you buy the right speakers

It's great that you can use your computer to make phone calls to people all over the world, or that you can use it as a videophone. But if you don't have the right sound hardware, you won't be able to do any of that. In this chapter, I'll clue you in on how to get and set up the right sound hardware. We'll talk sound cards, microphones, and speakers, with a side tour of things like headsets along the way. So come on along and get the rundown on what hardware can make your computer talk and sing.

Making Sure It's Sound: Getting the Right Sound Card

If you want to hear your best friend's voice instead of the sounds of silence when you try to use your computer as a telephone, you'll need a sound card.

There's good news, here: Any PC you buy these days has a sound card. So you'll be able to talk with friends, families, co-workers, passing acquaintances, raving lunatics...pretty much the whole gamut of whoever's on the Internet and wants to talk.

While there's a lot you need to know about sound cards if you're going to use them to listen to music, when it comes to things like making telephone calls over the Internet and using videophones, there's not much you really need to know. In fact, there's only one thing that's important: Your sound card should be *full duplex* instead of *half duplex*.

If you've bought your computer in the last five years or so, you can be pretty sure that your modem is full duplex. If your computer or sound card is older than five years, it might not be full duplex—although there's a chance that it is.

So how can you tell if your sound card is full duplex? Unfortunately, there's no simple way. The best thing to do is check the documentation. But what if the documentation doesn't give you help? (And given that most documentation appears to be written by people for whom English is a fourth language, don't count on it helping.) Head to the manufacturer's Web site or call technical support. (And if you head to technical support, have a good, thick book handy—you'll be put on hold for about two or three decades.) As a last resort, the thing to do is try it out. If you can't talk and listen at the same time, it's probably half duplex. If you can, it's full duplex.

If being able to talk and listen at the same time is important to you and you have a half-duplex sound card, then it's time to buy and install a full-duplex model. Depending on the model you buy, you can easily get one for under $100.

Cool Tips

Before You Buy a New Sound Card, See Whether a New Driver Solves the Problem

If you have a half-duplex sound card, you might be able to turn it into a full-duplex model without spending a penny. Any kind of hardware needs a piece of software called a *driver* to work properly. In many instances, simply by installing an updated driver, you can turn a half-duplex sound card into a full-duplex one. Head to the manufacturer's Web site, and look for the driver section for advice on how to download and install a new driver. It'll also tell you whether a new driver will turn your sound card into a full-duplex model.

Recording That Sound

You might be using your sound card for more than just using your PC as a telephone. You also might want to record your voice or a video, for doing things like sending voice messages in email. If you run into troubles doing this, there's something you can check out. Get to the Control Panel as I just described, and then double-click the **Multimedia** icon. Click the **Audio** tab and you'll see a screen like the one shown in Figure 3.1. You'll see two areas of the screen, one for Playback and one for Recording. If either of them doesn't have a Preferred device listed in the box, or if the device is grayed out, there's trouble in River City, my friend. Try reinstalling the driver or calling tech support.

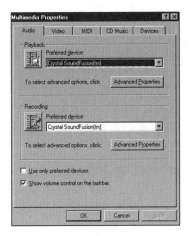

Figure 3.1

Here's how to make sure things are set up properly for recording and playing sound.

Making Sure to Get a Microphone

Many computers you buy have a microphone built into them. But just because there's a built-in microphone doesn't mean you should actually use it.

Unless you like scratchy and fuzzy sound, interference, and a lot of other noises mixing in with your voice, you need to buy a microphone for your computer. A microphone will give you far better sound quality, and you won't sound as if you're talking from the bottom of the ocean or the outer reaches of the solar system. And no one will think you said "Reebish hamaneuty frobash," when you were really saying, "How about lunch next Tuesday?"

Walkie
the Talkie

What's a Lapel Microphone?

You might see something called a *lapel microphone* advertised in magazines or on the Internet. It's a small microphone that you can clip onto your lapel (hence its name). It's quite handy, because when you clip it on this way, it picks up the sound of your voice quite well, and you don't need to hold the microphone in your hands.

Figure on spending from under $10 to about $25 for a microphone. Yes, you can buy a more expensive one, but you don't need to, unless you're planning on professional audio productions.

After you buy the microphone, plug it into the microphone port. How will you know which port on your computer is the microphone port? Easy. It's the one with a picture of a microphone. Bet you never thought hardware could be this easy.

Heady Times: Consider Getting a Head Set

Okay, crew. It's geek time. If you really, truly want to make the most effective use of your computer as a telephone, you need a headset.

Yes, *that* kind of headset. The one that makes you look like a nerd, or a NASA engineer communicating with astronauts lost in space, or that makes you look like a phone operator taking late-night phone orders for Ginsu knives.

Get rid of your vanity for a moment, though, and you'll find out that when it comes to talking with others over the Internet, these things are ideal. A headset places a microphone close to your mouth, so whomever you're talking to will hear your voice as clearly as possible. And the earphones you wear will deliver the clearest voice quality to you as well.

Don't count on using the same headset for your computer that you can use for a telephone. You'll need a specially designed set. They'll come with two plugs. One of those plugs connects to your microphone port, and the other plug connects to your speaker port. Just plug them in and you're ready to go. Just don't let your spouse or honey see you wearing them—they might place an order for some Ginsu knives.

How About the Speakers?

The final piece of equipment you'll need is a set of speakers. If all you're going to be using your speakers for is talking with your computer, pretty much any speakers will do. With an inexpensive set of speakers, the voice you hear will be tinny. (But then again, maybe the person you're talking to has a tinny voice.)

If you want to do other cool sound-and-music things with your computer—such as listening to music that someone sends you over email—you'll need a better set of speakers. Here's a brief rundown on what to keep in mind:

➤ **Get a subwoofer if you want the best sound quality with deep, bass sounds**   No, a subwoofer isn't some kind of precursor to a growl made by an angry guard dog. It's a small cube that plugs into your speakers and that adds a rich, deep bass to whatever you're listening to. You don't really need one for phone conversations—but it makes listening to music a whole lot more fun.

➤ **The speakers should be shielded**   Electromagnetic radiation comes out of speakers, which could interfere with your monitor. Pretty much any speaker sold today should be shielded, but better ask so you're safe rather than sorry.

➤ **With speakers, size doesn't matter** Sometimes very small cube speakers can produce beautiful sounds, while much larger speakers sound quite awful.

➤ **Look for speaker controls** There are a lot of different controls you can get. Make sure that in addition to controlling the volume, you can separately control the bass and treble.

➤ **The ears have it** The best judge of speaker quality is your own two ears. Listen to music on the speakers before buying to check out how it sounds.

No matter what speakers you buy, they'll be easy to install. You'll plug a wire from them into your speaker or headphone port, and then run wires between speakers, and to the sub-woofer if you have one.

Cool Tips

Here's Where to Get More Information on Buying Speakers

If you're serious about getting a good set of speakers, there's a lot more you should know than I can cover here. For a complete run-down on what to know before buying speakers—and, in fact, for buying any piece of hardware—get a copy of *The Complete Idiot's Guide to Buying a Computer*. Yes, you guessed it—it's another one of my books.

The Least You Need to Know

➤ It's best to have a full-duplex sound card, because that will let you talk and listen at the same time. If you have only a half-duplex sound card, you and the person you're communicating with will have to take turns talking.

➤ If you don't have a full-duplex sound card, you might not have to buy a new sound card. Instead, you might be able to download new drivers for your old card that will turn it into a full-duplex card. Check the manufacturer's Web site for information.

➤ If you need a new sound card, first take out your old sound card, then put the new one in the same spot where the old one was. Run the Add New Hardware Wizard to finish installation of the card.

➤ Even if your computer has a built-in microphone, you should buy a micro-phone to plug into your computer. The sound will be much clearer that way.

➤ Make sure that your speakers are shielded so that they won't cause interfer-ence with other parts of your computer, such as your monitor.

Chapter 4

How to Choose a Web Video Camera

In This Chapter

➤ A rundown of what kind of Web video cameras you can buy

➤ Looking at the different kinds of Netcams

➤ How to decide which Netcam to buy

➤ A look at digital video cameras

➤ Why you need the fastest Internet connection possible for using video

---

Before you can turn your computer into a Jetson-like videophone, participate in videoconferencing, or send videomail, you'll have to buy a Web video camera. For those uninitiated in the mysteries of hooking up video cameras to PCs, this can be an extremely confusing thing to do. There are so many choices, different specifications to consider, and so much variation in price that it can quickly become a frustrating experience.

But despair not, friend. I'm here to help. I'll walk you through what you need to know, step by step, and by the end, you'll be a master of all things having to do with buying the right camera. As you'll see in this chapter, it's not really that hard to make a decision about which Web video camera has your name written all over it.

What Kinds of Web Video Cameras Are There?

There's a lot of choices out there if you're interested in buying a Web video camera, and more become available each day (Everyone, it seems, wants to be a Web star.) But generally, there are three different kinds of video cameras you can hook up to your computer and use:

➤ **Netcams**   These are what most people use, and are the best choice for just about everyone. They're relatively inexpensive—you can get one for under $100, and even the better ones will cost you in the $150 range. They're also easy to set up and use, and usually come with a good assortment of software. They're also small and so fit nicely on your desk. One drawback to these cameras is that their video quality isn't nearly as high as digital video cameras (see the next bullet). And they can be used only when they're attached to your computer—you can't take them with you and record video away from your computer.

➤ **Digital video cameras (DV cameras)**   These are in many ways just like regular video cameras that record by using film—but instead of recording on film, they record onto what's in essence a hard disk. You can then transfer that recording to your computer and can send it as video mail. And you also can hook up DV cameras to your computer and use them for videoconferencing. DV cameras offer exceptionally high quality. Of course, they also cost an exceptional amount of money. And I mean some *serious* money. DV cameras can easily cost $1,000 and professional-level models can set you back $10,000 or more. So unless your bank account is bulging with spare cash, you probably won't buy one of these.

Netcams Can Double as Digital Cameras

Netcams can do more than play or record video—they also can do double-duty as a digital camera. You can take snapshots with them easily—most include a button you can push to do that. The picture quality won't be as high as when you use a digital camera, and you can only take snapshots when the camera is attached to a computer. Still, they're great in a pinch when you need a quick picture taken.

➤ **Normal video cameras with a video capture board**   Little-known fact: You can use your normal video camera with a special piece of hardware known as a video capture board—and faster than you can say Jack Robinson, you have a PC video camera. You'll be able to send either recorded video or live video to your PC, so they're great for creating video mail and for videoconferencing as well. A video capture board will set you back $150 or more. But keep in mind that setting up and using these boards can be problematic, and you can spend a whole lot of time doing troubleshooting if you go this route. However, you may be lucky without even knowing it. There's a chance that the existing video card in your computer has this capability already. Look for special video inputs and outputs on the back of your computer, and check your documentation to see if you have this capability already.

The First Choice: What Basic Type of Netcam to Buy?

Because of their balance between price, video quality, and ease of setup and use, Netcams are the best choice for most people. So you'll probably want to buy one.

There are a whole lot of specs and features to consider before deciding which Netcam to buy. But before looking at anything else, you have a very basic choice to make: How do you want to connect your Netcam to your computer? Netcams can connect to your computer via three basic methods:

➤ The Universal Serial Bus (USB) port

➤ A special card connected inside your computer

➤ A standard parallel or serial port

Sometimes the Same Netcam Can Connect to Your PC in More Than One Way

Sometimes, you can hook up a Netcam to your computer in several different ways. So you might buy a camera that has the option of connecting to your computer via the parallel port or the USB port, for example. In this instance, when you buy the camera, you usually have to make a choice of which model to get—the parallel port of the USB one.

There are pros and cons to each method. Here's how to decide which to buy:

➤ **USB Netcams**   USB Netcams are by far the easiest Netcams to set up. That's because the USB port and USB hardware has been specifically designed for ease of setup. There's no opening up your computer, and no weirdo installation woes. The USB port can send and receive data at higher rates than your parallel and serial ports, so USB Netcams tend to show video at a higher quality than cameras that attach via the parallel and serial ports. But they tend to show video at a lower quality than Netcams that plug into an add-in board on your computer. For most, a USB camera is the way to go. Of course, to use one, you'll need to have a USB port on your computer. Most computers manufactured in the past few years have USB port. You can see a picture of the USB port here in Figure 4.1—so check your PC to make sure that you have one.

USB 2.0 Offers a Very High-Speed Connection

A new standard for USB, called USB 2.0, enables devices like Netcams to have very fast connections to a computer—40 times the speed of previous USB connections. So if you're buying a new computer, or have recently bought one, look for USB 2.0—and make sure your Netcam can connect at the higher speed that the new USB allows.

Figure 4.1

To use a USB Netcam, you'll have to have a USB port on your computer.

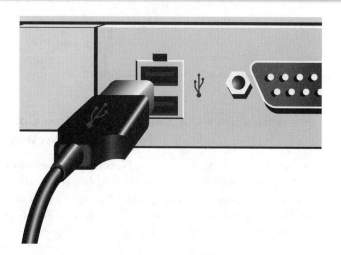

➤ **Netcams that connect to an add-in card on your computer** To use these kinds of Netcams, you'll have to open up your computer, install a special card inside it, close your computer back up, and then install software. If you're not very familiar with hardware, this can be a bit difficult to do—although I'll walk you through doing it, step by step, in the next chapter. These Netcams tend to be more expensive than USB Netcams, at least in part because they require more hardware—you're buying an add-in card as well as a Netcam when you buy one. Generally, the cards can transfer data faster than can USB ports, so these types of Netcams tend to display video at a higher quality than USB Netcams. But remember: They require more work to set up and troubleshoot.

If You Buy a Netcam with an Add-in Board, Make Sure It's PCI

If you decide to go the route of buying a Netcam that attaches to your PC, make sure to buy one that attaches via what's called a PCI card. Most, if not all, Netcams that attach to a card attach this way, but it can't hurt to check. PCI cards are easier to set up and are better than other kinds of cards.

➤ **Netcams that connect to the serial or parallel port of your PC** These types of Netcams used to be more common than they are today—to a great extent, they've been replaced with USB port Netcams. But they're still around. Although they're easier to set up than Netcams that connect to a card in your PC, they're harder to set up than USB Netcams. And, because serial and parallel connections are slower than a USB connection, the quality of their video isn't as good as a USB connection. Only consider buying one of these if you don't have a USB port and don't want the bother of opening your computer to add a card.

The Specs, the Whole Specs, and Nothing But the Specs: What to Know Before Buying a Netcam

So you've made your basic decision about what basic kind of Netcam to buy. Now it's time to get down to business: time to see what kind of specs and features your camera should have. Here's what to know before you buy:

➤ **What's the frame rate?** Frame rate refers to how many frames of motion the camera captures per second. In the acronym-crazy world of computing, it's often shortened to "fps" (frames per second). The higher the frame rate, the better. Generally, the more expensive the camera, the higher the frame rate. Don't settle for a frame rate of less than 25fps, and preferably 30fps or higher—up to 60fps and beyond.

➤ **What are the maximum colors it can display?**   Again, more is better. Look for a Netcam that can display what's called 24-bit color or what might be called 16.7 million colors—and that's a whole lot of colors.

➤ **What's the maximum resolution?**   Netcams display as a small frame inside a window on your computer. The resolution refers to the size of the frame—the more the resolution, the bigger the frame. And yes, you guessed it, bigger is better. Try to get a camera that can display at 320 by 240 pixels and preferably better—possibly 640 by 480. Keep in mind, though, that at 640 by 480 resolution, the image will have a lot of "lag" to it—it'll appear slow and out of synch with your voice. You'll mainly use that resolution for using the Netcam to take still pictures. Pictured in Figure 4.2 is what a 640-by-480 video image of my two kids looks like, taken with my trusty 3COM Home Connect USB Netcam.

Figure 4.2

Smile! You're on Candid Camera! At 640 by 480 pixels, the video image of Gabe and Mia looks pretty big.

What's a Pixel?

No, a pixel it not a male pixie. A *pixel* is a single dot on a computer monitor, and it's the basic measurement of screen resolution.

➤ **What's the focal range?**   You'd like a camera that can focus close-up as well as far away. Some Netcams can focus on objects within an inch of them; others can only focus on objects four inches or more away. The wider the range is, the better.

➤ **Does it automatically adjust to changes in the light?**   Especially in offices or rooms such as studies—where you most likely have your computer—the light can be very variable. You want a camera that automatically adjusts well to changes in lighting—and because you'll be using it indoors, you especially want one that displays well in indoor light.

➤ **What kinds of controls does it have?**   Mainly when you use a Netcam, you won't be touching the camera—you'll control most of what it does through software. But there are still some important controls you want it to have. You should be able to easily move the camera from side to side and up and down so that you can position it for the best pictures of you (closeup, please!). And you want as long a cord as possible that attaches the camera to your computer to give you the maximum amount of room for moving the camera and fiddling with it. There is often a focus control as well. Some cameras include a contrast control, although many of them automatically adjust the contrast and therefore don't require that control.

➤ **What kind of software comes with it?**   Any Netcam you buy will come with a variety of software that you can use for videoconferencing, and for other purposes as well. Look for a camera with as wide a range of software as possible. You want software that can capture video so that you can send video mail, and you'd also like software that enables you to capture single images as well, so that you can use your Netcam as a digital camera. And if you're planning to hook your Netcam to a Web site, you want Webcam software to do that. Popular ones are NetSpy and Webcam32. Pretty much any Netcam you buy should come with videoconferencing software. But you don't really need to worry if it doesn't come with any. Microsoft's NetMeeting videoconferencing software is free, and can be downloaded from the Microsoft Web site at http://www.microsoft.com/windows/netmeeting/.

If You Don't Have a High-Speed Connection...

If you're connecting to the Internet via a 56K modem or a slower one (Heaven forbid!), you don't need to think about frame rates or otherwise worry about the quality of your camera when buying. At that slow speed, the quality of your video won't be very good, and so one camera will do just as well as another. So if you're connecting to the Internet this way, consider buying only for ease of setup and what kind of software is bundled with the camera.

For Them That's Got: What About Digital Video Cameras?

If you're lucky enough to have oodles of spare money lying around, you should fork out the money for a digital video camera. These produce very high-quality video, and can be used as a regular camcorder, not just for videoconferencing.

Figure on spending at least $1,000 for one of these cameras and more if you want the absolutely best quality. Check for image quality before buying, and if possible, get a camera with more than one CCD (charged coupled device). A CCD is in essence a digital video camera's lens, and the more of them the better. Like any video camera, look for controls that make sense and are easy to use. And you'd like an LCD screen (the screen that shows you what your taking a picture of) that you can view from several different angles, and that can be viewed even in bright sunlight. Most of all, though, check the quality of the video. That's what you're really buying when you buy one of these cameras—and beauty, after all, is in the eye of the beholder.

The Least You Need to Know

➤ Netcams offer the best mix of price and image quality for hooking a video camera up to your computer.

➤ The easiest Netcams to set up are those that attach to your computer via the Universal Serial Bus (USB) port.

➤ When buying a Netcam, look for one with the fastest frame per second (fps) rate—at least 25fps and preferably higher, 60fps if you can.

➤ Look for a Netcam with the highest resolution and that can display the most colors—24-bit color (16.7 million colors) with a resolution of at least 320 by 240 pixels and 640 by 480 pixels if you're planning to use your Netcam to take still digital pictures.

➤ Software that comes with the Netcam should include video capture software for creating video mail, software that will capture still images, and software for posting pictures to a Web site.

Chapter 5

How to Set Up and Use a Web Video Camera

In This Chapter

➤ What to have ready before setting up a Netcam

➤ Five easy steps for setting up a Universal Serial Bus (USB) Netcam

➤ Seven easy steps for setting up a Netcam that requires you to install an add-in card

➤ Best tips for getting the most out of your Netcam

Time to get famous, to star in your own Web-based home video, to make videophone calls, participate in videoconferencing, broadcast your face to the world, and just all-around have a great time with Net-based video.

But before you do that, you'll have to set up a Web video camera—a Netcam. For those who are frightened of setting up hardware, stop hyperventilating and take a few deep breaths. It's actually easy to do, as I'll show you in this chapter.

In this chapter, I'll show you how to set up the most common kinds of Netcams, and then give advice on how to use a Netcam so that your face is as bright and beautiful as possible when you broadcast to the world.

What You'll Need to Get Started

In the previous chapter, we covered all the different kinds of Web video cameras you can buy. As I said then, the camera you want to buy is a Netcam—an inexpensive video camera that attaches to your PC.

The two best kinds of Netcams to get are those that use the Universal Serial Bus port (USB), and those that connect via an add-in card that you put in your computer. (For more information on the pros and cons of each, turn to Chapter 4, "How to Choose a Web Video Camera.")

Here's what you need to set up each type of Netcam before getting started.

For a USB Netcam, you'll need

➤ The camera

➤ A USB port on your computer

➤ A USB cable

➤ Installation software that comes with the camera

For a Netcam that uses an add-in card, you'll need

➤ The camera

➤ The add-in card

➤ A Phillips-head screwdriver or "hex nut driver" that can open up your computer

➤ Installation software that comes with the camera.

Walkie the Talkie

What's a Hex Nut Driver?

Sometimes nut drivers also are called hex nut drivers. That's because the cases of many computers are attached to the rest of the computer by six-sided screws called hex nuts. You use the hex nut driver to unscrew those nuts. Although you might be able to unscrew the case with a Phillips-head screwdriver, it's much better to use what's called a hex nut driver, because it's much less likely to strip the screws.

Okay, got what you need? Good. It's time to move on and install the camera. Don't worry—even if you've never installed anything on your computer, it's easy to do. Just follow my advice.

How to Install a USB Camera

One of the great advantages of USB cameras is how easy they are to set up. You won't even have to take the case off your PC—no muss, no fuss, and you'll be a video star within minutes of cracking open the camera's box. Here's how to do it. (By the way, follow these general directions, but also look for the directions that came with your camera.)

1. Make sure that you have a USB port. You can only install a USB camera if you have a USB port. Look for a small rectangular port on front, side, or rear of your PC that has a USB signal next to it. Figure 5.1 shows a USB port, along with the USB signal.

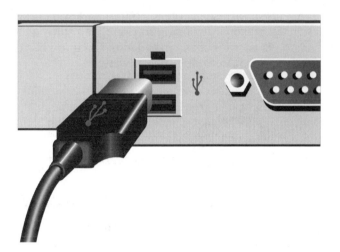

Figure 5.1

Yes, you've got one—here's what a USB port looks like.

2. Check your computer to make sure that USB is enabled. Most versions of Windows greater than Windows 95 support USB, although some versions of Windows 95 might cause some trouble. To make sure that yours properly supports it, check the Device Manager and look for the USB setting. To do that, right-click the **My Computer** icon, and then choose **Properties**. Next, click the **Device Manager** tab, and scroll down. You should see a USB controller entry, and there should be no exclamation point next to it. You can see the proper entry in Figure 5.2.

Figure 5.2

Here's how to make sure that USB is enabled on your computer.

3. Turn off your computer and plug one end of the USB cable into the camera, and the other end into the USB port on your computer. Make sure you plug the proper end of the cable into the camera and into your computer. The plug only goes one way, so don't force it—if you've got it right, it'll slip in easily.

4. Turn your computer back on and follow the directions that the Add New Hardware Wizard gives you. Your computer will automatically recognize that the new hardware has been added, and so launch the wizard. If the wizard asks if you have a disk from the manufacturer, put the disk in your computer.

5. Add any extra software that came with the camera. Your camera will come with extra software, such as Netcam videoconferencing software, and software for making videos you can send via email. Put the installation CD into your computer and follow the instructions for installing the software.

Cool Tips

You Can Download Extra Software for Your Web Video Camera

There's a lot of software you can use with your Web video camera, such as video-mail software, software for making videos, videoconferencing software, software for turning your camera into a Webcam, and much more. Most of this software you can download and try out for free before you decide whether to buy it. And some of it you'll be able to use for free, or pay a small fee, such as $5. To find this kind of software, go to an Internet download site, such as ZDNet Downloads at www.zddownloads.com.

How to Install a Video Camera that Uses an Add-In Card

If you buy a Web video camera that needs an add-in card to work, you'll have to do a little more work. You'll be taking off your computer's case, screwing in a card, and then attaching your Netcam to it. Don't worry, it's not as hard as it sounds. In fact, it's surprisingly easy, after you get used to the idea of mucking around inside your computer. Here's what to do, and how to do it. By the way, to make this easier on yourself make sure the add-in card is a PCI one, not an ISA one (check the camera for details before you buy).

1. Turn off and unplug your computer. Never do anything inside your computer before first turning it off and unplugging it.

2. With a Phillips-head screwdriver or nut driver, unscrew the screws holding the case onto your PC. Usually three to six screws hold on the case. Some newer computers, such as some made by Dell, have the cases held on by thumbscrews instead of regular screws. If that's how your computer is held on, consider yourself lucky, because you'll only need to loosen the thumbscrews to remove the case.

3. Remove the case. You usually remove it by sliding it toward the back of the computer and then lifting it up, off a set of rails. On some computers, the case slides out from the front instead of the back.

4. Find an empty "slot" in your computer and unscrew the metal tab protecting it. You'll see a series of empty slots with metal tabs plugged into them. Unscrew the screw holding the tab in place and remove the tab. Keep the screw nearby, because you'll need it in a few minutes.

5. Insert the add-in card by pressing down evenly on its connector so that it slides smoothly into the empty slot. Be sure that the card is tight, but don't press too hard; otherwise, you'll damage the card. Figure 5.3 shows you how you'll install the card. After you install the card, screw it in. Also make sure to connect any cables to your computer's sound card, if you have to.

Figure 5.3

See, it's not so hard. Here's how to insert the card into your computer.

6. Put the case back on the computer, turn it on, and follow the directions that the Add New Hardware Wizard gives you. Your computer will automatically recognize that the new hardware has been added, and will launch the wizard. If the wizard asks if you have a disk from the manufacturer, put the disk in your computer.

7. Add any extra software that came with the camera. Your camera will come with extra software, such as Netcam videoconferencing software, and software for making videos you can send via email. Put the installation CD into your computer and follow the instructions for installing the software.

That's it! Congratulations. See, that wasn't so hard. You're now ready to use your new video camera.

Top Tips for Using Your Web Video Camera

I've got news for you: Installing the Web video camera is the easy part. Now you've got to actually use the thing. Throughout the rest of the book, I'll show you how to do cool things like creating videos and sending video mail, doing videoconferencing, creating a Netcam, and other amazing stuff. But before you do that, there are some things you should know about using your video camera. Simple things. Things like how to make sure that you don't take a video of your scalp. Like making sure the lighting is right so you don't look like you're in a coal mine five hundred feet underground. (That is, unless you *are* in a coal mine five hundred feet underground.)

So before turning yourself into a video star, follow these tips:

➤ **Position your camera properly**   Believe it or not, one of the hardest things to figure out is where to put your camera. Many people put it on top of their monitor—but if you do that, more often than not, your camera will show a nice close-up of the top of your head, your bald spot, or dandruff front and center. I find the best place for a camera is just off to the side of the monitor. If you place it directly on the desk, it'll be pointed too low, so put something underneath it to raise it up.

➤ **Focus the camera**   Most video cameras come with a focus, even though you might not realize it. The focus will be on the front of the camera, around the camera's aperture. (Aperture is just a big word for the small hole on the front of the camera.) One of the main reasons for fuzzy video is a poorly focused camera.

➤ **Take note of what's in back of you**   If you have a white wall, a light, a window, or another light source in back of you, you're in trouble. You'll often appear as not much more than a shadow in a bright space. So position yourself and your camera so you don't have a light source in back of you.

Cool Tips

Adjust the Contrast Button

Some Netcams come with a contrast button—and if yours comes with one, it'll go a long way toward giving you the best quality video. If yours has a contrast button, adjust it properly for the best contrast. Make it a habit to adjust the contrast every time you turn on your camera, because lighting conditions change frequently.

➤ **Don't point a light at your face**   Do this and your face won't be a shadow—it'll be a blur of light. So unless you're after the ghostly, otherworldly effect, don't point a light directly at you. If you need more light, point it somewhere else to provide ambient light, such as upwards, but don't point it at you.

➤ **Experiment with lamps and lighting**   Try different types of indirect lighting, such as lamps and overhead lighting, until you get a clear image, free of shadows and bright blurs.

➤ **Don't rely on the camera's built-in microphone**   Some Netcams come with built-in microphones. Don't bother with them—they're a poor quality, and often let in background noise as well. Instead, buy a separate microphone or headset.

➤ **In videoconferencing, keep your movement to a minimum**   Especially if you have a slow connection, when possible avoid sudden, quick movements. Netcams don't do a great job of handling a great deal of movement, so if possible during videoconferences or videphone calls, be careful of sudden movements.

Cool Tips

The Smaller the Video Image, the Better the Quality

When you use videoconferencing software, you have a choice of what size to make your video image. The smaller you make your image, the better quality image you'll send. Making your image smaller can make a dramatic difference in the quality of the video. I'll show you how to change your image size in Chapter 15, "Using NetMeeting for Internet Video," and Chapter 16, "Using CU-SeeMe for Internet Video."

The Least You Need to Know

➤ If you're installing a Netcam that requires an add-in card, make sure to have a Phillips-head screwdriver or nut driver for opening up the case and installing the card.

➤ Before installing a USB Netcam, check the Windows Device Manager to make sure that USB is working properly on your computer.

➤ When plugging the USB cable into your Netcam and PC, don't force the cable—it goes in only one way and should slide in easily. If it doesn't, you're using the wrong end of the cable.

➤ When installing the add-in card for a Netcam, press firmly until the card is properly installed in the slot, but don't press too hard, or you could damage the card or your computer.

➤ Position your Netcam properly—be careful if you're putting it on top of your monitor that it doesn't point mainly at the top of your head.

➤ You shouldn't have a window, bright light, or white wall in back of you when using a Netcam—it will make you look like a bright blur.

➤ Every time you turn on a Netcam, focus it and adjust the lighting so that your face isn't in shadows or isn't a bright blur.

Chapter 6

How to Set Up Scanners and Digital Cameras

In This Chapter

➤ How to buy the best scanner for you

➤ How you'll install a scanner after you've bought it

➤ How to choose and install a digital camera

You want pictures? Pictures to send to your friends and family via email (they just can't *wait* to see photos of your summer vacation to Lake Winnetonka), and pictures to post on your Web site so that the world can see your brand-new baby?

Well, if you want pictures, you'll get pictures. The best way to get pictures into your computer is with scanners and digital cameras. In this chapter, I'll clue you in on how to buy and install both.

Choosing the Right Scanner

A scanner is a great way to get pictures into your computer. With a scanner, you're able to get pictures from magazines, photographs, or any other source, and put them into your computer. Scanners are a relatively inexpensive way to get good, quality photos and other pictures into your PC. Here's what you need to know about buying a scanner.

How Does It Connect to Your Computer?

First things first. You'll have to decide how to hook the scanner up to your computer. There are three ways you can connect a scanner:

➤ Via the Universal Serial Bus (USB)

➤ Via an add-in card

➤ Via the parallel (printer) port

Let me make this decision easy for you. Choose a scanner that connects to your computer via a USB port. It's simple, it's easy, it's fast, and it produces fast scans. It's much harder to install an add-in card, and parallel port scanners have the added drawback of being slower than USB scanners. They also interfere with printers.

Tech Specs and Other Vital Information

Next, you'll have to decide on what kind of specs your shiny new scanner should have. First, a note about filthy lucre; otherwise, known as money. Scanners have quite a wide price range—you can buy them for as little as under $100, and for well over $1,000. Generally, though, plan on paying from about $125 to $250 for one, depending on its quality. Here's what to know before buying:

➤ **Decide if you need a handheld, a sheetfed, or flatbed scanner** A handheld scanner is a small scanner that you pass over a page. It's the least-expensive scanner you can buy. Stay away; it generally produces low-quality pictures and is hard to use, and you might have to electronically "stitch" together large pictures if you use one. Sheetfed scanners are used primarily by people who need to scan many documents into the computer, one after the other. The great odds are that you don't need a sheetfed scanner. The best all-around scanner is a flatbed scanner—a rectangular device onto which you put the page or picture you need to scan. It's what you most likely should get.

➤ **Check out the resolution** One of the key specs for a scanner's quality is its *resolution*. No, I don't mean how determined your scanner is to do a good job for you. Resolution is a measurement of image quality, and is measured in dots per inch (dpi). There are two types of resolutions you need to worry about—the optical resolution and the interpolated resolution. A scanner with an optical resolution of 300dpi often has an interpolated resolution of 1,200dpi. (Why, oh, why, is hardware so complicated?) I'll spare you all the techie details, but the short version is this: the more dots per inch, the better. Look for a scanner with an optical resolution of at least 300dpi, and 600dpi if you can afford it. And look for an interpolated resolution of at least 1,200dpi.

What Is Optical Character Recognition (OCR)?

Scanners do more than put pictures into your PC. They also can convert a page of text into a document on your computer, such as a Word document. Scanners do this by using the magic of Optical Character Recognition (OCR). In optical character recognition, software looks at the scanned document and converts it to a file on your computer. If you want to use OCR on your scanner, make sure that it comes with OCR software. You can also buy it separately, if you'd like.

➤ **Get the greatest color depth** The other measure of a scanner's quality is its color depth. This is measured in the total number of colors the scanner can display. Don't buy a scanner that has less than what's called 24-bit color (that translates to 16.7 million colors). Even better is 30-bit or 36-bit color. The more colors, the more realistic photographs will be.

➤ **Check out the software that comes with it** After the picture is scanned into your computer, you're going to want to do things to it before you send it to others or post it online—add special effects, resize it, put the head of your loved one onto the body of a Sumo wrestler. To do all this, you need software. Check what kind of software comes with the scanner. You want to make sure it includes some kind of graphics software for manipulating images, at a minimum.

Installing a Scanner

Your best choice for a scanner is a USB scanner—so much so that I wouldn't suggest buying any other kind. If you really must install a different kind of scanner, follow the manual and instructions. Again, though, I'd stick with USB.

For instructions on how to install a USB scanner, or virtually any other USB device for that matter, turn back a chapter and read the section titled "How to Install a USB Camera." The steps are the same (keeping in mind that you are installing a scanner and not a camera).

Cool Tips

You Can Download Extra Software for Your Scanner

There's a lot of software you can use with your new scanner—especially many different kinds of graphics software. Most of this software you can download and try out for free before you decide whether to buy it. A great one is Paint Shop Pro that lets you manipulate pictures in ways you never thought possible. To get Paint Shop Pro, go to www.jasc.com. And for Paint Shop Pro as well as many other kinds of software, go to an Internet download site, such as ZDNet Downloads at www.zddownloads.com or www.softseek.com.

Say Cheese! How to Choose the Right Digital Camera

Another great way to get pictures into your computer so you can send them to friends, family, and complete strangers if you want, is to use a digital camera. Digital cameras work just like regular cameras, except that instead of using film, they use in essence small hard disks. You then transfer the pictures from your camera to your computer via a cable of some kind. Here's what you need to know about choosing the right digital camera for you:

➤ **It's best to get a USB camera** Digital cameras typically attach to your computer either via a USB port or via a serial port. You're much better off with a USB camera than with a serial port camera. USB cameras are easier to set up, and transfer data faster than do serial port cameras.

➤ **Set a price range and stick to it** Digital cameras can be very expensive pieces of equipment—far more expensive than scanners. You won't get a high-quality digital camera for under $250, and the top-notch models run to $1,000. So before buying a camera, decide on a price and stick to it—otherwise, you'll find yourself spending far more than you meant to on the camera.

➤ **Check out the camera's resolution** You measure a camera's image quality in resolution. You'll probably remember from earlier in this chapter that you measure a scanner's image quality in resolution as well. Unfortunately, the resolution each measures is different. (Once again, welcome to the wonderful world of hardware.) In the case of cameras, resolution is measured in the same way that a computer monitor's resolution is measured—in pixels for example, 640 by 480 pixels, 1,024 by 758 pixels, 1,280 by 1,124 pixels, and so on. (A pixel is a single dot on the screen, by the way). So what does all this mean? Just keep this in mind: The higher the resolution, the better quality the image. If you're only going to use your camera to take pictures that you post to a Web site, you can get away with a lower-quality camera, because Web images should be kept small.

➤ **Buy a zoom lens if you can afford it**
Especially if you plan on taking photos of people—and in particular, if you're going to be taking close-ups of faces. Without a zoom lens, taking photos of landscapes or groups of people or similar photos will be fine, but it'll be tough to get good quality close-up without a zoom. There are two kinds of zoom lenses—those with optical zoom, and those with digital zoom. I won't go into the gory details, but optical zoom is superior to digital zoom, so that's what you should get if you have the money.

➤ **Carefully examine the LCD panel** Most digital cameras include an LCD panel that you look at to show you what your photo will look like. See how slow they update the picture you're looking at if you or your subject moves, though; some of them take a while to update the picture, and so you won't know exactly what you're taking a photo of. And some LCDs look washed-out in bright light, and so can become almost unusable. So check before buying.

➤ **Find out how much memory the camera comes with** The more memory a camera has, the more pictures it can store. Many digital cameras come with cards that contain the memory that holds the pictures. Commonly, the cards come with 4MB or 8MB of memory, although you can buy cards that store much more—as much as 96MB. That'll hold a whole lot of pictures.

➤ **See what kind of software comes with the camera** A digital camera should come with image-editing software of some kind, so at a minimum you can get rid of the dreaded red-eye effect. Microsoft Picture It is a common one, and well worth using.

What's a Megapixel?

When shopping for cameras, you might well come across the term *megapixel*. A megapixel stands for one million pixels, and so a megapixel camera is one that can capture about one million pixels of information in a picture—which means a good quality picture.

Kids Love the JamCam

Kids love digital cameras. They can take pictures and send them to their friends via email, or post them on their Web sites. But a good digital camera can easily cost hundreds of dollars. The answer: Consider buying a JamCam. It's an inexpensive digital camera built to take abuse.

How to Install a Digital Camera

If you've read this far, you know by now what I have to say about USB digital cameras—they're the ones to buy. Installing a USB camera is quite simple. Just head back to earlier in the chapter, where I show you how to install a USB scanner. You'll install a camera in the same way, so follow the same general directions, and you'll be all set.

The Least You Need to Know

➤ It's best to buy a scanner that attaches to your PC via the USB port—it's the easiest to set up, and transfers images fast as well.

➤ When buying a scanner, find out its color depth and resolution. It should have at least a 24-bit color depth, and a resolution of 300 dots per inch (dpi) or better.

➤ Digital cameras can be expensive—reasonable quality ones generally cost $250 or so, and top-quality ones can top $1,000. Because of that, it's best to choose a price you plan to pay, and stick to that.

➤ If you can afford it, get a camera with an optical zoom lens, especially if you plan to take close-ups of people.

Part 3
Cool Ways to Communicate with Email

Email. Coolness. Somehow, I bet, those two words might not be necessarily associated in your mind.

But you're wrong, wrong, wrong, as you'll see in this section of the book. In fact, there are many super-cool ways you can communicate with email. You can use special fonts, colors, and pictures. You can add customized "signatures" to your email. You can send voice email, video emails, and a whole lot more.

Oh, yes, and did I mention that you also could get voice mail, faxing, and other cool things for free?

So head on into this part. It'll forever change the way you think about humble email.

Chapter 7

Tons of Fancy Email Tricks

In This Chapter

➤ What are email signatures?

➤ How to create fancy email signatures and put them into your email

➤ How to add smileys and emoticons to your email

➤ Dressing up your email with fonts, colors, and pictures

➤ How to use special email stationery

Sure, we all use email. It's useful, but it's certainly nobody's idea of cool. Ah, but that's because you haven't delved into the mysteries of email. In fact, as I'll show you in this chapter, there are seven ways from Sunday to make your email cool. In this chapter, I'll show you how you can add your own customized special signature to your emails; how you can use fonts, colors, and pictures in your email; how to use "smileys" to express emotions; and how to use fancy formatted stationery. So come on in—you'll never think of email the same way again.

Customizing Your Email with Special Signatures

When you sign a letter, your signature imparts its own personality. Your signature might be as big and bold as John Hancock's or as incomprehensible as a doctor's; you might sign it with cute little hearts and smiley faces, or with angry-looking scrawls meant to express your existential angst and utter disdain for the normal verities of life. (Then again, maybe you just have bad handwriting.) But, however you sign it, your signature reflects you to some degree.

Pity poor email. Most of us sign off with our name only. No personality there.

Fret not. Email programs let you create your own personalized signatures that can be put at the bottom of your email messages. These signatures aren't the kind that you sign in ink. Rather, it's text and keyboard characters that are added to the bottom of your email. It can be straightforward, like your name, email address, and similar contact information, formatted with text characters and spacing. Here's an example of what I mean:

```
I Preston Gralla          I  pg@walks.net       I 19 928th St.
I Minister of Silly Walks I  www.sillywalk.com  I Suite C
I Python, Inc.            I  Can U Walk the Walk? I New York, NY


     ******************** Other Cool Sites ********************
     ***         Stupid Shoe Tricks at www.stricks.com    ***
     ***         Dead Parrots at www.deadparrots.com      ***
     ********************************************************
```

Cool Tips

Why Can't You Just Use a Photo or Real Art in Your Signature?

Why bother to go to the trouble of creating special signatures with text and keyboard characters, when you can easily put in a real photo or real art in your email? Because when you do that, only people with email software that reads HTML will be able to see it. And pictures and photos tend to be large, so it will take a long time to send and receive email with photos and pictures in it.

When you create a signature like this, save it as a text file using a program such as Notepad. As I'll explain later, having signatures in text files makes it easier to include the signatures in your email.

Your art can be much fancier than what I just showed you. If you're a budding Chagall of the Computer, you can create a work of art to put in at the bottom, along with your contact information, like these.

```
   /       \                                         '&'
  / /     \ \                                         #
  \ \_(*)_/ /                                         #
   \_(~:~)_/                                         _#
    /-(:)-\                                         ( # )
   / / * \ \                                        / O \
   \ \   / /                                       ( === )
    \     /                                        `---'
The Spider Liberation Front                   GuitarMania
Arachne was a victim! Free the eight-legged prisoners   Don''t fret --- we sell guitars; strings attached.
www.slf.com
```

As with simpler signatures, save these in text files, because as I'll show you later in the chapter, that's the easiest way for including them in your email signature.

Where to Get Signatures

These pictures are certainly cool-looking. But what if you're not a Picasso of the keyboard or a Chagall of the computer and you can't use the keyboard to create all this stuff? Are you fated to having a signature that's as dull as dirt? Not at all. You can still create cool, outrageous, informative, or just plain silly signatures. How to do it? Simple...steal from the best. Well, I don't mean *really* steal. I mean just kind of borrow. There are a number of Web sites that are devoted to ASCII art—art created with keyboard characters. You can take the art from those pages and use them as part of your signature.

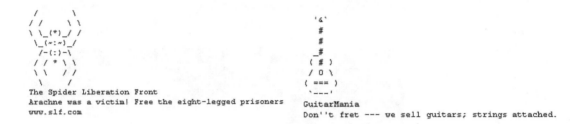

What Does ASCII Stand For?

ASCII stands for the *American Standard Code for Information Interchange*. It's a standard developed by the American National Standards Institute. Basically, ASCII characters are plain-text characters that you get by pressing keys on your keyboard.

It's easy to take the art from a Web page. Just highlight the art you want to use, copy it to the Windows Clipboard by pressing **Control+Insert**, and then copy it to a text file by using **Shift+Insert**. Figure 7.1 shows a piece of ASCII art on a Web site—and it shows the same picture copied to the Notepad, where it will be able to be used later in a signature.

Figure 7.1

Become an instant Picasso—here's how you can take ASCII art from a Web site and get it into a form that you can use in a signature.

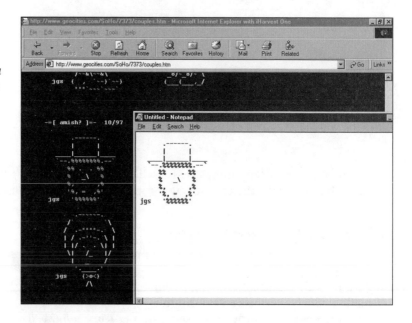

So where to get the art? Check out the following Web sites. By the way, you'll find all kinds of ASCII art at them. You should look only for the small pictures to use in your signature—larger pictures take up too much space to be suitable for signatures in your email.

Joan Stark's ASCII Art Gallery

http://www.ascii-art.com

This is a great site with a big collection of ASCII art created by one person. The art is clever, elegant, and above all, useful. All the art is copyrighted on this site, so you're using it at the discretion of the site owner. She asks that you leave the initials on the art, that you don't accept money for using the art, and a few other requests as well. The site will explain the details. You can see in Figure 7.2 some art from the site.

The Signature Museum

http://huizen.dds.nl/~mwpieter/sigs/

The Signature Museum is a big collection of ASCII art of all types, suitable for using in your signature. From animals to humor to sports and more, you'll find all kinds of art. In addition to art, there are quotes you can use in your signatures as well.

Christopher Johnson's ASCII Art Collection

http://chris.com/ascii/

This site contains a huge collection of ASCII art. A lot of it is too large to put into a signature file, but if you hunt around, you'll find something.

Figure 7.2

*Just Dragon around...
here's some of the great
art from the Joan Stark
ASCII Art Gallery.*

People Ask That You Leave Their Initials on Signature Art

When you go to these Web sites, you'll find art that many different people created and posted for all the world to see and use. On many of the pieces of art,
you'll see people's initials. It's generally considered good form to leave people's
initials on their art, even when you use it in your signature. After all, they're not
getting money for their work, but they would like some kind of recognition.

Create Your Own ASCII Art Even If You're Not an Artist

There's one other way to get ASCII art for your signatures—create it yourself with a
program designed to create ASCII art. A program called Email Effects is ideal for the
job. There are a set of tools that let you draw using ASII characters. And you also can
import simple drawings into it, and it will automatically convert the drawing into
ASCII art. Get it from Sig Software at www.sigsoftware.com. It's shareware, so you can
download it and try it out for free. If you decide to keep it, you should pay $15.

How to Put Signatures into Your Email

So, you've created a signature. Now it's time to use it. What do you do?

Pretty much any email program worth its salt (or its pepper, for that matter) includes an automated way to put signatures at the bottom of your email. I'll cover how to do it in Outlook. Check your email program, such as Eudora, for how to do it there. They all work fairly similarly.

You Can Use Fonts and Colors in Your Signature

There's a way to create a signature that includes not just text and keyboard characters, but fonts and colors. To do that, enable your email program to send HTML email as I outline later in this chapter. Then when you create a signature with the Signature Picker as you will see in this section, and you get to the Edit Signature screen, you can add fonts and colors.

To put in signatures in Outlook, first choose **Options** from the **Tools** menu, and then click the **Mail Format** tab. Near the bottom of the page, you'll see a box for **Signature Picker**. Click that—it'll let you create your first signature. When you click, you'll see a screen like the one pictured in Figure 7.3. Note that, depending on the version of Outlook or Outlook Express you use, the way you do this might differ slightly.

Figure 7.3

Your John Hancock goes here: Here's how to get started to create a signature in Outlook.

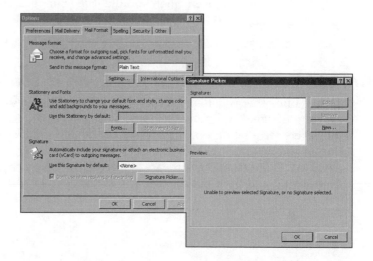

Click **New** and you'll see the screen pictured in Figure 7.4. Give the signature a name. Now you have a choice. You can either start off with a blank signature, or else use an existing file to create the signature. If you've been a good boy or girl, and saved your signature in a text file like I recommended previously, your work is pretty much done—click the button that lets you use a file as a template, choose the text file, and that's all she wrote—you're done. A signature file will now be created that will be put at the end of the emails you send out.

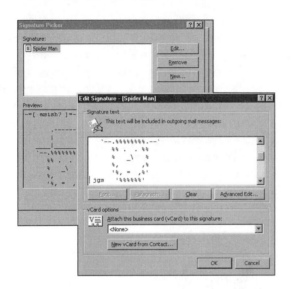

Figure 7.4

Getting down to the nitty-gritty: Here's how to create the signature.

If you haven't created the signature yet, or want to create it from scratch, click **Start with a blank signature**. Create the signature in the screen that appears. A word of warning here: The screen you're given doesn't work very well. So click the **Advanced Edit** button. That'll launch the Windows Notepad, where it will be much easier to create a signature. (Note: Depending on your version of Outlook, the menus for doing this might be in a different location.)

Create the signature in Notepad, save the file, and then exit the program. That's all there is to it. Your signature has been created.

No matter which way you create your signature, it will be automatically added to your email every time you create a message. You can create more than one signature and choose among them whenever you send out email, by using the Signature Picker. And if you don't want to use signatures on some emails, use the Signature Picker to choose to use no signature on them.

You Can Send a "vCard" as Your Signature

Outlook enables you to send what's called a vCard instead of your signature on email. A *vCard* contains your vital contact information, such as name, address, email address, phone number, and similar information. The vCard can be imported directly into a personal information manager such as Outlook, and will automatically create a contact for the person who sends a vCard. It's a very convenient way to send your contact information. To send a vCard as your signature, first create contact information about yourself in Outlook. Then, when you create a new signature, click **New vCard from Contact** in the Edit Signature screen from the Signature Picker. After that, choose your own contact information. Now, whenever you send an email, it will include your vCard.

How Much Information Should You Include in a Signature?

The perennial question: How much information should you include in your signature? Do you want to write a confessional and tell your whole life story, or be like Joe Friday and just include the facts, Ma'am? For business email, include as much contact information as possible, such as all your email addresses, various phone numbers, cell phones and pagers, and your real-life address. For your cool Net identity, you'll want to instead throw in as many confusing, mysterious-seeming ASCII characters as possible, and an anarchist slogan or two. As outlined in this chapter, most email software lets you create several email signatures, and then choose among them when sending email.

Put on a Happy Face: Using Smileys in Email

Have you ever noticed those cute little smiley faces like these—:] :) :) ;)—in email you've gotten? Yes, they suffer from terminal cuteness, I agree. But they also happen to be a very convenient way to express emotions in email. Smileys are also called *emoticons* because they're generally used to express emotions. Some people call them emoticons because they're a cross between emotion and icons.

There are zillions and zillions of smileys floating around in cyberspace. Here are just a few of them. Use them at will (or at Fred or at Hermione, for that matter). To use them, just create them with your keyboard and put them in your email. Check the tear card in this book for a list of emoticons. Here are a few of the most popular:

:-)	The original smiley; shows humor or happiness
:-(	A frown; shows sadness
=:-O	A frightened smiley
$-)	You just won the lottery

Cool Tips

Common Abbreviations and Cybershorthand You'll Use for Email

In addition to emoticons, many people use abbreviations and cybershorthand phrases in their email. Here are the common ones:

ASAP	As soon as possible	<g>	Grin> grin>
<bg>	Big grin big grin>>	IMHO	In my humble opinion
BTW	By the way	L8R	Later
F2F	Face to face	LOL	Laughing out loud
FWIW	For what it's worth	ROF	Rolling on the floor
FYI	For your information	ROFL	Rolling on the floor, laughing

Dressing Up Your Email with Fonts and Colors

There are other cool ways to dress up your email than to just use keyboard characters and ASCII art. You also can dress up your email with fonts and colors and more.

To do that, you'll need an email program that can handle HTML (Hypertext Markup Language). HTML is the language of the Web, and these days, most email programs—including Outlook, Outlook Express, Netscape Navigator's mail program, and Eudora, among others—can all handle HTML.

How you'll add fonts, colors, and other HTML-like things will vary depending on which program you use. Here I'll cover Outlook, so check your program to see how it works in yours.

Before you can use fonts, colors, and other HTML stuff, you need to set up Outlook's options properly. Considering how confusing a program Outlook can be, they're probably not already set up correctly. To use fonts and col-

Cool Tips

Check Out This Web Site for More Emoticons

For more emoticons than I have listed here, check out the Bronwen & Claire's Really Huge Emoticon Collection! on the Web at `http://www.angelfire.com/hi/hahakiam/emoticon.html`.

ors, you'll have to enable the program to send mail as HTML. To do that, choose **Options** from the **Tools** menu, then click the **Mail Format** tab. At the top part of the tab, where it says **Send in this message format**, choose **HTML**. (Depending on your version of Outlook, the menus might be located in different places.)

Now create a new message as you normally would in Outlook. To add fonts, colors, and other cool stuff to your message, you'll need to use a special formatting toolbar. Depending on how you've set up Outlook, it might or might not be visible. To make it visible, choose **Toolbars** from the **View** menu, and make sure the **Formatting** option is checked. When you do that, the toolbar appears as shown in Figure 7.5. Magic!

Figure 7.5

Here's the toolbar you'll use in Outlook to add fonts, colors, and other cool stuff to your email.

You use this toolbar just like any other toolbar in Windows. You change the font, font size, and text attributes (such as bold, italic, and so on) in the same way as you do in a word processor. To change the color, click the palette icon and choose a color.

After you're done fancying up your email, just send it off. Keep in mind that the person at the other end will only be able to see all your fonts and colors if he has an email reader that reads HTML.

Adding Links and Pictures in Your Email

Outlook and other email software also let you place pictures and hyperlinks in your email. It's easy to do. To place a picture in your email, choose **Picture** from the **Insert** menu and then browse to the picture you want to insert. It'll be placed directly into your email, as you can see in Figure 7.6. At times, people who receive your email won't see the picture in your email—instead they'll receive it as an attachment. There's nothing you can do about it; if that happens, it's because of the email program they use.

There are many ways you can get pictures to attach to your email, such as using a digital camera, a Netcam, and a scanner. They're all covered elsewhere throughout this book. One other way: When you have photos developed, check the box for using Kodak's PhotoNet. When you do that, your photos will be made available to you on the Web, and you can download them to your computer and use them in emails and for other purposes.

You create a link to a Web page in a similar way to how you insert a file. To create a link in your email, choose **Hyperlink** from the **Insert** menu and then follow the directions for inserting a link. You also can type the link directly into your mail message, and it'll be automatically created.

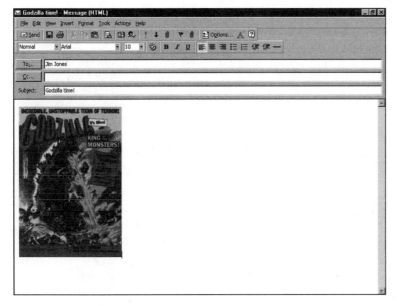

Figure 7.6

Here's what a picture looks like inserted into an email message in Outlook.

Walkie the Talkie

Don't Confuse Inserting a Picture with Inserting a File

Outlook can be very confusing when it comes to inserting pictures. If you follow the instructions I've given for inserting a picture, you'll insert a picture right into your email message so that people see it when they open your email. However, you also can send a picture or other file as an attachment—and in that case, they won't see the picture. Instead, it will be attached to the file. They can detach it and view it that way. Send files as attachments if you're not sure if the person has email software that reads HTML, because if he doesn't, he won't be able to see the picture. He will, however, be able to detach and view the picture. Turn to Chapter 8, "Tons of Fancy Multimedia Email Tricks," for more information about how to attach files to messages.

The Envelope, Please! Using Stationery in Your Email

Fonts, colors, and other fancy tricks are nice to use in your email. But let's say you want to get *really* fancy—you'd like your email to look as elegant, playful, or weird as you want.

It's easy to do, depending on email software. Some email software lets you do this, and others don't. Here I'll cover how to use stationery in Microsoft Outlook. Check your particular email program to see if it supports stationery, and if it does, how to use it.

What Is Stationery, Anyway?

To start off, let's get straight what stationery is. Email *stationery* is a lot like stationery for snail mail (that's shorthand for the U.S. Postal Service). It personalizes your email with a certain look—with a set of graphics, fonts, and colors that forms the background or border to your email. And best of all, you can alter your stationery depending on to whom you're sending the email.

In some instances, the stationery will be nothing more than a graphic at the top or side of your email, along with a set of colors and fonts that will be used whenever you type text. In other instances, the stationery is almost the entire email itself—you'll merely need to add a few words, and your email will be done. An example of this is a party invitation in which you only need to type your name, and the details of when the party is taking place (My house, New Year's Eve, you bring the champagne and the appetizers).

How to Use Stationery in Your Email

Outlook makes it easy to use stationery. (If you use a different piece of email software, check whether it uses stationery, and if so, how it uses it.) In fact, its use is built right into the program itself, and the program includes a lot of pre-built stationery ready for you to use.

Only HTML Email Software Can Read Stationery

Be forewarned that only email software that reads HTML will be able to make sense of the stationery you send out, and display the pictures, colors, and fonts you use. To software that doesn't read HTML, it'll just look like a bunch of code. Among the email software that can't read HTML is America Online's email.

Before you can use stationery, enable Outlook to send email as HTML, as I outlined earlier in the chapter. After you've done that, choose **Options** from the **Tools** menu, and then click the **Mail Format** tab. Now click **Stationery Picker**. You'll see the screen shown in Figure 7.7. (The menus may be located in different places depending on which version of Outlook you use.)

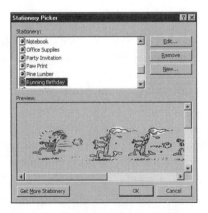

Figure 7.7

Pick a peck of stationery: Here's how to choose which stationery to use in Outlook email software.

As you scroll through the stationery, you'll see a preview of what the stationery will look like. Choose the stationery you want. Then the next time you create an email message, it'll create the message using the stationery. Shown in Figure 7.8 is an example of an email message created with stationery.

Figure 7.8

Happy birthday to who...here's an example of stationery used to create a birthday message.

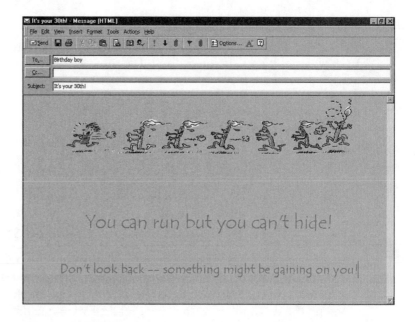

When you choose a piece of stationery using the Stationery Picker, that stationery will be used as your default—in other words, every time you create an email, it'll be used. To use different stationery, or none at all, use the Stationery Picker again and choose the stationery you want, or choose not to use any.

Creating Your Own Stationery

Feeling creative? I hope so. Because you're not limited to using the stationery built into Outlook. You also can create your own. To do that, get back to the handy-dandy Stationery Picker. Then click **New**. You'll see the following screen, which asks you to give a name to your stationery, and then asks how you're going to create it. You can start with a blank page, you can choose to start with an existing piece of stationery, or you can choose a file to use as the starting point for your stationery. If you choose a file, it has to be an HTML file that has pictures, colors, fonts, and other HTML commands built into it.

In the next screen, you'll be asked to choose the font you want to use and the picture or background color you want to include, as you can see in Figure 7.9. After you do that, you're done—you now have your own customized stationery (see Figure 7.10). It will show up in Stationery Picker, and you can use it in the same way that you can use any other kind of stationery.

Figure 7.9

Let your creative juices flow—here's how to start to create your own stationery in Outlook...

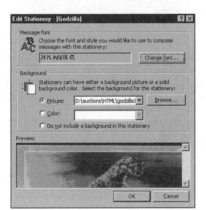

Figure 7.10

...and here's how to finish. You now have your own customized stationery.

Cool Tips

It's Easy to Get More Free Stationery

Outlook ships with a fair amount of stationery built into it. But if you want even *more* stationery to choose from, it's there for the taking. To get it from the Internet, click **Get More Stationery** from the Stationery Picker. You'll be sent to a Microsoft Web site that has free stationery you can download and use for free.

The Least You Need to Know

➤ Use email signatures to include contact information about yourself, and to customize your email with personal information and even pictures.

➤ The Web is an excellent source of art for your signatures. A good Web site to find signature art is http://www.ascii-art.com.

➤ Save your signature in a text file; most email programs will directly import signatures from them.

➤ Smileys or emoticons like this—:)—are a good way to dress up your email.

➤ To use fonts, colors, and pictures in your email, enable your email program to use HTML. Then use the toolbar for adding fonts, colors, and pictures.

➤ Stationery includes a set of pictures, colors, and fonts that customizes the way that your email looks to others.

HEY!!

Chapter 8

Tons of Fancy Multimedia Email Tricks

In This Chapter

➤ How to attach files to your email messages

➤ How to record videos for sending via email

➤ All the ways you can send video mail

➤ How you can record sounds and voices for sending via email

➤ All the ways you can send voice email

➤ How you can send free multimedia greeting cards via email

In the last chapter, you learned about fancy email tricks such as using fonts, colors, and pictures inside your email messages. Well, as the immortal Al Jolsen said (more or less): "You ain't seen nothing yet!"

There's all kinds of other amazing tricks you can do with email—fancy multimedia tricks. Things like sending talking email postcards or video mail. Things like sending voice email and greeting cards. And even things like sending and receiving email and email voice mail without even using a computer—you'll do it just by using your telephone.

You'll learn how to do all that and more in this chapter. What are you waiting for? Let's get started.

How to Send Attachments in Your Email

To do many fancy multimedia email tricks, you'll need to know how to attach files to mail messages, so we'll start there.

One of the simplest ways to send video mail and voice email is to attach a sound or video file to your email message. Then the person receiving it can detach the file and play it. Nothing could be easier.

How you attach files will vary according to what email program you use, but the general idea is the same, no matter which one is yours. Here I'll cover how to attach a file in Outlook.

Walkie the Talkie

Record Your Videos and Sounds in Popular Windows Formats

If you create your video or sound files in the most popular file formats—.wav for sound and .avi for video—you can be sure that whoever you send the files to will be able to play them. Windows includes programs that can automatically play .wav and .avi files.

To attach a file when you're creating a message, click the little **paper clip** icon in the toolbar on the top of your screen. You'll then be able to browse to the directory where you have the file you want to attach—and it can be any kind of file you want, not just video and sound files. When you click the icon, an **Insert File** box will come up that will let you browse to the file you want to add. Choose the file you want to add, click **OK**, and your file is ready to go. You can see the process in Figures 8.1 and 8.2.

Depending on how you've set up   Outlook, there's a chance that the little paper clip icon won't be in your toolbar. If it isn't, don't worry, you can still insert files. To do it, click the **Insert** menu and then choose **File** and then follow my previous instructions.

By the way, when sending voice, video, pictures, or any other kind of attachments via email, realize that some of these files can get big—and I mean *real* big, gargantuan, mammoth, super-sized...you get the idea. So be very careful what you send, because if you send a large file, it will tie up the computer of the person receiving your email for a very long time, and you'll have made someone very unhappy. So check the file size before you send.

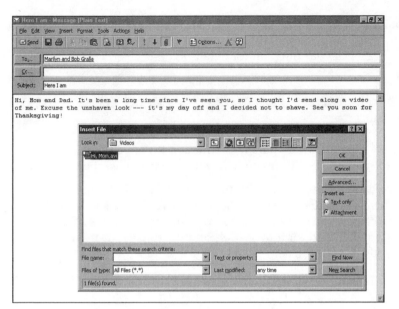

Figure 8.1

*As easy as one, two...After you click the **paper clip** icon, this dialog box appears, letting you choose the file you want to attach to your message.*

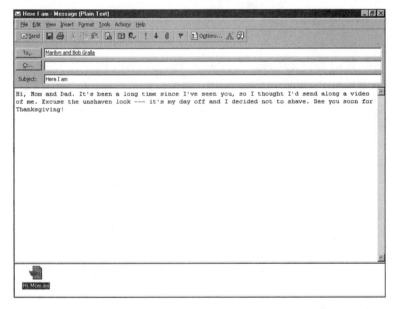

Figure 8.2

After you attach the file, here's what it looks like.

If you're lucky enough to be connected to the Internet at very high speeds, such as over a cable modem, pay particular attention to this. You'll be able to send a large file in very little time, so you might not realize how big the attachment is—and the person receiving it on a phone line will be tied up receiving the large file.

By the way, at any point before receiving email, you can make sure that large attachments won't tie up your PC. Some email software lets you limit the size of the email attachment you receive. Check your program for details.

Lights, Camera, Action! How to Record and Send a Video File

Makeup, please! If you're going to send video mail, the first thing you have to do is have a video to send to someone. So it's time for you to record a video file.

Don't break out in a cold sweat—it's actually quite easy to do. If you've installed a Netcam, you already have software on your PC that will let you record a video. (For information on how to choose the best camera for you, turn to Chapter 4, "How to Choose a Web Video Camera." And for information on how to set it up after you've bought it, turn to Chapter 5, "How to Set Up and Use a Web Video Camera.")

Mayday

Beware of the Installation Program for Software for 3Com's HomeConnect Camera

The Netcam I use is a 3Com HomeConnect USB camera. I love the camera, but the installation program that came with it was the worst I have ever seen. The program installed all the basic software—what I needed to get the camera running—with no problem. But then every time I used the built-in installer for installing the extra software—such as software for recording videos, and for putting a Webcam on a Web site—my computer crashed. Finally, I ignored the installer, and manually installed each program individually. So although I recommend buying the camera, I also recommend getting ready to call tech support when you install the extra software. Unless, that is, they've fixed the installation problem by now.

I'll show you how to record a video using the popular PictureWorks Live program that comes with the 3Com HomeConnect USB camera and others. If you have different software, follow the instructions on it for recording a video.

You'll find that it's quite simple to make a video. First start the program, in this instance PictureWorks Live. Smile! When you start the program, you'll see yourself—or whatever the camera is pointed at—in the program. You can see the camera pointed at some weird-looking guy in Figure 8.3.

Figure 8.3

Who is that handsome devil? Oh, that's me! When you launch PictureWorks Live, you'll immediately see whatever the camera is pointed at.

To record a video, click the **Record** button. You're on! As soon as you click that button, whatever you do and say—or whoever you point your camera at—will be recorded. When you're done recording, click **Stop**. Yes, you guessed it—the video will stop recording. The program will automatically put the video clip in an area where you can see it and preview it. You can keep making videos this way and can create multiple videos, one right after another. Figure 8.4 shows the program with several video clips.

Figure 8.4

Am I seeing in triplicate? Here's how you'll save one or more videos using PictureWorks Live.

To preview any of the clips, click it and then click **View**. You'll be able to preview what your video will look like. (Don't worry if you don't like how you look. No one except movie stars and egomaniacs can stand to watch videos of themselves.) When there's a video you want to save, click it, choose **Save As** from the **File** menu, and then save the file. After you've saved the file, you can attach it to an email message. You've done it! You've just sent your first piece of video mail. In PictureWorks, you'll save the video in a popular file format called AVI. Other programs may store them in AVI or other file formats.

There Are Several Video File Formats

When you record and play video clips on your computer, they'll be stored in one of several different file formats. Popular ones include QuickTime, MPG, and AVI. Before recording a file in one of those formats, make sure the person you're sending it to has the proper software for playing it.

Top Tips for Making a Video with a Netcam

When you make a video using a Netcam, you want to make sure that the lighting is right, that the camera is properly focused, and similar details. To get advice on all that and more, turn to Chapter 5.

How to Use Video Mail Programs

There's yet another way to send video mail to someone—use a program designed from the ground up for sending video mail. There are many of these programs out there. Some include components for recording the video as well as sending it in a special format, whereas others include only components for sending.

Check the software that came with your Netcam, because a lot of them ship with this kind of software. If yours doesn't come with one, you can get a free program, called NetCard, from the PictureWorks site at www.pictureworks.com.

NetCard takes a video and essentially puts it inside a kind of email postcard that includes a written message from you, and then sends the whole thing using your existing email program. When a person gets the video mail, they'll get it as an attachment to an email from you. All they need to do is detach the file, double-click it, and they'll see your video, along with your message, all inside a nice-looking postcard-like format. Figure 8.5 is an example of what NetCard sends.

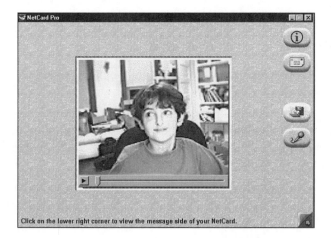

Figure 8.5

Here's a video mail of my son Gabe, sent with the NetCard program.

Cool Tips

There Are Other Video Mail Programs as Well

NetCard isn't the only video mail program—there are many others as well. You'll find many that you can try out for free before deciding whether you want to buy them. You can find them at Internet download sites such as ZDNet Downloads at www.zddownloads.com. Search on **video**, **videomail**, or **video mail** to find them.

Sound, Please! Recording and Sending Sound Files

One of the easiest ways to send voice email is to record a sound file, and send it, in the same way that you send video mail. To do this, you won't even need extra software—there's simple-to-use software to do this, built right into Windows. Clever of Microsoft to do that, wasn't it?

The program is called Sound Recorder, and in most versions of Windows you get to it by clicking the **Start** menu, then choosing **Programs**, **Accessories**, and then **Entertainment**, and finally **Sound Recorder**. If you want a shortcut to it, or if you can't find it for some reason, click the **Start** button, choose **Run**, and then run the file **sndrec32.exe**.

Whichever way you get there, it's easy to record your voice with the Sound Recorder. Click the little red **Record** button on the right side of the screen, and speak clearly into your microphone. As you record, you'll see a supercool oscilloscope-looking thing on the Sound Recorder that measures high-tech sound stuff as you record, as you can see in Figure 8.6.

Figure 8.6

*Here's the supercool-
looking oscilloscope-
display used by the Sound
Recorder as you record
your sounds.*

When you're done recording, click the **Stop** button. You can listen to what you've recorded by clicking the **Play** button. When you record something that you want to save for posterity, choose **Save** from the **File** menu, and save the file.

That's it! You're a recording star. To send voice email, just attach the file to an email message, and whoever gets the message will be able to listen to you loud and clear.

By the way, there's a chance that your microphone won't work because its settings are incorrect. If your microphone won't work, check your computer's documentation to see how to get to the Volume Controls and make sure that the microphone's volume control is not set to "mute." If it is, uncheck the "mute" box. If this still doesn't work, call tech support.

Make Sure You Have a Sound Card and a Microphone

Before you can record sound, you'll need to have a working sound card and microphone. The microphone might be one you plug into your computer, or it might be built into the computer itself. For more details on how to set up sound cards and microphones, turn to Chapter 3, "Setting Up Sound Hardware."

The Sound Recorder works fine for simple records of your voice. But if you're an audiophile, and want to do fancier stuff, there's a lot of software that can do that for you. My favorite is one called Cool Edit, available from Syntrillium Software at www.syntrillium.com. The software does amazing things—you can add sound effects, play around with the sound, and cut and paste sounds. Very cool. You can download a free version to try out, and if you decide to keep it, you can then pay Syntrillium.

How to Use Voice Email Programs

Many of the video mail programs I told you about earlier in the chapter also will let you send voice email as well, so it's worthwhile checking them out. Additionally, there are some programs, like RocketTalk, that are designed specifically to record and send voice email. You can get RocketTalk at www.rockettalk.com. And to find other, similar programs, go to an Internet download site such as www.zddownloads.com. These programs all work differently. Many work in concert with your own email program, whereas others go their own way and do it all themselves. Choose the one right for you, try it out for free, and you'll be on your way.

Supercool Web-Based Voice Email Services

There's an even cooler way to send voice email than by sending files as attachments. You can go to one of the free Web-based services that let you send voice email directly from them, or more amazing still, let you send voice email from your telephone, or even have your email read to you over the telephone when you're away from the Internet. (If you're like me, though, you're *never* away from the Internet, except perhaps when you sleep.)

Cool Tips

A Benefit of Web-Based Voice Email Is That No Large Files Are Sent

One of the benefits of using Web-based voice email such as the ones I cover here is that usually the sound files themselves are not sent over the Internet, and so the recipient doesn't have his computer tied up for a long time. Instead, a link is sent, so the person can follow the link and then listen to the mail at their leisure.

These services are all different, all idiosyncratic, and all pretty amazingly cool. I'll cover two of them in this chapter. For more information about other free, cool communication services such as free faxing, free email, free voice mail, and more, turn to Chapter 10, "Getting and Using Free Email, Voice Mail, Faxes, and Other Services." With many of them, you don't send the sound file itself over the Internet. Instead, you send a link via email. The person clicks a link, and is then sent to a Web page where they can listen or else the file is delivered to them via the link.

Sending Voice Email with OneBox

My favorite way to send voice email on the Web is with an amazing free service called OneBox. I'll cover all the ins and outs and ups and downs of OneBox in Chapter 10 because it does a lot more for you than just let you send voice email. But here, I'll show you how to send voice email using it.

Head to the OneBox site at www.onebox.com, or else to one of the OneBox's partner sites, such as www.zdnetonebox.com. After registering for the service, you'll have your own free email box that, among many other things, lets you send and receive voice email.

When you compose a message using OneBox to send a voice email, click the **Compose As Voice** button. Then when a new screen appears, click **Record**. Your voice will be automatically recorded. All the usual rules apply: Click **Stop** to stop, click **Playback** to listen to what you've recorded, and click **Send** when you're happy with the voice email you've composed. When you send the voice email, the actual voice file doesn't get sent over the Internet. Instead, the person you're sending the message to gets a notice they have a voice email and a link to it. When they click the link, they're sent to a page where they can listen to the voice email. Figures 8.7 and 8.8 show how you compose a message, and then how the person listens to it, after he follows the link he's received in the mail.

Figure 8.7

Here's how you compose a voice email with OneBox...

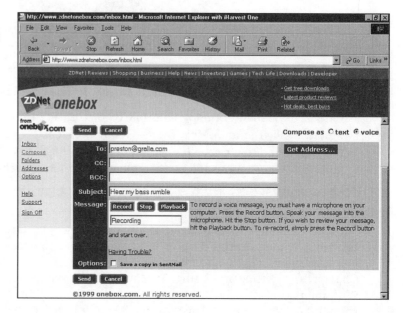

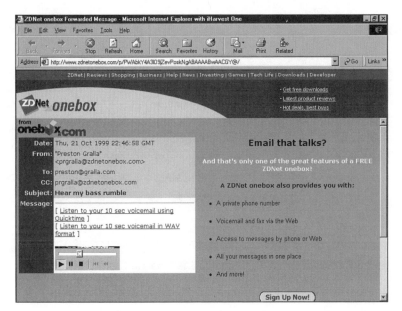

Figure 8.8
...and after the email is sent, and the recipient follows the link, here's where he will hear your message.

Using the Mind-Bending Voice Email Services of ShoutMail

ShoutMail, another free voice email service, is even more amazing than OneBox. The twist on this one is that you can send and receive email and voice email without even using a computer! No, you don't have to be the amazing Kreskin or Harry Houdini to pull off this trick—it's all built into the service itself.

Here's how it works. After you register, if you want to send a voice email, but you're not at your computer, you dial a toll-free (800) number. Then, with your telephone touchpad, you address an email to someone. (Be prepared for a long process—touchpads weren't built to do this. But still, amazingly enough, it works, if you just persevere.) After you've addressed the email, record your message by talking into the telephone. (Telephones were built for *this* part of the process, so it's easy to do.) When you're done, send your email on its merry way. Believe it or not, you've just sent a voice email to someone—and you didn't even have to use a computer keyboard.

The recipient will get an email with a link to listen to the file. They can listen to the file in two ways: Either as a .wav file, or else using a piece of free software called RealPlayer. RealPlayer streams the message to a computer—that is, it plays the file while it's being downloaded, so that the person doesn't have to wait until the whole file downloads before listening to it. RealPlayer is free, and can be gotten at www.realnetworks.com. You can see RealPlayer and ShoutMail in Figure 8.9—in the background you can see the message sent by ShoutMail, and in front, you can see the RealPlayer playing the voice email.

Figure 8.9

Shout it from the rooftops: When you send a voice email to someone with ShoutMail, they'll be able to listen to what you said using RealPlayer, pictured here, or by listening to it as a normal .wav file.

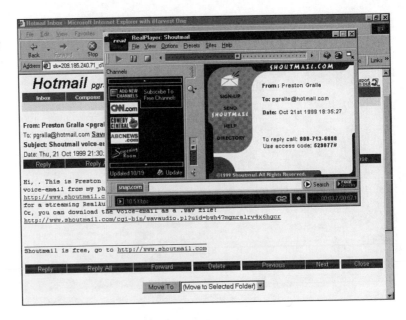

There are a whole lot more crazy tricks ShoutMail can do for you. Not near a computer, but you want to get your email? No problema. Call an (800) number, key in your username and password, and you can have your email read to you. True, it's read to you by a robot voice and takes a long time. And hearing your email spoken out loud makes you realize just how pointless some of your messages are. Still, it's an amazing way to catch up on email.

By the way, there are even more cool tricks that ShoutMail can do for you. To find out about more of them, turn to Chapter 10.

Cool Tips

RealPlayer Plays Video Files, Too

RealPlayer does more than just play sound files—it can play video files as well. It's one of the most popular ways to play video files from the Internet. Many news sites let you watch videos using RealPlayer.

How to Send Multimedia Greeting Cards

Birthdays. Anniversaries. Passover. Kwanzaa. Bela Lugosi's Birthday. National Mole Day. There are countless holidays celebrated every year. Aren't you tired of sending the same old greeting cards the old-fashioned way, via snail mail? (Hmmn…is there a National Snail Day?)

Jazz up your next greeting card. Instead of sending it via the mail, send it over the Internet. And send one that includes music, sounds, and animations. Oh, yes, and send it for free—you won't even have to pay postage.

You do this by heading to greeting card Web sites. Whereas some charge a fee, there are so many that offer the service free of charge, that I frankly think you'd have to be a bit loony to pay for one. After all, free is free.

The services all work pretty much the same. You head to a Web site, pick out a card, type your customized greeting, and then send it to whom you want to get the greeting. The person will get an email with a link in it (starting to sound familiar, isn't it?). When they click the link, they'll see the card, complete with art and, depending on the service, with animations and music and sound effects as well.

There are a whole lot of services like these on the Web. Here are some of the best.

American Greetings

www.americangreetings.com

One of the big real-world greeting card companies comes to the Internet. In addition to free email greeting cards, there are those you can pay for as well. (Although why you would want to do that, I don't know.)

Blue Mountain Arts

www.bluemountain.com

Here it is—the greeting card motherlode. You'll find more cards here than you can count, complete with pictures, music, sound, and animations. There's a card for every occasion, purpose, and holiday that you can possibly imagine—and in multiple languages. Figure 8.10 shows an example of part of a greeting card sent from the site.

Figure 8.10

One of the many multimedia greeting cards you can send from www.bluemountain.com.

Cool Tips

You Can Create Your Own Greeting Card in Your Email Program

If you know how to use HTML, the language of the Web, you can make your own greeting cards if you and the recipient have software that can read HTML. Use an HTML editor or Notepad to create a greeting card, paste it into an email message, and send it along. That's all it takes.

E-cards

www.e-cards.com

Here's a greeting card site with a twist—many of the cards offer environmental themes, and when you send cards, the company donates money to environmental groups, such as The Nature Conservancy.

Hallmark

www.hallmark.com

The greeting card giant whose name is synonymous with greeting cards comes to the Web. Big site, many multimedia cards. Free. Need I say more? Figure 8.11 shows how you create a card on the site.

USA Greetings

www.usagreetings.com

This site features many cards, most of which feature photographs. There's no multimedia here, but you'll be able to send greetings in several languages.

Figure 8.11

Hallmark, the greeting card giant, comes to the Internet. Here's how to create a greeting card on the site.

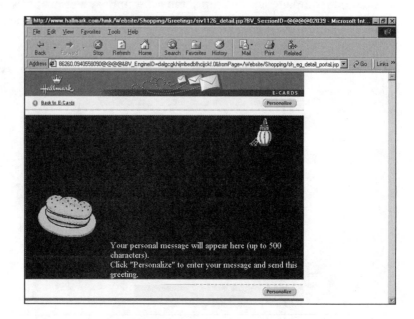

The Least You Need to Know

➤ When creating video clips or sound clips to send to others with email, create them in common Windows formats such as .avi for video files and .wav for sound files.

➤ To record a video, use the software that came with your Netcam.

➤ You can send video mail by attaching a video clip to an email message, or by using special software built especially for sending video mail, such as NetCard, which is available for free at www.pictureworks.com.

➤ You can send voice email by attaching a sound clip to an email message, or by using special software built especially for sending voice email. The software is available at many Internet download sites, including www.zddownloads.com.

➤ Some Web sites, including www.onebox.com and www.shoutmail.com, let you record and send voice email for free.

➤ You can send multimedia greeting cards for free from many Web sites, including www.bluemountain.com and www.hallmark.com.

Chapter 9

Fancy Email on America Online

In This Chapter

➤ How to add fonts and colors to your email

➤ Adding pictures to your email

➤ How you can add an attachment to email

➤ Dressing up your email with smileys, signatures, and stationery

➤ Adding hyperlinks to your email

➤ How to use You've Got Pictures

➤ Other cool, fancy email tricks

All you America Online users have probably looked at all the other chapters covering cool things to do with email and thought: Why not me? Why can't I do all those supercool things?

There's good news—you can. In this chapter, I'll show you how to fancy up your email with pictures, colors, fonts, and more. I'm not going to cover the basics of email here, because I assume you already know how to do things like create and read messages. Instead, we'll focus on the fancy stuff. By the way, this chapter was written about version 5.0 of America Online. If you have an earlier version, you might not be able to get the software to do all this stuff, or the options might be available in locations other than the ones I refer to, so check what version you have before starting. And consider upgrading to the newest version of America Online—it's free!

Dressing Up Your Email with Fonts and Colors

Plain everyday text on a white background? *Boooring!* Why bother with simple black-on-white text when America Online lets you go color-mad and font-crazy? You can express yourself in Technicolor and crazy (and not-so-crazy) fonts with America Online email.

It's simple to do. Start off by creating a new email message by clicking the **Write** icon on top of the screen. Figure 9.1 shows you what you'll see when you create a new message.

Figure 9.1

They've got mail! Here's how you'll create mail on America Online—and where you'll be able to add colors and fancy fonts to your email.

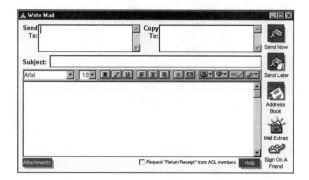

Right here you have all the controls you need for changing fonts and colors. Here's how to do it.

Getting Fancy with Fonts

Dressing up your email with fonts is easy. To change fonts, use the toolbar just underneath the Subject line. You change fonts in America Online the same way you do when changing fonts in any Windows document. (By the way, when you take the actions outlined here, it'll affect all text you type from then on. If you want to just affect certain text, first highlight the text, and then follow these instructions.) Here's how to do it:

➤ To change the font, click the leftmost downward arrow and choose the font from the list that appears. You'll be able to choose any font on your system.

➤ To change the font size, click the next downward arrow to the left and choose the size from the list that appears. Note that you can only choose from these sizes—unlike in Windows, you can't type a different size from the ones that are listed.

➤ To change the type to bold, italic, or underlined, choose the corresponding icons marked as **B**, **I**, and **U**.

➤ To change whether the text should be aligned left, center, or right, choose the proper icon.

Who Are You Calling a Dingbat?

If you'd like, you can insert special small pictures in your America Online email called *dingbats*. There are many different kinds of dingbats, ranging from a tiny mailbox to a small sign of the Zodiac to a small picture of the mouse, and many others. To insert a dingbat, change the font to **Wingdings** and press a key. Instead of a letter, there will be a dingbat. Unfortunately, there's no list of what letters create what dingbats, so you'll have to either accept getting a random picture, or memorize your favorite ones.

That's all there is to it. So go hog wild—dress up your email with crazy fonts and dingbats.

Colorizing Your America Online Email

It's just as easy to add colors to your America Online email as it is to change fonts. You'll use the same toolbar as you do for changing fonts. To change color of text before you start typing, click the button with the blue-colored **A**, and choose your color. If you have text that you want to change the color of, first highlight the text, and then change the color in the way I just explained. To change the background color of your email, click the button that has the gray-colored **A** against a blue square background, and you'll be able to change the background color of the email. If you want to change the background color of a portion of your email, define it and then choose a color, and just the area you defined will be given the new color.

Figure 9.2 shows how to change colors in your email in America Online.

Figure 9.2

Easier than a coloring book: Here's how to change email colors on America Online.

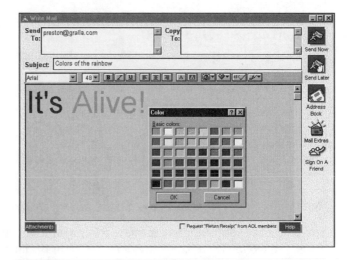

Worth a Thousand Words: Adding Pictures to America Online Email

Got a picture of your pet llama you want to send to your mama? A picture of your hen to send to your friend? No matter what the picture, it's amazingly easy to send them in email using America Online. There are two ways you can send pictures: You can either embed them right in the email message itself, so that the person sees the picture right in the email message, or else you can send the picture as an attachment. Here's how to do each:

➤ **To embed the picture directly in the email** Create a mail message, then click the **camera** icon in the America Online email toolbar. Put your cursor where you want the picture to appear. Then choose **Insert a Picture** from the drop-down menu that appears, and use the box that pops up to go to the folder where your picture is and choose it. You'll be able to preview the picture before putting it into your email. After you choose it, it will be put into your email. You can see in Figure 9.3 and Figure 9.4 how to choose the picture, and what the picture looks like in the email message.

➤ **To attach a picture to your America Online email** Click the **Attachments** button at the bottom of the email screen. From the screen that appears, click **Attachments** again (sheesh! Couldn't they save a few steps here?) and browse until you get the file you want to attach. Then choose it and send it. It'll be attached to your mail message, so it won't be visible in the message itself. Instead, someone will have to detach the picture to view it. You can send any kind of attachments, including video clips or other files. By the way, when you get a message with an attachment in it, you click the **Attach** button at the bottom of the email screen, then click **Detach** to detach the message.

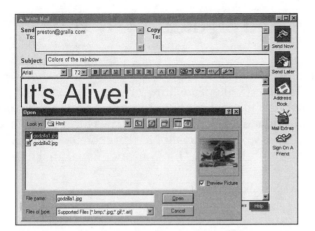

Figure 9.3

It's monstrously easy to embed a picture into America Online email. First you choose the file...

Figure 9.4

...and then it appears in your email. Godzilla rules!

Cool Tips

Use a Picture as a Background for Your Email

On America Online, you can use a picture as a background to your message. When you do that, the picture will appear instead of the normal background white, and whatever you type in your message will be typed over the picture. To add a picture as a background, click the **camera** icon in the email toolbar, and choose **Background Picture**. Then choose the picture you want to appear as a background and it'll be put in as the background.

Smile! Using Smileys and Signatures in Your AOL Email

You don't need to use pictures and fancy fonts to dress up your email in cool ways. You also can use *smileys* and *signatures*. Smileys are little pictures you can make with your keyboard that express emotions, like this one—:)—to express a joke or happiness. Signatures are quotes, contact information, or pictures you draw with your keyboard that you use to sign your email as a way to personalize it. (For more information about smileys and signatures, turn to Chapter 7, "Tons of Fancy Email Tricks.")

Only America Online Users Can See the Fonts, Colors, and Pictures You Choose

It's fun using colors, fonts, and pictures in your America Online email. But be forewarned: If you're sending the email to non–America Online users, they won't see them. Instead, they'll just see your message as plain text. So if you're sending email to people who aren't on America Online, don't bother dressing it up with colors and fonts. And only users of America Online version 3.0 or better can see them as well.

You can add smileys to your America Online email like you do any other—by using the right keyboard combination. But there's a faster way as well. Here's how to do it:

1. Click **Mail Extras** after you choose to create a message, and then click **Smileys**.

2. Double-click the smiley you want to add to your message.

3. You'll see a preview window that shows you what the smiley will look like. There will be instructions on that window to tell you how to add the smiley.

4. Instead of following the directions, you can highlight the smiley, copy it to the Windows clipboard by pressing **Control+Insert**, and then paste it into your message by going to the message and pressing **Shift+Insert**.

That's all there is to it. You can now express yourself with abandon (or with whoever else you want, for that matter) whenever you want.

It's just as easy to add a signature to your email. America Online, in fact, lets you create many signatures, and then choose among them for each email you send out. Here's how to create a signature, and then how to insert it into your email:

1. Create a mail message, click the **pencil** icon, and choose **Set Up Signatures**.

2. From the box that appears, click **Create**.

3. Create your signature. You can use fonts, colors, links, keyboard characters—the whole nine yards (and even more than nine yards if you want). In Figure 9.5 you can see a signature being created.

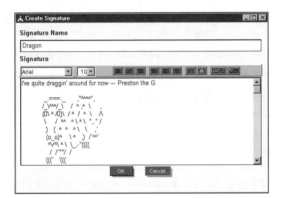

Figure 9.5

Here's how to create your personalized signature on America Online.

4. Save the signature. If you want, create more signatures this way. In fact, if you suffer from multiple personality disorder, create a whole *lot* of signatures, one for each of your personalities.

5. The next time you create an email, and you want to put in a signature, click the **pencil** icon and choose the signature you want to put at the bottom of your message. It will automatically be put at the bottom of your message.

The Envelope, Please: Using Stationery on America Online

So, signatures, smileys, colors, fonts, and graphics aren't enough for you, are they? No? Never satisfied, are you? You want *more* ways to customize your mail in cool ways on America Online, don't you?

I thought so. Well, there's more as well. America Online lets you use what it calls stationery—a set of colors and fonts, that includes your name and contact information. As with all things AOL-ish, it's easy to do. Here's how to do it:

1. Create a new mail message, click **Mail Extras**, and then click **Stationery**.

2. Double-click the stationery you want to use. You'll see a preview of what the stationery will look like in your message.

3. When you've chosen which stationary to use, click **Create**.

4. A form will appear, enabling you to personalize your stationery with things like your name, mail address, and business name. Fill out the information.

5. The stationery will now appear at the top of your email message.

You'll Have to Put in Personal Information Each Time You Create Stationery

Sometimes America Online isn't so swift and doesn't have much of a memory. Unfortunately, when you create stationery is one of those times. You would think that the first time you create stationery and put in your personal information, America Online would remember all your information. You'd think that, but it wouldn't be true. Every time you create stationery, you'll have to input your name, contact information, and any other personal information. In this case, AOL has no memory.

Using Hyperlinks in America Online Email

There are a lot of times when you'll want to send a hyperlink to a Web site when you're sending someone email on America Online. It's easy to do. After you've created a new email message, right-click the message, and then choose **Insert a Hyperlink**. You'll see the screen pictured in Figure 9.6. Fill in the description of the link (this is the text that will appear in the message), and then the location of the Web site, such as www.zdnetdownloads.com. Then, when someone clicks the link, they'll be sent to the location.

You also can insert hyperlinks that America Online has chosen for you. To do that, choose **Mail Extras** when you create a message, click **Hyperlinks**, and follow the instructions for creating a link.

Figure 9.6

Here's how to create a hyperlink in an America Online message.

How to Shut Up the "You've Got Mail" Voice

Okay, already! I get it! I've got mail, I've got mail, I've got a whole lot of goshdarned mail! Do you have to keep telling me that every time I open America Online! And why are you so cheery about it—don't you know most of it is junk mail offering to sell me a bridge in Brooklyn or swamp real estate in Southern Florida?

Whew! Sorry for that rant, but I'm glad I got it off my chest. If you're like me, you're sick to death of the ubiquitous voice intoning "You've Got Mail," every time you log on to America Online. Well, guess what, friends? You don't have to put up with it anymore. You can fight back and turn it off, or instead have a different sound greeting you whenever you get mail. So as an added bonus, and just because I like you, here's my advice on how to do it:

1. Open the Control Panel by clicking the **Start** menu, and then choosing **Control Panel** from **Settings**.

2. Double-click the **Sounds** icon and scroll down to the America Online section.

3. Highlight the **You've Got Mail** entry. To silence the "You've Got Mail" voice, click the arrow in the box marked **Name** and choose **None**. You can see how to do that in Figure 9.7. Now, whenever you've got mail, you won't hear his annoying voice.

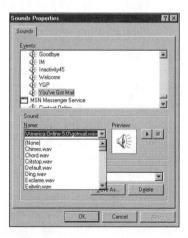

Figure 9.7

Sounds of silence: Here's how to silence the America Online "You've Got Mail" guy.

4. If you want, you can substitute a different sound to notify you that you've got mail. To do that, when you click the arrow, choose a different sound file. (They have to be in a .wav file format.) You can use sound files from any directory, by clicking the **Browse** button and browsing to that directory. After you choose the sound, you can preview it by clicking the **Preview** button. By the way, you can use this process to substitute sounds for other America Online sounds, such as the welcome or instant message notification.

Cool Tips

You Can Use HTML in Your Email

If you know how to use Hypertext Markup Language (HTML), the language of the Web, you can use it in your America Online email. HTML lets you get a great deal of control over pictures, fonts, colors, and many other things. To use HTML in your America Online email, create an HTML file with a program such as Notepad, or an HTML editor. Then right-click your email message, choose **Insert Text File** from the menu that appears, and choose the HTML file that you created. Your email will now display the HTML just like a text editor will.

Worth a Thousand Words: How to Use You've Got Pictures

It's not always easy to get pictures into your computer so that you can send them to others via email. You'll usually need a scanner, digital camera, or Netcam. (For information on how to use a scanner, digital camera, and a Netcam, turn to Chapter 5, "How to Set Up and Use a Web Video Camera," and Chapter 6, "How to Set Up Scanners and Digital Cameras.")

But what if you don't have that hardware? No problem. America Online has come up with a simple way to get pictures into your computer, with its "You've Got Pictures" feature. It's a breeze to get pictures into your computer with this feature, and you can then send those pictures to friends and family.

Just take your pictures with your camera as you normally would. Then, when you drop off your film for processing, check the AOL box. When your film is ready, pick it up as you normally would. But at the same time your film is ready, it also will be available to you online, in the "You've Got Mail" area of America Online. Just click the icon when you log on and follow the instructions.

Cool Tips

How to Find Out if You've Got Pictures Is in Your Area

The "You've Got Pictures" feature isn't available in every part of the country yet. To see if there's a film processor near you, click **You've Got Pictures** in America Online, and then click the link that gives a list of retailers that work with You've Got Pictures.

After you're in the area, you can preview the pictures, download them to your computer, and more. Including the pictures in email is easy—click the **E-Mail Picture** button, and they'll be put into an America Online email for you automatically, and you can send them to who you want. And after you save them to your computer, you can send them in email the same way you send any other pictures, as outlined earlier in the chapter.

Turning Your Address Book into a Picture Album

You no doubt use your America Online Address Book to keep the email addresses of people you often correspond with. But you probably never realized that you also can use it as a picture album—you also can keep pictures of people in there as well. It's easy to do it. For any contact whose picture you want to add, click **Picture** tab on their listing in the Address Book. Then click **Select Picture** and browse to the directory where you put the picture (pictures can be in .gif, .jpg, or .bmp formats). Select the picture and, along with the person's contact information, you'll have a photo of them as well. Pictured in Figure 9.8 you can see one of the larger friends in my Address Book.

Figure 9.8

A picture of one of my favorite buddies in my America Online Address Book.

Cool Tips

Create a Mailing List in Your Address Book

Let's say that you need to often send out an email to a group of people—family, friends, a PTA group, your CIA sewing circle. It's a pain to individually address that email message to many people. Instead, create a mailing list, so that you'll only need to send the mail to a single address, which will then automatically send the mail to everyone on your list. To do it, click **New Group** in your Address Book. Name the group (such as **CIA Sewing Circle**). Then in the **Addresses** box, put in the screen names and Internet email addresses of everyone who you want to include on the list. Make sure to separate each name with a comma. That's it—you've just created a mailing list.

The Least You Need to Know

➤ To change fonts and colors in your email and to insert pictures and do other cool things, use the toolbar across the top of the email message you're creating.

➤ When you add a picture to your email, you can either embed it directly in the email message itself, or include it as an attachment. Only people who use America Online will be able to see the picture if you embed it in the message.

➤ Only America Online users can see the colors and fonts you use in your email—when you send the message to anyone else, they'll see it as plain text.

➤ You can change the "You've Got Mail" greeting if you want, by using the **Sounds** portion of the Windows Control Panel.

➤ The "You've Got Pictures" feature is an excellent way to get pictures into your computer that you can then send via email. Check on America Online to see if it's available in your area.

WANT SOME?
DON'T COST
NOTHIN'...

Chapter 10

Getting and Using Free Email, Voice Mail, Faxes, and Other Services

---

In This Chapter

➤ The reasons why free email accounts are useful

➤ How to get free email accounts

➤ Best sites on the Internet for getting free email accounts

➤ How to send and receive faxes for free using the Web

➤ How to send and receive free voice mail and other communication services online

---

What's many people's favorite four-letter word in the English language? Hint: It starts with an "f." No, it's not that one. I'm talking about the word "free."

There are all kinds of ways that you can communicate for free online. You can get free email boxes. You can send and receive faxes for free. You can even get your own personal voice mail box, and send and receive voice mail messages for free. I'll show you how to do all that and more in this chapter.

Why You Should Get Free Email Accounts

Free email accounts these days are a dime a dozen...well, actually, they're free, so they won't even cost you a dime. But the point is, there are a whole lot of free email accounts available to you. I have about a half-dozen of them myself.

If you're on the Internet, there's a good chance you already have an email account. So why get another one, even if it's free?

There are many reasons you might want to get a free account. Here are the main ones:

➤ **You want to be able to check your email when you're away from your own computer, but you can still get onto the Web** The free email accounts you get are all Web-based, which means that you can check your mail on them from any computer, not just your own. So if you travel without a computer, or want to check your email when using someone else's computer, it's easy to do with a free Web-based email account.

➤ **You would like to have a backup email account, in case your primary one goes down** Face it: The Internet isn't exactly the most stable and dependable technology that's ever been created. So it's possible that at times you won't be able to get to your email on your Internet service provider (ISP). If you're like me, and can't live without email, you'll want at least one backup account. A free email account will do that for you.

➤ **You want a way to stop getting spam in your email inbox** If you go to Web sites and fill out registration forms, you'll usually be asked for your email address. And after you provide it, you'll often be deluged with *spam*—unwanted junk mail that the site and its marketing partners send you. Use a free email account to stop the spam. Whenever you fill out a registration form, give the address of your free account, and the junk mail will be routed there. Pictured in Figure 10.1 is the free account I use at www.hotmail.com for that very purpose. As you can see, it's a spam magnet.

Figure 10.1

Here's my free HotMail account at www. hotmail.com, filled with spam. I use it when filling out Web registration forms, so that the junk mail heads there instead of to my main email account.

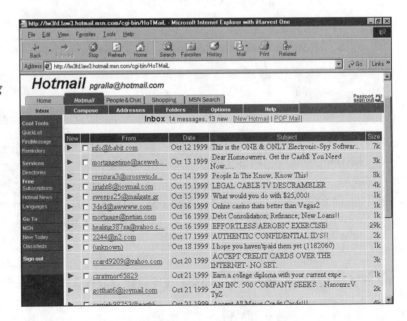

➤ **You have an email account at work, but don't have a private one**

Perhaps your office provides an email account and Internet access for you as part of your job, but you don't have a personal email account. It's generally a no-no to use your work account for private matters. And all the messages in your work email account can legally be read by your boss. (So remember, stop calling him a overpaid, overweight, overbearing son of a baboon—even if he is one.)

➤ **You just plain like to get free stuff**

Everyone likes to get something for free, even if they never use it. For what other reason would grown men and women, who make big money, stand for hours in line at trade shows to get free T-shirts from companies they've never heard of?

So even if you never use it, you might want to get a free email account. After all, there's nothing for you to pay, so what have you got to lose?

How You'll Get Free Email Accounts

The email accounts you get for free on the Web are different from the normal email accounts you're used to. With your normal email account, you use an email program like Outlook or Eudora, which connects to an email server at your Internet service provider. You send and receive email using the software on your computer, which interacts with the mail server. So when you receive mail, for example, it's transferred from the mail server to your own computer. And when you send mail, it's transferred from your own computer to the mail server.

The free email you'll get on the Web works differently. You don't use a piece of email software to send and receive mail. Instead, you

Cool Tips

There Are Many Other Ways to Combat Spam

Pitch alert! If you're annoyed by spam, and want ways to combat it other than getting a free email account, get a copy of my book *The Complete Idiot's Guide to Protecting Yourself Online*. It'll teach you how to kill spam and protect yourself in many other ways when you go online.

Walkie the Talkie

What Are POP3 and SMTP?

Spend much time around an email program, and you'll probably come across the terms *POP3* and *SMTP*. POP stands for *Post Office Protocol*, and it's what's used by most email servers to deliver mail to you. SMTP stands for *Simple Mail Transfer Protocol*, and it's what's used by email servers to send mail from you to other people.

visit a Web page. You send and receive mail directly from that Web page, not from a separate piece of email software. Pictured in Figure 10.2 is the free email account you can get at the www.zdnet.com Web site.

Figure 10.2

Free email at ZDNet: One of the many sites on the Internet that offer you a free email account.

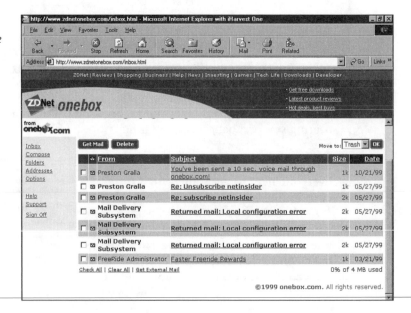

To get the free email account, you have to register at the site, and fill out a registration form of some kind. You'll then get the service for free.

Now, you've no doubt been brought up on the saying, "There is no free lunch." And you're no doubt wondering, "What's the catch?" and you're certainly wondering, "How in the world can these companies keep giving this service away?"

Good questions, all. In this case, though, there is a free lunch, and there really is no catch—the email account is truly free. As to how the companies can keep giving the service away—they make money every time you log in to send or receive email. They sell advertising on the Web pages you view when you visit them, and make money in other ways as well. That's why the free email services require you to visit a Web page rather than use a piece of email software—so they can show you ads.

To get these free accounts, all you'll have to do is sign up for them. So where to go? In the next section, I'll clue you in on some of the top free email spots on the Internet.

Cool Tips

There Is One Drawback to Free Email on the Web

There's one drawback to the free email accounts you get on the Web—you can only read and compose email when you are on the Web site. With an email program, you can read your mail when you're not connected to the Internet, and you can compose mail when you're not connected. Not so with Web email—you can only compose and read mail when you are at the site.

Where to Get Free Email Accounts

There are many places on the Internet where you can get free email accounts. Here are some of the best. There are many more than I can include here—just about anywhere you go seems to offer free email—but start off here and you won't go wrong.

Bigfoot

www.bigfoot.com

Whether you have big feet, small feet, or something in between, you can still get free email here. There are some nice, clever extra services here. You can, for example, have all your email sent to you from here automatically forwarded to any other email address of yours—and can even forward the mail to more than one account.

Excite Email

www.excite.com

Click **Free Voice mail/Email**. Excite Email offers good mail service, and it offers free voice mail as well. Especially if you're a fan of Excite, check this one out.

HotMail

www.hotmail.com

This is probably the largest free email service you'll find. It's simple to use, offers good email management, and is all-around a top pick. One of the nice features here is that you can also check your regular POP3 email accounts from this site as well, so you can check all your email in one place.

MailCity

www.mailcity.com

Free email, along with 4MB of storage space for storing your messages. It's simple to use, and it's connected to the various services offered by the www.lycos.com Web portal.

Cool Tips

You Also Can Get Free Email from Sites that Offer Free Web Pages

Some sites that let you build free Web pages, such as www.xoom.com, also offer you free email accounts. So if you frequently use one of those services, check to see if they have free email for you. For more information about sites that offer free Web pages, turn to Chapter 18, "Broadcast for Free: How to Get and Use Free Web Pages."

OneBox

www.onebox.com

This site offers more than just free email—it also offers you free faxing, free voice mail, and the capability to send voice email. I cover it in more detail in the following sections on free faxing and other services.

Yahoo! Mail

www.yahoo.com

Click **Yahoo! Mail** and use my favorite free email service, and also the one I use more than all the others. In addition to all the usual features you'd expect, it has one other very big benefit—you can configure it like your normal POP3 email, and so you can check mail from it using your normal email program. And you also can check it the normal way, from the Web. There's a lot more here as well, such as the capability to check your other email accounts from this one spot, and the capability to send greeting cards. Figure 10.3 shows how you send mail using Yahoo! Mail.

ZDNet Mail

www.zdnetonebox.com

The email on this well-known technology site is the same as that offered by OneBox, and includes all the extras that OneBox provides, including voice mail and more.

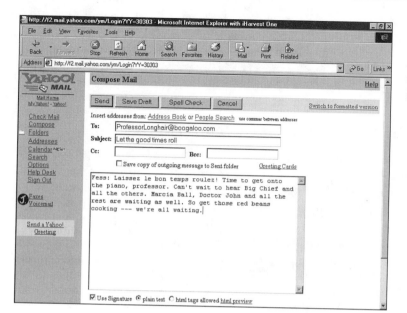

Figure 10.3

Yahoo for Yahoo! mail! Here's how you'll send mail with this excellent free email service.

Just the Fax, Ma'am. How You Can Send and Receive Faxes for Free

Here's one of the better-kept secrets of the Web: You can send and receive faxes for free. Forget fiddling around with fax machines and second phone lines, having to use and install faxing software, or having to pay a service like Mailboxes Etc. to send and receive faxes for you. You can do it for free, using sites on the Web.

Most free faxing services give you a personal fax number that's yours and yours alone. When you're sent a fax using that number, the fax is automatically converted to a graphics file, and that file is then sent to you as an attachment to an email. To view the fax, you view the attachment.

Many of these services, though, don't let you send faxes. That's where they get their money from—to send faxes, they'll ask you to pay a monthly fee. But as you'll see next, I've found services that let you send faxes for free as well.

These services are great (after all, they're free), but they have some drawbacks. When you receive a fax, for example, you won't be able to mark it up, sign it, and fax it back to someone—you can only view it or print it out. So you might be forced to print it out, mark it up, and send it via a fax machine. And when you send a fax, you can only send a document on your computer, so you'll need a scanner if you have a paper document that you want to fax to someone. Most of these sites offer for-pay services that let you mark up and send faxes, and that give you toll-free (800) numbers for your private fax line. So if you want to pay, you'll get around some of the problems offered by free fax services.

You Also Can Get Free Internet Access

Why stop at getting free email, faxes, and voice mail? Why not get Internet access for free? In fact, several companies now offer free Internet access. The main drawback is that when you dial in, you'll see ads on your screen all the time. If ads annoy you, you won't like these services. But if you can put up with them, you'll get one of the all-time great deals. Among the places that offer free Internet access are www.netzero.com and www.altavista.com.

Still, let's get real here: These services *are* free, so don't start complaining. I use them all the time. One of their great benefits is that you don't have to be near a fax machine to receive faxes—wherever you can receive email, you'll be able to pick up your faxes.

Sites Where You Can Get Free Fax Services

So here they are—great sites where you can get free fax services. In this section I list sites that offer free fax services, but don't cover the sites that offer free voice mail and free email in addition to faxing services—for that, turn to the end of the chapter.

eFax

I have accounts with at least five free fax services, but this is the one I use all the time. To view the faxes you're sent via email, you use a small program called a microviewer to see them. That's why I like this site—it has a great microviewer, and the fax attachments tend to be small. Figure 10.4 shows the microviewer in action, viewing a fax I've received via email.

FaxWave

www.faxwave.com

Here's another free faxing site. Just sign up and start receiving your faxes. It's that simple. As with eFax, you can't send faxes from this site. To do that, you'll have to pay extra.

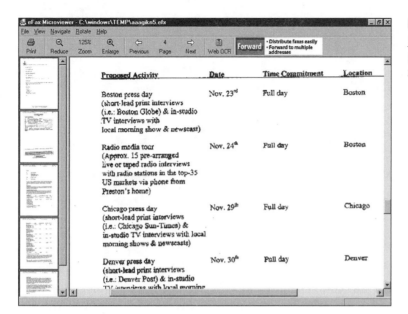

Figure 10.4

Here's a way to get just the fax, using the eFax microviewer.

Fax4Free

www.fax4free.com

You don't receive faxes from this site. instead, you can send faxes from it for free. Unlike the other faxing sites, you don't have to register to get an account here. Just visit the site, and compose a fax. You can fax a document that's already on your computer, such as a Word or Excel document. Or you can instead use a form that uses word processor–like features and compose faxes to send.

Free All-in-One and Voice Mail Sites

Now for the weird and amazing stuff. There are many sites that combine free email with faxing and voice mail, and even other, weirder services. With free voice mail boxes, you get a free phone number, and people can call and leave you voice mail. When they do that, it kicks off an email sent to your email inbox. The email usually has a link that you follow—when you click the link, you're sent to a site where you can listen to a voice mail message. (For more information about voice email, turn to Chapter 8, "Tons of Fancy Multimedia Email Tricks.") In some instances, the actual voice mail file will be sent straight to your inbox.

Here's a list of the best all-in-one and voice mail sites on the Internet.

GetMessage

www.getmessage.com

This site combines email, faxing, and voice mail in one site. It's not as good as OneBox, which I cover later in this chapter, but it's free, and so worth checking out.

jfax

www.jfax.com

This started off as one of the first free faxing services, and has since added voice mail as well. I've been using this one for a long time, and I can vouch for it—it's a good, solid service.

MyTalk

www.mytalk.com

This one offers free email and voice email with a twist. You can call a phone number and have your email read to you, and can then record a message to respond to the email. And it also lets you place a free real-life telephone call—that's right, a free one—to anywhere in the U.S. for two minutes. The catch is that you have to listen to three ads first, and you can only talk for two minutes. Still, free is free.

OneBox

www.onebox.com

Here's a superb, all-in-one service. From one place, you'll be able to get free email, free voice mail, and free receiving of faxes. It's simple, easy, and free…what more is there to say?

ShoutMail

www.shoutmail.com

This site offers many different kinds of services, some of them a bit hard to believe or even understand. So let's start straight. It gives you free email. But it does far more as well. You'll be able to send voice emails with the service—and without using your computer. Just call a toll-free phone number, address your message using the telephone keypad, and record your message, and it'll get sent as voice email. You also can call a toll-free phone number and have your email messages read to you over the telephone. And there's more, still—for example, it will notify you when other users of the popular ICQ chat program are online.

TeleBot

www.telebot.com

Like OneBox, this site offers free email, free receiving of faxes, and free voice mail. There are some limits, though—for example, voice mail is limited to 20 seconds per call. But it also has a service that will alert your pager when you receive a voice mail or fax message.

The Least You Need to Know

➤ Free email accounts are useful because they'll let you check your mail using someone else's computer, and because they're a good backup if your normal email account goes down.

➤ Most free email accounts are based on the Web, so you'll send and receive email by visiting a Web site such as www.hotmail.com.

➤ When you receive a free fax account, you'll get a personal phone number that people can send faxes to. The fax is then converted to a file, and sent to you as an attachment to an email message.

➤ Not many sites let you send faxes for free. One that does is www.fax4free.com.

➤ Free voice mail sites give you a phone number where people can leave you voice mail. You'll then get an email message notifying you that you have a voice mail. You can visit a page that will play the voice mail, although in some instances it will be sent to your email inbox as an attachment.

Part 4

Can We Talk? Using the Internet as Your Telephone

Want to talk to a friend in Tokyo from your PC to his PC for free—no strings attached? How about making phone calls from your PC to real telephones in the U.S. or anywhere in the world—at a cost of only a few pennies a minute? And how about using your PC for real chat with your buddies—voice-to-voice?

Amazingly enough, you can do all that and more. You can make telephone calls over the Internet, either to people sitting at other computers or to people's real-life telephones.

It's all easy to do. It's not only cool, but it'll save you money big time—and that might be the coolest thing of all.

Chapter 11

How You Can Use the Internet to Make Telephone Calls

In This Chapter

➤ Understanding how you use the Internet to make phone calls

➤ The different ways you can make PC-to-PC phone calls

➤ How you can call a telephone from your PC

➤ How much money you can save by making a call to a telephone from your PC

When you sit down in front of your computer, you're sitting down in front of a finely tuned, expensive, complicated piece of machinery that's the result of the work of thousands of different patents, technological advances, and manufacturing prowess.

So why in the world can't you do something simple with it, like make a phone call to your mother in Florida? After all, you can get a phone these days for about $5.99, and they work perfectly fine. Why can't your $1,500 PC do as well?

In fact, it can—you probably just didn't know about it. That fancy piece of equipment you use every day can do double-duty as a telephone. And not only that, it can save you big bucks when you use it. As I'll explain in this chapter, you can make calls to other people at their computers for free, no matter where they are in the world. And you can even use your computer to make phone calls to telephones, and save a significant amount of money compared to a normal phone call.

How Does Internet Telephony Work?

Okay, crew, let's get ready for another of those big, fancy-sounding words that the Web is so famous for creating. Here it is: *Internet telephony*.

Sounds very cool, cutting-edge and high-tech, doesn't it? Well, that's good, because it is all those things. But it also might sound complicated and forbidding, and it really isn't. All Internet telephony really means is that you use the Internet to make telephone calls. Pretty simple.

But before you go ahead and use the Internet to make phone calls all over the world, it's a good idea to get some kind of background understanding of how it all works. So here goes.

There are two ways you'll use the Internet to make phone calls—when you talk to someone from computer to computer, so that no telephone is actually involved, and when you talk to someone on the telephone using your computer. In the following sections, we'll take a look at what you need to know about each.

Walkie the Talkie

What Is IP Telephony?

IP telephony is merely another term that means the same thing as Internet telephony. IP refers to Internet Protocol, which is a way that computers communicate with each other over the Internet.

How Computer-to-Computer Phone Calls Work

The best way to save money on phone calls is to make them for free. And you can do that, using your computer and the Internet. You'll only be able to make them for free if you talk to another computer user—talking computer to computer.

When you talk computer to computer, your microphone takes your voice, and sends it to your computer, which *digitizes* it—turns it into the bits and bytes that your computer and the Internet understand. The computer takes those bits and bytes and sends them out over the Internet to another computer. That computer in turn takes the bits and bytes and coverts them back into speech, which is heard using speakers or a headset. It all happens just about instantaneously. Voilà! You're now making an Internet phone call.

When you talk to someone over the Internet this way, you don't actually use a telephone—in fact, you don't use the telephone system at all. Everything gets sent over the Internet. That's why you won't pay a penny to talk to someone this way, no matter where they're located.

However, that's also why sometimes the voice quality leaves a lot to be desired. Depending on the speed of your Internet connection, your specific hardware, the amount of traffic on the Internet, and sometimes, it seems, the phase of the moon, there can be a big variance. Sometimes it sounds as if you're making something that resembles a normal phone call. Other times it seems as if you're talking to an alien race, or someone at the bottom of the ocean.

There are several different ways you can talk computer-to-computer over the Internet. Here's what you need to know about each:

➤ **By using Internet telephone software** You can get software that will let you talk person-to-person over the Internet. Popular software for doing this includes MediaRing Net2Phone and BuddyPhone, among others. Here's the good news—the software is free. Here's the bad news—you'll only be able to talk to other people who use the exact same software that you do. So, for example, if you use MediaRing and someone else uses BuddyPhone, you won't be able to talk to one another. You'll each have to use the same software. Figure 11.1 shows how you'll make a phone call to someone using BuddyPhone.

Figure 11.1

Hey, buddy, can you hear me? Here's how to make a PC-to-PC telephone call using the free BuddyPhone phone software.

➤ **By using PC-to-telephone software** You can get software for free over the Internet that lets you make a call to a telephone from your PC . You'll have to pay for that kind of call. But some of this software also lets you make PC-to-PC calls for free, in the same way that Internet telephone software works. As with Internet telephone software, you'll both have to use the same software in order for this to work. Net2Phone is a popular piece of software of this type. MediaRing also enables you to make calls like this.

➤ **By using instant messenger and chat programs** Some instant messenger– and chat-type programs also let you communicate with others not just using your keyboard, but also by voice. With Yahoo! Messenger, for example, when one of your buddies is online, you can talk via your voice, rather than having to type with your keyboard. You can see how you make a call like that in Figure 11.2. And you also can use the popular chat program ICQ to find people who are online—and then you can launch your telephone software to talk directly to them. You can get Yahoo! Messenger from—surprise!—the Yahoo! site at www.yahoo.com.

Where to Get Free Internet Telephone Software

It's easy to get free Internet telephone software on the Internet. For Net2Phone, go to `www.net2phone.com` . For BuddyPhone, go to `www.buddyphone.com`. And for MediaRing, go to `www.mediaring.com`. Notice a pattern here? You also can download these and other Internet telephone software from download sites such as `www.zddownloads.com`.

Figure 11.2

Are you there? Here's how to use Yahoo! Messenger to start a voice chat with a buddy.

➤ **From Web sites**   Some Web sites have been *voice-enabled*, which means that you can chat directly from the site, without having to install any kind of extra software. An example of this is the chat area on the popular Excite site at www.excite.com. Go to the chat area, and when you're chatting, there's a phone button you can click that will let you voice chat with someone else.

➤ **By using videoconferencing software**   It's not much of a well-known fact that you can use videoconferencing software even if you don't have a Netcam. Strange, but true. You can use videoconferencing software such as Microsoft NetMeeting or Cu-SeeMe to talk to others over the Internet, even if you can't see them. For information on how to use videoconferencing software, turn to Part 5, "The Eyes Have It: Doing Video Over the Internet."

How Computer-to-Telephone Phone Calls Work

You can't turn on the TV without seeing the ads: Use AT&T for cheap phone calls...no use MCI...no call 10-10 this and call 10-10 that. Stop already! After being barraged by these ads, and by their hectoring telemarketers who are determined to bug me just at the moment I'm sitting down to dinner, I never want to use the telephone again.

There must be a better way! In fact, there is. If you *really* want to save on your phone bills big time, forget all that hype. Instead, turn to your PC. You'll be able to make calls to telephones very inexpensively—in fact, at costs well below anything you'll see advertised on TV. You won't be able to make the phone calls for free, but you will get them cheaply.

But how, you might well wonder, can you make a call to a telephone from a computer? In fact, it's not that hard. All you'll need is special software.

Cool Tips

You Should Use a Full-Duplex Sound Card for Talking Over the Internet

If when you talk to someone, you want to both be able to speak at the same time, you'll need a full-duplex sound card. Without a full-duplex sound card, you'll have to take turns talking—pretty much an impossibility with anyone who has anything more to say than did a former president, the famously reticent "Silent Cal" Coolidge. So check to make sure your sound card is full duplex. If it's not, either buy a new one, or else check the Web site of the manufacturer. They might have posted special driver software that will turn your sound card into a full-duplex one.

Here's how it works. When you want to make a call to a telephone, you run the software, and it "dials" the number for you, makes the connection, and you can then talk with the person, as if you were both on the telephone. What happens is that when you talk to someone, your microphone takes your voice and sends it to your computer, which digitizes it—turns it into the bits and bytes that your computer and the Internet understands. The computer takes those bits and bytes and sends them to the Internet. If you have a good memory, this will sound familiar—up until this point, it works just like PC-to-PC phone calls. But now things change. Instead of those bits and bytes going to a computer, they go instead to a special Internet "gateway," which takes those bits and bytes, converts them into speech, and then sends them over the normal telephone system to the telephone.

When the person talks to you, the whole procedure is reversed—his voice goes over the phone system, and is sent to an Internet gateway that converts speech into bits and bytes, and sends them to your computer. You computer then converts those bits and bytes back into voice. Once again, Internet magic rules!

But What About the Rates?

You'll save big time making phone calls like this, especially when you're calling internationally. But even when you call within the United States, you'll save money.

How much? Here are some sample rates from Net2Phone, which might be the most popular software for making computer-to-telephone phone calls. Let's start off at home: All calls within the U.S. are 3.9 cents a minute. And if you're calling the U.S. from anywhere out of the country, it'll cost from 10 cents to 15 cents a minute, depending on where you're making the call from. Many overseas rates are quite inexpensive, such as calling the U.K. for 9.9 cents a minute. Of course, if you need to call Afghanistan, you'll have to pay a bit more—$1.13 per minute. But hey, I've heard the Taliban aren't big talkers anyway, so you probably won't get much beyond "I beg to disagree. The United States is *not* the Great Satan that you think it is." You'll be able to find out all the calling rates on the www.net2phone.com site, spelled out in black and white (with some blue and red thrown in for good measure). Figure 11.3 shows a sample of more rates from the site.

Figure 11.3

As you can see here on the www.net2phone.com *site, calling from computer to phone can save you big money: Not only is it only 3.9 cents a minute within the U.S., but the next time you call Uzbekistan, you'll only have to pay 72 cents a minute. What a deal!*

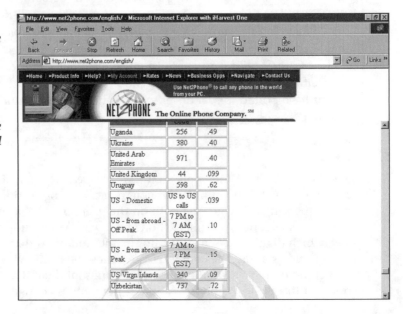

Uganda	256	.49
Ukraine	380	.40
United Arab Emirates	971	.40
United Kingdom	44	.099
Uruguay	598	.62
US - Domestic	US to US calls	.039
US - from abroad - Off Peak	7 PM to 7 AM (EST)	.10
US - from abroad - Peak	7 AM to 7 PM (EST)	.15
US Virgn Islands	340	.09
Uzbekistan	737	.72

What Kinds of Hardware and Software You'll Need to Make Phone Calls

So I bet by now you're raring to join the chattering classes and would like to make phone calls with your PC. As I'll show you in the next several chapters, it's easy to do.

Get the right software, as I outlined earlier in the chapter, or head to a Web site that is voice enabled. And check out the CD at the back of this book for cool voice software as well. For the right hardware, head to Chapter 3, "Setting Up Sound Hardware."

So what are you waiting for? Head to the next chapters—it's time to talk!

The Least You Need to Know

➤ When you talk to a person at another computer from your computer, your voice is digitized into bits and bytes by the computer, and sent over the Internet to the other person's computer, which then turns those bits and bytes back into a voice that the person can hear.

➤ When you call a telephone from your PC, your voice at first travels over the Internet, just like it does when you talk to a person on a computer. But then it gets sent over the normal phone system.

➤ It's free to talk to people at other computers over the Internet—the software you'll use is free, and there's no charge for using the Internet in this way. Popular software includes BuddyPhone, MediaRing, and Net2Phone.

➤ You can use videoconferencing software such as Microsoft NetMeeting and CU-SeeMe to make phone calls to other PC users on the Internet.

➤ When you call a telephone from your computer, you'll have to pay for it, but the costs are less than when you make a normal phone call—for example, 3.9 cents a minute within the United States.

125

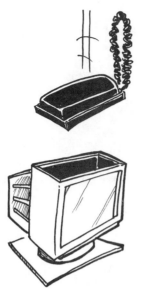

Chapter 12

Setting Up the Telephone Software

In This Chapter

➤ What kind of software you should get for making telephone calls

➤ Why telephone software is so often given away for free

➤ How to set up Net2Phone telephone software

➤ How to troubleshoot hardware if it gives you trouble during the setup

➤ Other software for making telephone calls using your PC

When you buy a telephone, there's not a whole lot you need to know about how to set it up. Take the phone line, plug it into a wall jack, and you're done.

If only the Internet could be so easy.

Before you can make telephone calls using your PC, you'll have to set up telephone software. In this chapter, I'll take you on a step-by-step tour to teach you how to do it. True, it's not quite as easy as plugging a line into a jack, but you'll be surprised how easy it is to do.

What Kind of Software You Should Get

You've gotten to this chapter, so you know what kind of hardware you'll need for making phone calls. Now it's time to get down to business and install the software for making phone calls.

A reminder here: There are two different ways you'll use software to make telephone calls with your computer. You'll be able to make a phone call from your PC to another PC, and you'll be able to do that for free. And you'll also be able to make phone calls from your PC to a real-life telephone. For that, you'll pay, but you'll pay less than you normally would for a long-distance phone call, because for most of the call you're not using the telephone system—the call gets routed for free over the Internet.

There's a lot of different software that will do one or the other, or both, for you. My favorite—and the one I'll show you how to install in this chapter, and use in the next chapter—is Net2Phone. It has more features than all the others. With it, you can

➤ Make PC-to-PC phone calls

➤ Make phone calls from your PC to a telephone

➤ Send faxes

➤ Record and send voicemail

➤ Talk to others who use the popular ICQ instant messenger program. To do this, you and others will have to both have Net2Phone and ICQ.

Later in this chapter, I'll tell you about other Internet telephone software as well.

Cool Tips

Some Instant Messenger Programs Let You Talk to Others with Your Voice

PC telephone software isn't the only way to talk to others with your voice over the Internet. Some instant messenger software lets you do the same thing as well. Yahoo! Messenger and AOL Instant Messenger, for example, both let you do voice chats with other users of the same program.

Why Are They Giving It Away for Free?

One of the more amazing facts about Net2Phone and similar software: You can get it for free. Just head to a download site or the Net2Phone or similar site, and you'll get it at no cost.

How can they do this? Once again, it's Internet economics at work. Remember, when you use the software to make a phone call, you'll have to pay. And that's where these companies make their money. You pay them when you make a phone call to a real-life telephone, and they get that revenue. So the more software they give away, the more money they make, because the more people will be using it to make phone calls. Keep in mind that you'll still be able to use the software for free to make PC-to-PC telephone calls, so you don't ever have to pay a penny if you want to use the software to talk to other people who have the same software and want to talk.

How to Set Up the Software

Enough talk! Let's get some work done around here! Time to set up the software.

I'll show you how to set up Net2Phone software, which lets you talk PC-to-PC, make telephone calls from your PC to regular telephones, and even lets you fax files from your PC. Later on in this chapter, I'll tell you about other PC telephone software.

Keep in mind that although I'll be showing you how to set up Net2Phone, other telephone software is often installed similarly, so even if you're installing a different kind of software than Net2Phone, it'll be worth your while to check out this section of the chapter.

Let's start at the beginning—how you'll get Net2Phone. There are two ways you'll get Net2Phone—either form a CD, or from a site on the Web. Many download sites carry Net2Phone, and it's also available from the Net2Phone site at `http://www.net2phone.com`.

Cool Tips

You Might Need an "Unzipping" Program if You Download Net2Phone from an Internet Download Site

Many Internet download sites "zip" the programs you're going to download—shrink them using a special program so that they're smaller when they're transferred to you over the Internet, and so take less time to transfer. To "unzip" them, you'll need a special unzip utility. The best is WinZip, available at many download sites and at `http://www.winzip.com`. Install WinZip on your computer. Then download Net2Phone, unzip the file with WinZip, and then install the program normally. It will now work fine.

In either case, run the installation program, which is fairly straightforward at first. I'll clue you in on the most important part of the installation process—these three tests:

➤ **A playback test**   To check whether your sound card is working with the program properly, and to adjust the speakers and sound card if the sound quality isn't right.

➤ **A record test**   To make sure your microphone is working properly.

➤ **A network test**   To make sure that Net2Phone can work properly with your particular Internet connection.

In the following sections, I'll show you what you need to know about each.

129

Playing with the Playback Test

When you use a telephone, there's something pretty basic that better work—you have to be able to hear the person on the other end of the line. The playback test checks to make sure that your sound card is working properly with Net2Phone. When the test runs, you'll see the screen pictured in Figure 12.1.

Figure 12.1

Testing, testing…here's the screen that will test to make sure your speakers are working properly.

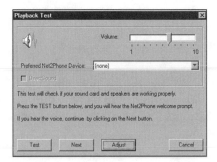

Click the test button, and you should hear a voice saying "Welcome to Net2Phone!" It's a pretty chipper, bright voice, not the kind of voice you'd like to hear first thing in the morning when you roll out of bed. But for testing purposes, it'll do.

There's a slider across the top of the screen that lets you adjust the volume. One suggestion: When adjusting the volume, make it louder than you normally think you'll need it. I've noticed that often when making phone calls over the Internet, voices seem faint and far away (yes, I know they're *physically* far away, but there's no reason they have to *sound* that way). So making the volume a little louder than you need it is often a good idea. Don't worry if you don't get it right—when you use the program itself you also can adjust the sound.

Mayday

Don't Worry if Your "Preferred Device" Shows Up as "None"

You might notice on the playback test screen that there's an entry for "Preferred Net2Phone Device," and that right next to it, it says "none." Don't be alarmed—that doesn't mean your system is set up incorrectly. In fact, it means it's set up right. (Go figure. But this is computers we're talking about, so everything is topsy-turvy.) When "none" shows up, it means only that Net2Phone will choose which is the best "device" (meaning a sound card) to use.

If you don't hear a sound when you test, turn up the volume. That might solve the problem. If you still don't hear a sound, it means your sound card isn't set up properly. If you run into that problem, turn to Chapter 3, "Setting Up Sound Hardware," for what to do.

Doing the Record Test

So far, so good. You've confirmed that you can hear other people when you talk to them. But can they hear *you*?

That's where the record test comes in. It will test that your microphone is working properly. After you complete the playback test, you'll get to the screen pictured in Figure 12.2.

Figure 12.2

Can you hear me? That's what you'll test in the record test, pictured here.

This one's simple. Click **Test**, speak into the microphone, and then wait to see if what you said was recorded. If it was, you pass. If it doesn't, there's trouble in River City.

If there's trouble, the first thing to check for is whether the microphone is plugged into the proper spot on your computer. The microphone will fit into several different jacks located next to each other. You might, for example, have plugged it into the headphone jack. After double-checking that it's plugged into the right jack, make sure it's pushed in all the way. If the connection isn't made securely, the microphone won't work.

If neither of these things helps, get in touch with the manufacturer of the microphone, who might be able to provide technical support.

Time for the Network Test

Great work—if you've gotten this far you're two for two. Now it's time to see if you can score a perfect 100. After you pass the record test you get to the network test. This tests whether you can properly access the Internet with Net2Phone. You can see it pictured in Figure 12.3.

Figure 12.3

Two down, one to go...here's the network test, the final test you need to run to make sure you can use Net2Phone on your computer.

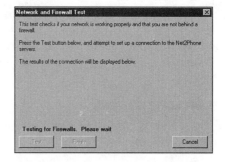

This is the only test that is fairly confusing. Because even if you use the Internet every day for browsing the Web, sending and receiving email, and similar things, you still might not be able to use Net2Phone. That's because Net2Phone uses a different kind of Internet technology than email and the Web, and there's a possibility that the technology that it uses won't be able to be used with the way you get onto the Internet. If you use Net2Phone at work, for example, you might be behind something called a firewall that blocks certain kinds of Internet technology, and it might block you from using Net2Phone.

Walkie the Talkie

What's a Firewall?

Businesses are worried that their computer networks might be hacked or attacked by malicious people looking to spy on them or damage computers. Because of this, businesses put up what's called a *firewall* between the company network and the Internet. A firewall is a computer and hardware designed to stop malicious attacks. Depending on how a firewall is set up, it also can stop legitimate uses of the Internet, such as Net2Phone.

To run the test, click the test button and wait. After a short amount of time, you'll get a message back, either telling you that you passed the test, or telling you that the test failed. If the test fails, you won't be able to solve this one on your own. It involves some pretty complex technology. The best thing to do is get in touch with Net2Phone's technical support people, and have them work with you to get around the problem. Head to http://www.net2phone.com and look for the **Help** area, or call 1-800-438-8879.

What Happens After You Install the Software

After the tests, you'll finish installing the software. A key part of the process is getting a personal account number. It's a long number—it has 12 digits in it—so don't think that you'll be able to remember it off the top of your head. You'll need that account number to identify you when you make any kind of phone call. The number will be put into the Net2Phone program, but if for some reason it gets erased, you'll need it to put back into the program. Write it down so that you can remember it if you need to.

You'll also choose your own PIN (personal information number). It's essentially a password that you'll need to make phone calls with the program. You have the option of saving the PIN inside the software, so that you don't have to enter it each time you make a call, or instead require that the PIN be entered each time a phone call is made. If you're the only person using your computer, and you're sure no one else will be able to break into it and use it, you might want to store the PIN inside the program so that you don't have to type it each time you use the program. However, if other people use the computer, you'll probably want to require that it be typed every time a phone call needs to be made.

So that's it. You've installed the software, tested the hardware, and gotten the numbers you'll need to call. You're set to go. Head to the next chapter to see how to use Net2Phone. Before you do that, though, check out the other software that does similar things, covered at the end of this chapter.

Other Software for Making Internet Phone Calls

As I told you earlier in the chapter, Net2Phone isn't the only software that lets you make phone calls from your PC. There are others as well. Here are my favorites:

➤ **MediaRing** It lets you make PC-to-PC phone calls as well as PC-to-telephone calls. It'll also let you create voice mail. You can see it shown in Figure 12.4. You can get it for free at http://www.mediaring.com.

Figure 12.4

MediaRing is another program that lets you make telephone calls over the Internet.

Walkie the Talkie

You'll Have to Use the Same Software as Your Friends to Make PC-to-PC Phone Calls

There's one downside to using software to make PC-to-PC phone calls—you'll both have to use the same software. So if one of you uses BuddyPhone and the other uses MediaRing, you're out of luck. You both have to have the same program to talk to one another.

➤ **BuddyPhone** This one is for making PC-to-PC calls only, not for making calls to real-life telephones. Like Net2Phone, it also works in concert with ICQ. It'll even work as a kind of answering machine, so that if someone tries to call you with it, but you're not online, it'll take a message for you. You can get it at `http://www.buddyphone.com`.

➤ **Really Easy Voice** This one also only lets you make PC-to-PC phone calls. It's exceedingly easy to set up and use. That's the good news. The bad news is that although you can try it out for free, if you want to continue using it after the tryout period, you'll have to pay $24.95. Get it at `http://www.really-easy.com`.

The Least You Need to Know

➤ To talk PC-to-PC with telephone software, you and your friend will both have to have the same telephone software.

➤ Net2Phone is the best telephone software—it gives you the broadest range of services and features.

➤ You'll have to pay when making calls to a telephone from your PC, although PC-to-PC calls are free.

➤ The most important part of the Net2Phone setup is its tests of your sound card, microphone, and type of Internet access. You won't be able to use the program unless you pass all three tests.

➤ After you install Net2Phone, make sure to write down your account number and PIN number—you'll need them to make phone calls.

➤ Other software for making phone calls over the Internet are MediaRing, BuddyPhone, and Really Easy Voice.

TOMMY, CAN YOU HEAR ME?

Chapter 13

Now Let's Talk: Communicating by Voice Over the Internet

In This Chapter

➤ How to call telephones using your PC with Net2Phone

➤ How to set up Net2Phone Speed Dial calls

➤ How you can make PC-to-PC calls using Net2Phone

➤ Sending faxes with Net2Phone

➤ Sending voice emails with Net2Phone

➤ Using ICQ to alert you when buddies are available for Net2Phone calls

Get ready to save some money—you're about to make phone calls from your PC. You'll be able to call other people at their PCs for free, and save big bucks on long-distance and international phone calls.

Before heading into the chapter, I'd suggest first reading Chapter 11, "How You Can Use the Internet to Make Telephone Calls," and Chapter 12, "Setting Up the Telephone Software"—it'll help you know what to do.

After you do that, you're ready to do one of the cooler things you can do on your computer—save some money.

How You'll Call Others from Your PC

Before we get started, I figured we might have a brief remedial course here. As a reminder, here's the basics of what to know about making phone calls from your PC:

➤ **You can make PC-to-PC phone calls for free** No matter how far away the two of you are located from one another, the phone call will be for free. But the two of you will have to use the same telephone software.

➤ **You can make a call to any telephone from your PC** You can connect to any telephone by using PC telephone software. You'll have to pay for the calls, although you'll pay much-reduced rates.

➤ **You can download telephone software for free** Most telephone software you can get free of charge. (And check the CD in the back of this book for free telephone software.) What a deal!

Okay, we've got that out of the way. Time to make some phone calls.

Cool Tips

Some Instant Messenger Programs Will Let You Voice Chat

Here's another quick way to talk to others over the Internet: Use an instant messenger program that lets you voice chat as well. Several of them do, including Yahoo! Instant Messenger. Turn to Chapter 20, "'IM Me': How to Use Chat and Messenger Programs," for information on how to voice chat with it.

Making a PC-to-Telephone Call with Net2Phone

As I explained in the last chapter, I find Net2Phone the best software overall for making any kind of phone calls with your PC. And, of course, you can't beat the price—it's free. So throughout this chapter, I'll show you how to make calls with Net2Phone. But other software will do it for you as well. If you want to find out about other telephone software, turn to Chapter 12. And that chapter also will tell you how to install and customize Net2Phone. After you install the software, you're ready to start making calls.

First You'll Have to Pay the Piper

With Net2Phone, you'll pay less for making phone calls than you would if you were calling with a telephone. But the calls aren't free—you do have to pay. And unlike with the telephone company, you pre-pay for your calls. So after installing the software and establishing an account (I show you how to do that in the previous chapter), you'll have to go the Net2Phone site and buy time with your credit card. You can choose how much to buy. Usually, Net2Phone has some pretty great deals when you first buy time, such as giving you a free hour of phone calls and a free headset, so I'd suggest going with one of those deals. As I'll show you, you can always add to the account when you want.

After you've paid the piper, you can start making phone calls to telephones. Read on for how to do it.

One Ringy-Dingy: Now You Can Make Some Calls

Making a phone call with Net2Phone is about as easy as it gets. Using either your keyboard, or the numeric keypad on Net2Phone, key in the phone number you want to call, then click the **Call** button. A note will pop up, as you can see pictured in Figure 13.1, telling you how much money you have in your account, and telling you for how long you can talk to the number you're calling, based on how much money is in your account. Click **OK**, and your call will be on its way. Note that you can call internationally as well as long-distance—and the savings are particularly big when you call overseas.

Figure 13.1

Yes, I want to make the call...although I don't think I'll need to talk for more than six hours. I'm calling my parents, and even they can't talk for that long.

You'll hear the phone ring, just as your normally would, and from here on in, it's just like making a normal telephone call.

Mayday

Be Careful Where Your Microphone Is and Make Sure Your Speakers Don't Give Feedback

When you're making a phone call, be careful where you microphone is in relation to your speakers, and make sure your speakers aren't turned up too high. If the microphone is close to your speakers, and the speakers are too loud, the person to whom you're calling will be able to hear themselves talking through your microphone, and will get a feedback effect.

As you can see in Figure 13.2, Net2Phone will show you the number you're calling, and how much time you can spend on the call, based on the time left in your account. To hang up, click the **Hang Up** button.

Figure 13.2

Here's what Net2Phone looks like as you're talking on the phone. It'll tell you the number you're calling as well as how much time you can spend on the call, based on the money in your account.

Using the Phone Book and Speed Dial

If there are people you call all the time, such as your mother (and if you don't call her all the time you should—call her now!), you'll want to use Net2Phone's Speed Dial feature. With Speed Dial, you'll just need a click or two and you can make the call—you won't have to fiddle around with your keyboard or Net2Phone's keypad.

To set a number up for Speed Dial, click the **My Phone Book** button, choose **Program Speed Dial**, and then **Create New Entry**. You'll fill in a name and phone number and click **OK**. When you do that, you're ready to use Speed Dial. Now to make a Speed Dial call, click **Speed Dial**, choose the person you want to call, highlight and choose the number, and the number will be dialed automatically. You can see it in action in Figure 13.3.

Figure 13.3

Make it speedy: Here's how to use Speed Dial with Net2Phone.

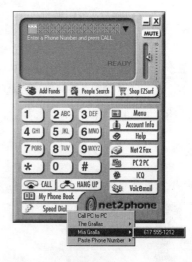

138

I Want More! Checking Your Account and Buying More Time

If you're a hard-core yakker, you might burn pretty quickly through the time you've bought. It's easy to check how much money you have left in your account—click the **Account Info** button and choose **Account Balance**. You'll be told how much money you have left. And as you might guess, Net2Phone has made it extremely easy to buy more time. After you click **Account Info**, choose **Purchase Time** and you'll be sent to a Web page where you can buy more time.

Cool Tips

It's Easy to Find Out the Long-Distance and International Rates Charged by Net2Phone

Net2Phone offers inexpensive rates when you call long-distance or overseas. To check the rates before calling, head to http://www.net2phone.com and click **Rates**.

Calling a PC from Net2Phone

It's as easy to call another PC with Net2Phone as it is to call a telephone—and you won't have to pay when you make a PC-to-PC phone call. To do it, though, the person who you're calling will have to have installed Net2Phone. And he'll have to be running Net2Phone as well—you won't be able to call him unless it's running on his computer.

To make a PC-to-PC phone call, click the **PC2PC** button and then type the person's "nickname" or "virtual number." When you set up Net2Phone, you can type a nickname and virtual number. When someone wants to call you, they'll contact you via either the nickname or number. So to make a PC-to-PC call, you'll have to know your friend's nickname or virtual number. If you don't have it, you're out of luck.

Mayday

Internet Telephone Calls Are Often of a Poor Quality

A word of warning: When you make phone calls from your PC, the quality can be quite poor. The faster your connection, the better will be the quality of your call. Even with fast connections such as cable modems, though, the quality isn't as good as when you talk on the telephone. Also, at some times Net congestion can be quite bad, and the conversation can be thoroughly garbled. If that happens to you, call again at a different time to see if the connection is better. To test for Net congestion, first make a toll-free call, such as to the Net2Phone operators, to see whether quality is generally good. If it is, go ahead and make your regular call.

When you connect PC-to-PC like this, the software works just as it does when you make a regular phone call. And it doesn't cost you a cent.

Just the Fax: Sending a Fax with Net2Phone

Net2Phone makes it easy to send faxes as well as make phone calls. You can only fax documents you have on your computer, such as Word documents. To fax a document, click the **Net2Fax** button, browse to the file you want to send, and select it. When you do that, the file will open and the print command will be automatically executed—although it won't be sent to a printer. Instead, it'll be send to a fax machine. Fill in the form enabling you to fax, as you can see in Figure 13.4, and you'll send it on its merry way. When you fax, by the way, you have to fill in a phone number in the "To" field, not a name. And if you're sending to a fax outside your area code, make sure to put a **1** in front of the number.

Figure 13.4

It's a breeze to send a fax with Net2Phone. Here's how to do it.

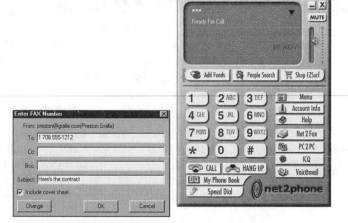

When you send a fax, it's sent over the Internet to a fax machine, and delivered just like any other fax. You'll be charged for the time, just as you would for a telephone call. If you want to find out how to send faxes for free, instead of being charged for them, turn to Chapter 10, "Getting and Using Free Email, Voice Mail, Faxes, and Other Services."

Sending Voice Mail with Net2Phone

One of Net2Phone's cooler features is its capability to send voice email. You can use it to record your voice, and then send an email to anyone that they can listen to. Click **voicemail**, and you'll see the screen shown here in Figure 13.5.

Figure 13.5

Here's how to record a voice email you can send to anyone.

Record your message and when it's done, fill in the email address of the person who you want to send it to. That's all it takes—you're done. You can send voice mail this way for free. Free? Why do they let you send it for free? Because there's a catch with this kind of voice email. The only way the recipient can listen to it is if he has Net2Phone. So if they don't have Net2Phone, they'll have to download and install it. If you want ways to send voice email where people won't need special software to listen to the golden tones of your voice, turn to Chapter 10.

I Seek You to Talk: Using Net2Phone with ICQ

If you want to make PC-to-PC phone calls with telephone software like Net2Phone, it can be a frustrating experience. You'll only be able to talk to others with it if both of you happen to be running the software at the same time.

There's a way around the problem. You can use the program along with the instant messenger and buddy-list program ICQ. ICQ will alert you whenever one of your friends is online, and when you get that alert, you can then connect to them in a PC-to-PC phone conversation.

To be alerted when they're online, and connect to them in a call, run ICQ and et2Phone.

Mayday

It's Best to Close All Other Programs When Running Net2Phone

One way to make sure that Net2Phone works as well as possible is to close all other applications when you make phone calls with Net2Phone. You'll run into fewer problems when you do that.

Then click Net2Phone's **ICQ** button. Whenever one of your buddies is online, you'll be notified of his presence in Net2Phone, and you can then connect to him via a PC-to-PC phone call with Net2Phone.

141

The Least You Need to Know

➤ To make a PC-to-PC phone call to someone else with Net2Phone, you'll both have to have the software installed and running.

➤ You'll have to pay for PC-to-telephone calls with Net2Phone, although you'll pay much less than with normal long-distance calls.

➤ Before you can make PC-to-telephone calls, you'll have to pay with your credit card.

➤ The quickest way to make calls from Net2Phone is to use its Speed Dial feature.

➤ Net2Phone lets you send faxes and voice email.

➤ Use ICQ along with Net2Phone if you want to be alerted when buddies are online so you can talk for free PC to PC.

Part 5

The Eyes Have It: Doing Video Over the Internet

Fans of The Jetsons *might remember the great videophones they used. For years before and since that cartoon series began running, futurists have been promising that we'll all soon be using the videophone, if not now, then certainly by the millenium.*

Well the millenium is here. Where are the videophones?

They're in your computer. It's easy to make videophone calls with your PC, as I'll show you in this section. And you can do more than just make videophone calls. You can participate in videoconferences, do video chat, and more. I'll show you how. So brush down that cowlick, and make sure you shave or put on your makeup before you sit down at your computer. After all, you want to look your best for your friends.

Chapter 14

I See You: How You'll Use Video Over the Internet

In This Chapter

➤ How videoconferencing and videochat work

➤ What kind of hardware you'll need for video over the Internet

➤ What kind of software you'll need for video over the Internet

➤ Learning how to do videoconferences and videochats over the Internet

➤ The etiquette of videoconferencing and videochats

Lights! Camera! Action! Get ready for your closeup (and make sure the makeup people get that shine off your nose). It's time to learn about video communications on the Internet.

With the right equipment, it's easy to see and talk to people around the world. You'll be able to have one-on-one videochats, participate in videoconferences with several people, broadcast to the world the view outside your windows, send videos to your friends via email, and more.

In this chapter, you'll learn how you'll be able to do video communications on the Internet. After reading this chapter, turn to Chapter 15, "Using NetMeeting for Internet Video," and Chapter 16, "Using CU-SeeMe for Internet Video," for details on how to use videoconferencing software.

The Rundown on Internet Video Communications

Understanding how you'll communicate using video and your PC is often very confusing. So let's start off with the basics: Here's the rundown on all the different ways you can communicate using video on your PC. Later on in this chapter, I'll go into more detail on what you need to know about each.

➤ **Videoconferencing** This allows you to see and talk to others over the Internet using a Netcam, microphone and speakers, or a headset. You also can collaborate with others using what's called a "whiteboard"—everyone can mark up a common virtual "board" that you all see and comment on, just as if you were all in the same room at a real whiteboard. You'll need special software, such as Microsoft NetMeeting or CU-SeeMe, to videoconference with others. In a videoconference, two or more people can participate, so you can have many people on the same videoconference. To make the most use of videoconferencing, you should make sure that you have a sound card.

Walkie the Talkie

What's the Difference Between Videochat, Videophone Calls, and Videoconferencing?

You'll often see all three terms used interchangeably. In general, though, videochat and videophone calls mean the same thing—a one-on-one communication between two people using Netcams and microphones. Videoconferencing, on the other hand, can involve more than two people communicating with one another. So although all three terms are often used similarly, generally videoconferencing means more than two people are communicating, whereas videophone and videochat usually means it's a one-on-one chat.

➤ **Videochat and videophone calls** These terms are often used interchangeably. You can use a Netcam to see and talk one-on-one with others. To do that, you use videoconferencing software such as NetMeeting or Cu-SeeMe—you just connect to an individual rather than a group of people. Pictured in Figure 14.1 is an example of a videochat using NetMeeting.

Figure 14.1

Where's George Jetson? Here's an example of a one-on-one videochat using Microsoft NetMeeting. If you look closely enough, you'll see that I'm using a telephone, as is the person I'm talking to. That's because the computer sound quality was so poor—an occasional problem with videochats.

➤ **Video mail** You can use a Netcam to record video, and then send it to friends, family, and others via email. To learn how to do that, turn to Chapter 8, "Tons of Fancy Multimedia Email Tricks."

➤ **Webcam** A Webcam will take a picture or video of anything you aim it at, and then upload that picture to your Web site. In that way, you can broadcast the view outside your window, your own face, or anything else you can aim a camera at, to the world. Some computers also have standard video connections on them that allow you to plug in a normal video camera and take video pictures that way.

For the rest of this chapter, I'll explain what you need to know about videoconferencing, videochat, videophone calls, and Webcams. I covered video mail in Chapter 8.

What Hardware and Software You'll Need

Unless you're telepathic (and even if you are telepathic), you'll need hardware and software when you use video on the Internet. It's not expensive to get hardware and software—in many instances, it comes with your computer, or else the software is free or inexpensive. Here's what you need to know.

Hardware's Not Hard: The Rundown on Internet Video Hardware

The hardware you'll need for doing video over the Internet isn't particularly complicated. Here's what you'll need:

➤ **A Netcam or other video camera** As my daughter would say, *"Helllllooooo!"* If you're going to transmit pictures of yourself, you need some kind of video camera that attaches to your computer, such as a Netcam. For more information, turn to Chapter 4, "How to Choose a Web Video Camera," and Chapter 5, "How to Set Up and Use a Web Video Camera."

147

➤ **A microphone**   If people are going to hear you when you talk, you'll need a microphone. On many laptops and on some desktop PCs, a microphone is built in, although the quality isn't very good. Normally, you'll connect a microphone into a plug on the computer (often on the sound card) that will let you talk with others. (For information about how to buy microphones as well as other sound equipment, turn to Chapter 3, "Setting Up Sound Hardware."

You Can Watch Videoconferences Even if You Don't Have a Video Camera

You can still watch videoconferences or be on the receiving end of video chat, even if you don't have a microphone. Software like NetMeeting will let you watch meetings, and speak during them, even if you don't have a video camera.

➤ **A sound card**   To send and receive voice along with video, you'll need a sound card. It should be a full-duplex card, which means that you'll be able to send and receive sound at the same time—in other words, more than one person can talk at a time. (Around the Gralla household, no conversation is considered complete unless at least two people talk simultaneously.)

➤ **Speakers**   You're not a politician, so you'd like to listen as well as speak during your video-conferences or videochats. To do that, you'll need speakers.

➤ **Headset**   Instead of a microphone and speakers, you can get a headset. No, you won't look fashionable, but you'll hear better, sound better, and be more comfortable. In Figure 14.2 you can see me wearing a microphone during a videochat.

Figure 14.2

Operators are standing by…You'll be a bit geeky-looking when you wear a headset, but still, they're great for videoconferencing because you'll be able to hear and be heard clearly.

Be a Softie: The Rundown on Video Software

Hardware by itself won't do you much good without software. If you're going to do video on the Internet, you'll need software, too. Here's what you'll need:

➤ **Videoconferencing software**   This software lets you participate in videoconferences as well as in videochats. Microsoft NetMeeting is a popular one, and is available for free at many download sites as well as on Microsoft's site at `http://www.microsoft.com/windows/netmeeting/`. Another popular piece of videoconferencing software is CU-SeeMe, but you'll have to pay for it. You can buy it at `http://www.wpine.com` or on online software-selling sites such as `http://www.beyond.com` and at retail stores. For information on how to use NetMeeting, turn to Chapter 15. For details on CU-SeeMe, turn to Chapter 16.

Cool Tips

NetMeeting Only Lets You See One Other Person at a Time

There's one drawback to videoconferencing with NetMeeting— it lets only two people send video and audio in a videoconference. The other people in the conference can see and listen to the two people, but they can't transmit video or voice. They can only text chat. CU-SeeMe, on the other hand, lets multiple people send and receive video and audio in a videoconference, so it's a better bet for videoconferencing in which more than two people participate. Of course, you'll have to pay for CU-SeeMe, and NetMeeting is free. In this case, at least, you really *do* get what you pay for.

➤ **Webcam software**   If you want to broadcast from your Netcam to the world via a Web page, you'll have to get Webcam software, which will take your Netcam images and post them on your site. Popular ones are SpyCam and Webcam32. They're both available at Internet download sites such as `http://www.zddownloads.com`. You also can get SpyCam at `http://www. netacc.net/~waterbry/SpyCam/SpyCam.htm`, and Webcam32 at `http://www. surveyorcorp.com/webcam32/`.

➤ **Video capture software**   If you're going to send video to others via email, you'll need software that will capture video images and sounds from your Netcam and turn them into video files. Often, this software will come with your Netcam. A good one is PictureWorks Live. Get it at `http://www. pictureworks.com`. You can see it in action in Figure 14.3. For more details on how to use video capture software, turn to Chapter 8.

Figure 14.3

Quiet on the set! Here's how you can record a video and turn it into a file using PictureWorks Live, a type of video capture software.

How You'll Videoconference and Videochat Over the Internet

So you're armed with a Netcam and with videoconferencing software such as NetMeeting or CU-SeeMe. Now what?

I'll show you how to use each of these pieces of software in detail in the next two chapters. But before you head there, you should know the basic ways you'll participate in videoconferences and videochats, no matter what kind of software you use. Here's the rundown (later in this section I'll talk in more detail about each of these ways of participating in video):

➤ **Using an Internet videoconference server**   There are free, public videoconference servers you can connect to as a way of finding other people to chat with. These are often called "ils" servers, which stands for Internet Locator Service. I'll detail where to find these and similar servers later in this chapter, and what you need to know before connecting.

➤ **Connecting directly to other people**   You don't need to connect to a server to do video with others over the Internet. Instead, you can connect directly to another person or people. I'll show you how it's done later on in this chapter, and in the chapters on NetMeeting and CU-SeeMe.

➤ **Using an instant messenger program**   Some instant messenger programs will alert you when one of your "buddies" is online, and then will allow you to connect directly via videoconferencing software. Later in this chapter, I'll clue you in on how you can do it.

What Does H.323 Stand For?

Spend any time videoconferencing or hanging around videoconferencing servers and you'll inevitably come across the term "H.323." No, it's not the name of a public high school in New York City. Rather, it refers to a standard that is supposed to allow people using different videoconferencing software to communicate with each other on the same server. So, for example, if you used NetMeeting and someone else used CU-SeeMe, you should be able to communicate on a server that meets the H.323 standards.

Got the basics down? Good. Let's go into a little more detail about each of the ways to do video. Smile, please! You're about to be on camera.

Connecting Using a Videoconferencing Server

In many cases, the best way for doing video-conferences or videochats is to log on to a server, and find partners that way. When you log on to a server, two things happen. Information about you is listed in a public directory, so that others can connect to you for a videoconference. And after you're on the server, you'll be able to see a listing of other people logged on to a server, so that you can videoconference with them.

Many Public Servers Are R-Rated or X-Rated

Beware! Many public videoconferencing servers host videoconferences and videochats that are R-rated or worse. Most servers include descriptions of the kind of conferences and videochats they host, so check before logging on.

Clearly, if you're looking to find videochat partners who you don't know yet, you'll want to log on to these servers. But even if you want to videoconference with people you already know, these servers are often the best way to go.

The reason for that has to do with some peculiarities of the Internet. To connect to have a videoconference with someone, you need to connect to him or her using what's called an IP address. An IP address is a set of four numbers, separated by dots, like this: 209.78.241.160. Lucky you: I'll spare you the gory details of what an IP address is and how it works. (Pitch alert! If you want to learn all the gory details of IP addresses and anything else having to do with the Internet, get a copy of my book *How the Internet Works*.) In short, though, an IP address is what lets you hop onto the Internet and do all the cool Internet things you like to do. It identifies you with the Internet.

When it comes to videoconferencing, think of this IP address as a kind of video phone number. If someone wants to call you by telephone, in the real world they just need to dial your telephone number. In the same way, if someone wants to videoconference with you, they need to connect to your IP number.

So far, so good. So why, after you know someone's IP address, can't you just connect directly to him or her? Because this is the Internet we're talking about, that's why, and nothing—and I mean absolutely *nothing*—is simple. In most cases, when you connect to the Internet, you're given a different IP address each time. Log on this morning, and your address might be 209.78.241.160. Log in later in the day and it might be 209.78.241.121. It's as if every time someone wanted to call you on the telephone, your telephone number was different.

ils servers solve the problem. When you log on to one, it puts you in a directory listing, and finds your current IP address. When anyone wants to do a videoconference with you, they'll just need to click your name—they won't need to know your IP address. So that means that any time you go onto the Internet and log on to a server, other people can immediately contact you, without having to know your IP address. And you can contact them similarly. So think of ils servers as the directory assistance of the videoconferencing world—they'll get you a direct line to whomever you want to videoconference with.

There are a lot of ils servers out there—and it's easy to find a list of them. One good site with a big list of ils servers is the NetMeeting Zone at http://www.netmeet.net/. When you get there, click the link to the list of ils servers. Another good list of ils servers is provided by CU-SeeMe at http://www.cuseeme.com. When you get there, log on and go to the Meeting Point Directory. You can use either NetMeeting or CU-SeeMe to connect to any ils server listed in either directory. (For more information on how to connect to ils servers, read the next two chapters, which will show you how to use NetMeeting and CU-SeeMe.) In Figure 14.4 you can see the CU-SeeMe Meeting Point Directory, and in Figure 14.5 you can see the list of ils servers at the NetMeeting Zone.

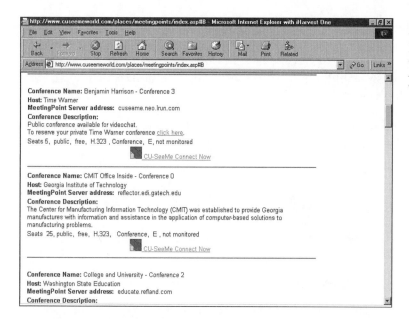

Figure 14.4

Check out the list of servers at the Meeting Point Directory at `http://www.cuseeme.com`.

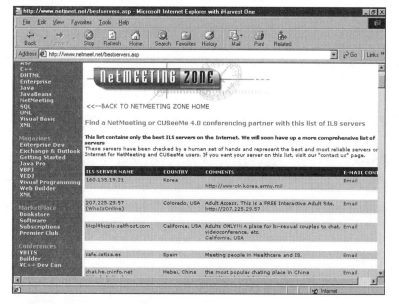

Figure 14.5

A great place to find ils servers is the NetMeeting Zone at `http://www.netmeet.net`.

Making a Direct Video Connection

You don't need to connect to an ils server to have a videochat—you can instead connect directly to the person over the Internet, or they can connect directly to you. To do that, you'll need to know the IP address of the person to whom you want to connect. Arrange ahead of time to get the IP address of the person, and then use your videoconferencing software to connect. In the next two chapters, I'll show you how to do that with NetMeeting and CU-SeeMe.

Cool Tips

It's Easy to Find Out Your IP Address with NetMeeting

If you want people to connect to you via NetMeeting, you'll need to know your IP address. What! You say you don't know your IP address? Join the club. Not many people do—it's not that easy to find out. However, there's a trick you can use in NetMeeting to find out your IP address. Choose **About NetMeeting** from NetMeeting's **Help** menu, and at the bottom of the screen that appears, you'll see your IP address. You can give that out to anyone, who can then connect to you via NetMeeting. Keep in mind that the IP address will probably change every time you log on to the Internet, so check it each time you log on.

Are You There? How to Use Instant Messenger Programs to Locate Video Partners

What might be the best way to videochat with your friends is to use instant messenger programs in concert with your videoconferencing software. That way, you don't need to deal with ils servers, you don't need to wonder when a friend is online or not. What happens is simple: The Instant Messenger program tells you when a friend comes online, and you can then use the Instant Messenger program to launch your videoconferencing software and connect to your friend. No fuss, no muss, no mucking around. Simple.

The best program to use for this is ICQ. (For more information about ICQ, turn to Chapter 21, "I Seek You: How to Use ICQ, the World's Most Popular Chat Program.") Most other chat programs don't include this feature, and ICQ is great at doing this. It's easy to do. Here's how to do it:

1. Put your list of buddies into ICQ as you normally would. (Again, turn to Chapter 21 for how to do it).

2. When someone comes online, and you want to videochat with him, highlight his name, choose **Internet Telephony/Games** from the menu, and then choose **Other**.

3. From the menu that appears, choose the videoconferencing software you want to videochat with, such as NetMeeting or CU-SeeMe. (Any videoconferencing software you've installed will be automatically listed.)

4. A screen will appear, like the one pictured in Figure 14.6. Write a note to your friend. It will be sent to him, requesting a videoconference. If he accepts, you'll be able to connect to one another.

Note that you can send a request like this to someone in ICQ even when they're not online. The request will be delivered to them when you log on to ICQ. Figure 14.6 shows that kind of request.

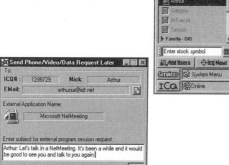

Figure 14.6

I Seek You for a NetMeeting. Here's how you can use ICQ to request to have a video-chat with someone.

You also can use the MSN Messenger to do the same thing. It works only with NetMeeting, however. Highlight the person's name, and then from the **Tools** menu choose **Send an Invitation** and then **To Start a NetMeeting**. It will send a request to the person to start a NetMeeting. If he accepts, you'll be able to have a videochat.

155

Mayday

Bugs Might Interfere with ICQ Working with NetMeeting

Some people have reported a bug that interferes with the capability of ICQ to connect to people with NetMeeting. There is a way around the problem, however. ICQ reports to you someone's IP address when she goes onto the Internet. So you can get the person's IP address from ICQ, and then connect to her by making a direct video connection using the IP number. To get someone's IP number in ICQ, right-click the person's name and choose **Info**. You'll see his IP address. Again, keep in mind that this IP address will usually change each time the person logs on, so check it each time the person logs on to ICQ.

Minding Your Video Manners: The Etiquette of Videoconferencing and Videochat

Just as there are rules about how you communicate in the real world, so there are rules about how you communicate online, especially when you videoconference. So if you'd like to do the right thing, and be considered a good video pal, and not a gauche, obnoxious slob, follow this advice:

➤ **Respect the rules of the site or room you're visiting**   Servers and sites have rules and etiquette that you should follow—both written and unwritten. If you're visiting a business-oriented site, don't send video images of your cat coughing up hairballs. (Unless it's a videoconferencing site for veterinarians who specialize in the digestive upsets of domesticated felines.) If you're visiting a family-oriented site, don't tell off-color jokes or send R-rated material.

➤ **Respect the copyright laws**   On videochat sites, you can leave videos for other people to download and play, or have them played live. If you've captured any video from broadcast or cable TV, or music from audio CDs, you're not legally allowed to have them available over the Internet. So be careful what you send out for others to view and listen to.

➤ **Don't slander people or businesses**   There are legal consequences to what you say online. If you slander people or businesses, you can be legally liable. Businesses, in particular, pay attention to things said about them online. So unless you want to end up on the receiving end of a lawsuit, keep what you say within the bounds of the law. You can certainly express your opinions, but be careful not to slander—so make sure what you say is true.

Cool Tips

You Can Text Chat While in a Videoconference

Most videoconferencing software, such as NetMeeting, allows you to text chat at the same time that you're holding a videoconference. So you can send and receive text messages while a videoconference is going on. This is useful because in some videoconferencing software, such as NetMeeting, only two people at a time can be using the video and audio conferencing. With text chat, everyone can participate. And for those people who always used to sit in the back of the classroom and pass nasty notes about the teacher—you can chat with only one specific individual, not the entire videoconference. So you can call your boss all the nasty names you want, and laugh at his choice of ties. Just make sure when you send your chat message, you click the right button and send it to one individual. If you instead send it to the whole group, you'll be in big trouble.

➤ **You're not required to give out your email address to others**   Often, people will ask for each other's email addresses when they have videochats. Feel free to not give it out or give it out. It's up to you.

➤ **Be aware that a lot of video servers are X-rated**   It's an unfortunate rule of life that many video servers are X-rated. People who visit there are looking for others also interested in X-rated videochat. So be careful to read the description of the server before you visit so that you'll know the kind of people and chats you'll find when you get there.

➤ **Don't broadcast still images**   If you're in a videoconference, don't point your camera at the wall, ceiling, or floor. It should be pointed at you, or something else of interest (that's assuming that you're of interest, of course). When you're in a videoconference, you're sharing Internet bandwidth with other people, and wasting it on an unmoving image of your blank wall is considered bad form.

The Least You Need to Know

➤ In a videoconference, you communicate with two or more people via video, whereas in videochat, you communicate with only one other person.

➤ You'll need a Netcam, microphone, sound card, speakers, and videoconferencing software such as NetMeeting or CU-SeeMe to participate in video-conferences and videochats.

➤ The most common way to connect to others with video is to log on to a videoconferencing server, often called an ils server.

➤ You can directly connect to another person for a video chat if you know his IP address, or he knows yours.

➤ Instant messaging software such as ICQ can be used to alert you when some-one is online who you want to have a videochat with, and can then connect you to him with your videoconferencing software.

➤ When you're in a videoconference or videochat, respect the rules of the server or room, don't slander others, and respect the copyright laws by not sending out copyrighted material.

Using NetMeeting for Internet Video

Let's do a meeting. A NetMeeting that is. It's time to get down to business or have fun while meeting over the Internet.

NetMeeting lets you do all kinds of things: participate in videoconferences, mark up a virtual whiteboard with other people, send and receive files, and more. In this chapter, I'll give you the rundown on how to install and use NetMeeting, how to become master of your meetings, and how to troubleshoot any problems you might have with the program. If you haven't yet read Chapter 14, "I See You: How You'll Use Video Over the Internet," it's a good idea to head there now. It'll clue you in on all the basics of how videoconferencing works, and give you tips and tricks as well as a basic rundown of videoconferencing etiquette.

What You'll Use NetMeeting For

NetMeeting is the most popular piece of videoconferencing software available (due at least in part, I have no doubt, to the mere fact that it's free—who can pass up a deal like that?—and that as a component of Internet Explorer, it comes installed on many computers). There's all kinds of reasons you might want to use NetMeeting. Here, though, are the main reasons to use it:

➤ **To do one-to-one videoconferencing**   In essence, you can use it like a videophone or for videochat. You and someone else can see each other and talk to each other while seated at your PCs.

➤ **For group videoconferencing**   Maybe you have a group of people scattered all over the country (or the globe) who need to have a meeting. Forget flying—use NetMeeting instead.

NetMeeting Isn't the Best Program for Group Videoconferencing

NetMeeting allows you to have group videoconferences, but it's not the best program for doing it. That's because with NetMeeting, you can only see and talk to one other person at a time in the videoconference—in essence, people have to take turns, because not everyone can participate at once. With CU-SeeMe, on the other hand, multiple people can take part in a videoconference. For details on how to use CU-SeeMe, turn to the next chapter, Chapter 16, "Using CU-SeeMe for Internet Video."

➤ **To share a "whiteboard"**   Real-life whiteboards have become ubiquitous in the business world, even though sometimes it seems the main reason they're being used is for grocery lists. Still, businesspeople love whiteboards. You can use NetMeeting as a virtual whiteboard—people in far-flung places can all see the same whiteboard and mark it up together. What fun—you can even compose group grocery lists!

➤ **To send files and share applications**   With NetMeeting you can send files directly to one another, which is certainly useful. You also can "share" programs. So, for example, everyone together can work on the same Word document. Why would you want to do this? Beats me. In fact, I've never heard of anyone actually doing this in real life. On the other hand, it certainly sounds cool, and it's nice to know it's there even if you never use it.

Installing NetMeeting

Decided you want to videochat, do videoconferences, or for whatever oddball reason want to share applications over the Internet? All you'll need to do next is install NetMeeting. If you don't have a copy on CD, head to http://www.microsoft.com/windows/netmeeting, find the file, and run the installation program. Installation is pretty straightforward (well, as straightforward as installing any piece of software can be), but there's a few things you should know before getting started. Read on—I'll clue you in on what you need to know.

What to Know Before Getting Started

Before installing NetMeeting, it's good to get a basic idea about how videoconferencing works—it'll help you understand the setup a little better. (For more details, turn to Chapter 14.)

When you use a videoconferencing program, you can connect to people in two different ways. You can connect to them through a videoconferencing server, called an *ils* server. Or you can bypass a server completely, and connect directly to the person if you know his Internet address.

After you connect to the person, you establish a connection directly between the two (or more) of you. Video and audio flow directly from computer to computer.

Pretty simple, right? Okay, time to move on and start installing the program.

What Does "ils" Stand For?

The term *ils* stands for *Internet Locator Service*. It's a computer, with special software, that keeps track of people and allows them to contact each other for videoconferencing.

You're Off to See the Wizard

As with many Microsoft programs, when you run the NetMeeting installation program, a wizard will do your work for you. It'll ask you a series of questions and then install the program on your computer. Most of the questions are pretty simple and self-explanatory, so I won't walk through them step by step. But there are a few trick questions there, so here's what to know about certain of the setup screens:

➤ **You'll have to fill in your name and email address, even if you don't want them to be visible on a videoconferencing server** The program won't go on unless you fill in certain information. Don't worry, though, you can choose to hide information later on if you want.

Mayday

If You're a Woman, Consider Using a Male-Sounding Name

Sad but true: There are creeps and weirdoes on the Internet. Sadder and truer: Almost every one of them is a male. If you're a woman and list your real name on a public server with NetMeeting, you can be sure that you'll be bothered by these creeps and weirdoes, trying to contact you for unpleasant purposes. So consider using a pseudonym or male-sounding name when you fill in your name on NetMeeting. That way, the creeps and weirdoes won't know you're a woman, and so are less likely to bother you.

➤ **You can choose which server to log on to and whether to log on to one at all** You'll be asked which videoconferencing server to log on to, whether you should even log on to a server, and whether your name should be shown when you log on. By default, the server will be one run by Microsoft, and unless you happen to know another server to log on to, I suggest using the default one. If you want to log on to a server, but don't want to be bothered by strangers requesting meetings with you, check the box that says not to list your name in the server. You can see how to do all this on the screen pictured in Figure 15.1. Later on in the chapter, I'll show you how to find servers other than the default one suggested by Microsoft.

Figure 15.1

Here's the screen that lets you choose whether to log on to a server when you start NetMeeting.

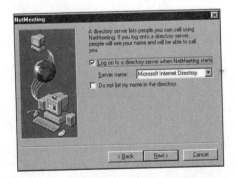

Fine-Tuning NetMeeting Once You've Installed It

Sending and receiving video over the Internet is, at best, a sometimes flaky task. Your Internet connection speed, what kind of computer you have, the Netcam you use, and sometimes, it seems, the phase of the moon, all affect video quality.

Because of that, after you install NetMeeting, you'll probably want to fine-tune your video setting. To do that, choose **Options** from the **Tools** menu and click the **Video** tab. You'll see the screen pictured in Figure 15.2.

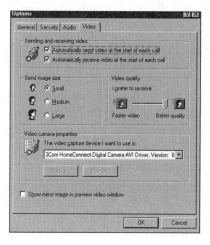

Figure 15.2

Here's how to fine-tune NetMeeting after you've installed it.

There are two important things to look at on this screen—the Send Image Size area and the Video Quality area. Here's what you need to know about each:

➤ **If you have a slow Internet connection, or your video camera has a slow frame rate, choose the smallest image size**   There are three options for image size: small, medium, and large. The larger the image, the more data is being transmitted over the Internet. If you have a slow connection, and choose to send a large image, the image you send will appear to be stop-motion—you'll send a frame at a time, and it won't look like video at all. So for a slow connection, make sure to use the smallest size. Use the medium size if you have a reasonably fast Internet connection, such as a cable modem, DSL connection, or are on a local area network. Even in that case, though, you might want to choose the small image size, depending on how the image appears on the receiving end. Only choose the large size if you have a powerful computer and an extremely fast connection to the Internet. And only choose the large size if you have a top-of-the-line Netcam, a very powerful computer, and a high-speed connection to the Internet.

➤ **Adjust the video quality settings to fine-tune your video image**   In NetMeeting, you have to strike a balance between the quality of the video you send and how smooth the video motion is on the receiving end. When you make the image fuzzier, the video will appear smoother; when you sharpen the image, the video appears jerkier. Test moving the slider in the Video Quality area to find the best medium for your particular computer and Internet connection.

163

Cool Tips

Get the Latest Copy of NetMeeting

Even if you already have NetMeeting installed, it's a good idea to make sure you have the latest copy installed. To find out which copy you have of NetMeeting, click the **Help** menu, and choose **About NetMeeting**. You'll be shown what version of the program you're running. Then check the Microsoft Web site at www.microsoft.com/windows/netmeeting to see if you have the latest version. If you don't, download and install it.

How to Make Videoconferencing Calls with NetMeeting

Finally, you've got NetMeeting set up, you've fine-tuned it, and you're ready to make your first videoconferencing call. You'll make calls in two different ways: Either through a videoconferencing server, or directly to another NetMeeting user. Here's how to do both.

How to Videoconference Using the Microsoft Directory

As I showed you before in this chapter (you were paying attention, weren't you?), when you set up NetMeeting, by default you're logged on to the Microsoft Directory. That means that when you start NetMeeting, you're automatically listed in the directory, and available for a videoconference. Note that you won't actually be informed that you're logged on to the directory—it happens automatically without you doing anything or being told about it.

Because you're logged on automatically, that means that you can search the directory for people with whom you want to videoconference.

To find someone with whom you want to videoconference, click the **Directory** button (it looks like a small picture of an address book on the right side of the screen). When you do that, you'll get a form allowing you to search the Directory, as you can see in Figure 15.3.

Microsoft's Videoconferencing Directory Is Often Down

Here's one big problem with NetMeeting—Microsoft's Directory is frequently down or overburdened so that you won't be able to log on. So when you start NetMeeting, you'll get an error message saying that you can't connect to the videoconferencing server. The solution? Keep trying to log on, or use another ils server (I'll show you how later in this chapter), or bypass servers entirely and connect directly to someone (again, I'll show you how to do that later in this chapter).

When the person you're looking for is connected to the directory, a link to the person will be displayed. To connect to the person via NetMeeting, click the link, and you'll send a request to them to connect, as you can see in Figure 15.4. When they agree to the meeting, you'll be connected, and you can talk and videoconference to your heart's content, as you can see in Figure 15.5.

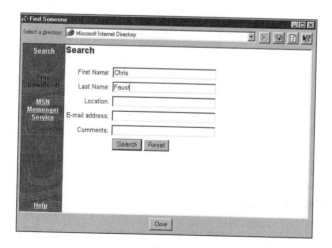

Figure 15.3

As easy as 1-2-3. Get ready to connect. Here's how you'll search for a videoconferencing partner using the Microsoft Directory.

Figure 15.4

Once you locate them, you send a request to hold a videoconference...

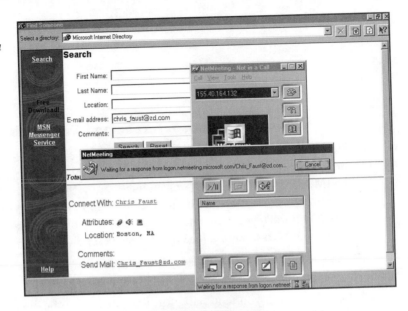

Figure 15.5

...and when they accept the request you're off yacking.

Connecting Using Other Videoconferencing Servers

Microsoft's directory isn't the only server that lets you find other people who want to videoconference. There are many others out there. So if the Microsoft server isn't working (a very common occurrence, I can tell you, based on much personal experience), or if you just want a wider audience of people to videoconference with, you'll have to go to other servers.

For the best list of ils servers, head to the NetMeeting Zone at http://www.netmeet.net. Look for the page that lists ils servers. You'll get the best list on the Internet of servers you can use to connect to other NetMeeting users. Figure 15.6 shows the first part of the listing.

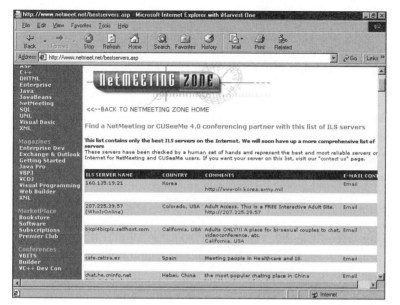

Figure 15.6

The NetMeeting Zone: The best place on the Internet for finding ils servers.

So far, so good. But now things get complicated. There are two ways you can use these ils servers to videoconference with others. Look closely at Figure 15.6. Notice that all servers have their Internet address listed, such as 160.35.19.21 or ils.byte-beam.com. And beneath that address, for some ils servers, there are the words **WhoIsOnline**. The easiest way to find people to videoconference is to click those words. When you do that, you'll be sent to a Web page that lists everyone on the server, as you can see here in Figure 15.7.

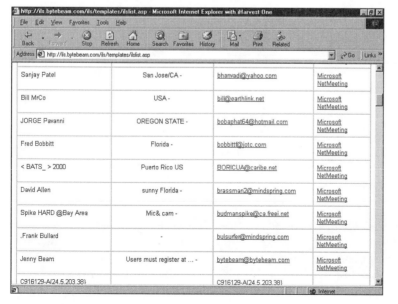

Figure 15.7

*Click **WhoIsOnline** and you'll get a complete listing of everyone on the server. It's a quick and simple way to find others to videoconference with.*

167

Many ils Servers Include a Great Deal of Adult Content

Be aware that many ils servers you'll find at the NetMeeting Zone and elsewhere on the Internet are often frequented by people interested in "adult"-type videoconferencing. So check the server description carefully before logging on.

To videoconference with someone, click the **Microsoft NetMeeting** link across from her name, and you'll send that person a request to hold a videoconference.

Ah, but things aren't always that easy—after all, we're talking about the Internet here. Sometimes, there is no WhoIsOnline link next to a server. So to connect to that server, you'll have to do a little more work. Choose **Options** from NetMeeting's **Tools** menu and on the **General** tab, go to the Directory Settings area. In the box next to **Directory**, type the ils location, such as **160.35.19.21** or **ils.bytebeam.com**. Click **OK** and when you're asked if you want to connect to the server, say you want to. When that happens, you'll connect to the server, and see a screen like that pictured in Figure 15.8. Double-click anyone in the directory listing, and you'll send that person a request to hold a videoconference. Not simple, not easy, but it can be done.

Figure 15.8

Not easy, but it can be done: Here's another way to connect to an ils directory with NetMeeting.

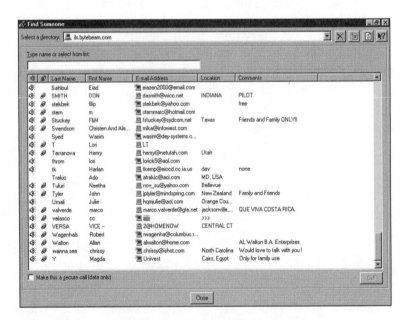

Videoconferencing with a Direct Connection

If you want to videoconference, you don't only have to use a server—instead you can go by the direct route and connect directly to people. In fact, if you're looking to set up a videoconference ahead of time, this is a much more efficient way of working—

you won't have to deal with connecting to servers, searching for your friends on them, and similar matters.

Making a direct connection is quite easy. Just to the left of the icon of a telephone in NetMeeting is a place where you can input the IP address of someone. When you input that address and press **Enter**, you'll send that person a request to have a video-conference via NetMeeting. And if you want someone to connect to you, just give them your IP address, and they'll send you a request for a videoconference.

How to Host a NetMeeting

If you're planning on several people joining a videoconference, the best way to all connect is to have one participant host the meeting, and then have the others join in. Everyone should agree on a time, and on who will host the meeting. The host should send out his IP address to everyone.

Then, at the time the meeting is about to start, the host should choose **Host Meeting** from the **Call** menu. The host can give the meeting a name and can require a password. There are several other options as well for hosting a meeting, such as the ability to say that only the host can place or accept calls. Everyone can now call the host—let the meeting begin!

It's best if the host of the meeting has the fastest computer and the fastest connection to the Internet, because to a great extent the speed and connection of the host will determine the quality of the meeting's video and audio.

Cool Tips

It's Easy to Find Out Your IP Address in NetMeeting

Don't know your IP address, or your friends don't know theirs, and so you can't hook up via NetMeeting? No problem. It's easy to find out. Choose **About Windows NetMeeting** from the **Help** menu and you'll see your current IP address. Check it each time you log on, because your IP address might be different every time you get onto the Internet.

One Ringy-Dingy: How to Accept an Invitation to a NetMeeting

Up until now, I've talked about how you can send invitations to others to participate in videoconferences. But how about if someone asks you to join one?

Well, this will be just about the shortest section of the book, because it's easy to do. When you get an invitation to a videoconference, all you need to do is accept if you want to join, and not accept if you don't. It's that simple. And if you want to always accept a call automatically, then choose **Call** from the menu and select **Automatically accept calls**.

I Didn't Know That: Other Cool Things You Can Do with NetMeeting

As I mentioned earlier in the chapter, in addition to plain-Jane videoconferencing, NetMeeting can do some other cool things, too. Here's a brief rundown on what they are and how to do them.

Using the Whiteboard

The whiteboard lets you and others share ideas by drawing on a virtual "whiteboard" that everyone in the videoconference can see. Figure 15.9 shows you the whiteboard in action.

Figure 15.9

Here's an example of a virtual whiteboard being used in NetMeeting.

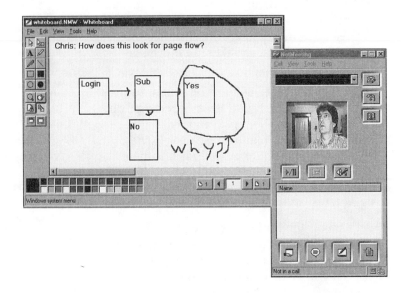

To use the whiteboard, choose **Whiteboard** from the **Tools** menu, or press **Control+W**. You can draw on the whiteboard, write text in a variety of fonts and colors, paste pictures, and more—pretty much do whatever you can on a real-life whiteboard. Multiple people can work on the whiteboard at once, and you can open up multiple whiteboards at once.

You Can Save the Contents of the Whiteboard and Use it Again Later

There are times that you might want to save a whiteboard, and open it up again later so that everyone can take a second look at the work, or even work on it a second time. To do that when there's a whiteboard you want to save, choose **Save** from the **File** menu, save the whiteboard, and then later on when you want to work on it again, use the **File**, **Open** command to open it.

Using Chat

Only two people at a time can send and receive audio and video images. If you have several people in a videoconference, that leaves other people out. Everyone can participate, though, by using the chat feature that lets you type messages via the keyboard, and see messages that other have left. And for those who still haven't outgrown throwing spitballs from the back rows of a classroom, using chat is a great way to taunt other videoconferencing participants! To chat, choose **Chat** from the **Tools** menu, or press **Control+T**.

Share and Share Alike: Using Sharing

Your mother always taught you to share, didn't she? Well, now you can put that teaching to good use. You can "share" applications in NetMeeting. That means that you can show what's on your computer screen to all the other participants, and they can see what you do as you make changes to a file—for example, working on a Word document. And you can even let them work inside the same document. To do that, choose **Sharing** from the **Tools** menu, or press **Control+S**.

Special Delivery: Transferring Files

Have a file you want to send to someone in the videoconference? Or perhaps they have a file to send to you. To send a file in NetMeeting, choose **File Transfer** from the **Tools** menu and then follow the screen for sending files.

Virus-Check All Files that Are Sent to You

If someone sends you a file, never open it unless you first virus-check it with a good virus-checker like Norton Utilities. Anyone can have viruses in files they send to you, and you don't want inadvertent damage to be done to your files or computer.

Troubleshooting NetMeeting

As I've mentioned before, video and audio over the Internet can be quite flaky, and you might well run into problems when setting up and running NetMeeting. Here are some common things to keep in mind when troubleshooting:

➤ **Your Windows colors should be set to 16-bit color or higher** The quality of NetMeeting video at 256 colors is extremely poor. So when using NetMeeting, always set your colors to 16-bit colors or greater. To set your Windows colors, right-click the desktop, choose **Properties**, click **Settings**, and then choose 16-bit color or better from the Color Palette area.

➤ **If you can't connect to an IP address, check the number again** Because IP addresses such as 150.34.221.23 contain many numbers, it's easy to copy one down incorrectly. If you can't connect to a given IP address, make sure you copied it down right.

➤ **Keep in mind that ils servers are frequently down or filled with traffic** There's more NetMeeting traffic than most servers can handle. That means that servers are often down, or else have the maximum number of people they can handle. Keep trying different servers until you find one that lets you in.

Use ICQ to Connect to Others with NetMeeting

A good way to connect to your friends and co-workers is to use ICQ. ICQ, a popular instant messenger program, will alert you when friends and co-workers are online. It also includes a feature that allows you to connect to them via NetMeeting. Turn to Chapter 14 for details on how to do it.

➤ **Audio quality is often poor in NetMeeting** When you're in a NetMeeting, you might notice that the audio quality is so poor that it's difficult to understand other members of the meeting. They might sound as if they have marbles in their mouths. (Then again, maybe they *do* have marbles in their mouths. If so, there's not much you can do, except find friends who haven't gone off the deep end.) Have everyone use the **Audio Tuning Wizard** from the **Tools** menu to fine-tune his or her audio. If that doesn't work, sometimes the only way to solve the problem is an old-fashioned way—use the telephone for audio, while using NetMeeting for video..

➤ **If you're having audio or video problems, download the latest drivers from hardware manufacturers** Often hardware problems with microphones or Netcams can be solved by downloading and installing the latest drivers from the manufacturers' Web sites. Make it a habit to keep your drivers up to date.

The Least You Need to Know

➤ When you install NetMeeting, you'll have to include a name and email address, although if you're a woman, you might want to choose a male-sounding name so that you're not badgered when you log on.

➤ Fine-tune your NetMeeting video by choosing the smallest video size if you have a slow Internet connection, and the medium video size if you have a fast one. Only choose the largest image if you have a very fast computer and a very fast connection.

➤ To connect to someone using the Microsoft ils server, click the **Directory** button after you've logged on to the server, and then search for the name. After you find the person, click the name to connect.

➤ You can use other servers to find people to connect to. Go to the www.netmeet.net site for a list of servers.

➤ To connect to someone directly, type his or her IP address. To find out your own IP address, choose **About Windows NetMeeting** from the **Help** menu.

➤ Your Windows colors should be set to 16–bit color or higher if you want to have a reasonable video quality during the meeting.

Chapter 16

Using CU-SeeMe for Internet Video

In This Chapter

➤ All the reasons to use CU-SeeMe

➤ How to install CU-SeeMe

➤ Connecting to videoconferences and videochats with CU-SeeMe

➤ How to use the Conferencing Companion to get the most out of NetMeeting

➤ Using the whiteboard, sharing applications, and sending and receiving files

➤ Troubleshooting CU-SeeMe problems

Time for a meeting—a video meeting, that is. You'll be able to use CU-SeeMe for videoconferencing and videochats, and do all kinds of other neat stuff as well. You'll be able to mark up a virtual whiteboard with other people, send and receive files, work together on the same file, and do true videoconferencing with multiple people.

In this chapter, I'll give you the rundown on how to install and use CU-SeeMe and how to master it and troubleshoot any problems you might have with the program. If you haven't yet read Chapter 14, "I See You: How You'll Use Video Over the Internet," it's a good idea to head there now. It'll clue you in on all the basics of how videoconferencing works, and give you tips and tricks as well as a basic rundown of videoconferencing etiquette.

Why Use CU-SeeMe?

As you've learned in the previous chapter, NetMeeting is the most popular piece of videoconferencing software. In large part that's because it's free. It's a pretty hard deal to pass up.

CU-SeeMe, on the other hand, costs money—figure on paying about $70 or so for it. So why would anyone pay $70 for a piece of videoconferencing software when they can get one for free? And no, insanity is not a correct answer.

You'd pay $70 if you need some of CU-SeeMe's features that NetMeeting doesn't have. Here are the reasons you'd want to fork out $70 of your hard-earned cash for CU-SeeMe instead of getting NetMeeting for free:

➤ **It does true group videoconferencing** NetMeeting doesn't really allow groups of people to do true videoconferencing—only two people can be using the video or audio at a time. CU-SeeMe, on the other hand, allows many people to vidoeconference together so that everyone can see and talk to everyone else in the videoconference.

➤ **It allows for "cybercasting"** With CU-SeeMe, the Internet can be used in the same way as a television station, to broadcast to many people. A single server can send video, audio, and even text and graphics. Examples of this are NASA shuttle launches and live cybercasts from outer space using CU-SeeMe. If there is a cybercast done with CU-SeeMe, you won't be able to view it with NetMeeting.

➤ **It's easier to find and connect to video-conferences than with NetMeeting** It's not particularly easy to connect to videoconferencing servers and other people with NetMeeting—there's no easy way to organize all your contacts and all the servers you like to connect with. In CU-SeeMe, on the other hand, it's very easy to organize all that, using the Conferencing Companion, shown here in Figure 16.1.

➤ **It's easier to use than NetMeeting** In general, CU-SeeMe offers a wider number of features presented more elegantly and simply. It's simply a nicer-looking program.

Cool Tips

CU-SeeMe Lets You Do Everything that NetMeeting Does

You don't give up anything when you use CU-SeeMe instead of NetMeeting. It lets you share applications, work on a group whiteboard, and all the other things that NetMeeting does.

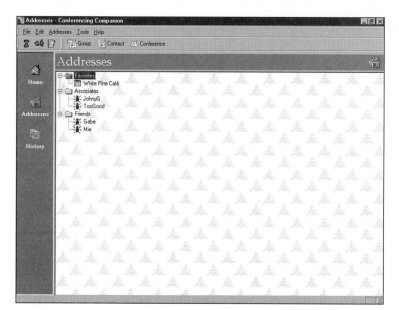

Figure 16.1

*Can you see me?
CU-SeeMe makes it easy
to organize all the people
you like to videoconference
with, and the servers
you like to connect with,
using the Conferencing
Companion.*

So should you take the plunge and pay the $70 extra for CU-SeeMe? Certainly if you need to do group videoconferencing you should. As for the rest—it depends upon how much time you spend videoconferencing. If you're a casual user, it probably doesn't make sense to spend the money. But if you videoconference with any regularity, consider dipping into your pocket.

Installing CU-SeeMe

So you've decided that it's worth the extra money to get a videoconferencing program. Now it's time to install. Here's what you need to know about installing the software before you start videoconferencing.

How Did You Buy the Program? Installation Advice for Downloaders and Store Buyers

You can buy CU-SeeMe at a store or online shopping site, and get the program shipped to you on a CD, or you can instead buy it at an online site where, after you pay, you download the software and you don't get a box or documentation. Here's some installation advice for each:

➤ **If you install from a CD**   Copy down your serial number and keep it in a safe place. That way, you won't have trouble if you need to re-install the software—during installation CU-SeeMe requires that you type a serial number.

177

➤ **If you install from a downloaded file** Keep a copy of the file on disk somewhere so that you will still have a copy of it if your computer crashes for some reason. And print out and copy the confirmation page you received when buying the program. That way, if something goes wrong, you'll be able to prove that you bought the program, and so can get a new copy, if need be. And also keep your serial number in a safe place as well.

Getting Assistance from the Assistants

It's pretty straightforward to install CU-SeeMe; install it just like any other piece of software. After the basic program has been installed, you should run the **Setup Assistant**, which will walk you through the process of completing and customizing the installation. It's pretty easy to do, but there are some things to keep in mind during installation:

➤ **If you want to be notified whenever someone tries to connect to you for a videoconference, check the box that says "Incoming call notification"** That way, you won't miss a videoconference call.

**If You Have an Earlier Version of CU-SeeMe,
Install into a Different Directory**

If you have an earlier version of CU-SeeMe than the one you've just bought, make sure to install it to a different directory from your earlier versions. If you don't, you might lose some of your contact information. And if you're running CU-SeeMe Listener, make sure to disable it, so that you don't cause any problems.

➤ **You'll have to put in your name and email address to use the program** You won't be able to connect to a server or directly to other people unless you fill this in. You also can choose to put in a *nickname*, which will be the name other people will see when you're in a videoconference.

➤ **Pay attention to how you connect to videoconferencing directories** In the Directory Services screen, you'll choose how to connect to directories. By default, you'll automatically connect to a CU-SeeMe ils directory. (For more information about ils directories, turn to Chapter 14, "I See You: How You'll Use

Video Over the Internet," and Chapter 15, "Using NetMeeting for Internet Video.") You can choose a different server to connect to if you want. On this screen, you'll also be able to have your listing hidden when you log on to a directory. And you can choose whether information about you will be published in the **Personal**, **Business**, or **Adults only** category. You can see the Directory Services screen pictured in Figure 16.2.

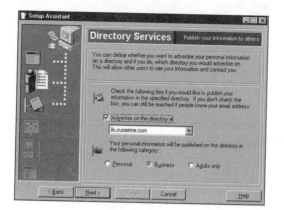

Figure 16.2

Here's how to customize how you'll connect to videoconferencing servers.

If You're a Woman, Consider Using a Male-Sounding Name

As I've mentioned earlier in this videoconferencing section of the book, it's a sad fact of life that there are creeps and weirdoes on the Internet. And they're almost all male. If you're a woman and you don't want to be contacted by this kind of slime, consider using a pseudonym or male-sounding name when you fill in your name. That way, the creeps and weirdoes won't know you're a woman, and so are less likely to bother you.

Fine-Tuning Your Video Settings

Video tends to be flaky over the Internet. Your connection speed, the speed of your computer, Internet congestion, and anything else you can imagine will affect the quality of the video image you send and receive. Because of that, you should fine-tune how you send video with CU-SeeMe. To fine-tune video, you'll use the Performance screen pictured here in Figure 16.3.

Figure 16.3

Make it picture perfect: Here's how to fine-tune your video settings.

Pay close attention to the Video Encoding section of this screen. You'll be able to adjust the size of the video image that you send, as well as the video quality you send. First pick your connection speed. After that, fine-tune. Here's what you need to know:

> ➤ **If you have a slow Internet connection, or your video camera has a slow frame rate, choose the smallest image size** There are three options for image size: small, medium, and large. The larger the image, the more data is being transmitted over the Internet. If you have a slow connection, and choose to send a large image, the image you send will appear to be stop-motion—you'll send a frame at a time, and it won't look like video at all. So for a slow connection, make sure to use the smallest size. Use the medium size if you have a reasonably fast Internet connection, such as a cable modem, DSL connection, or are on a local area network. Even in that case, though, you might want to choose the small image size, depending on how the image appears on the receiving end. Only choose the large size if you have a powerful computer and an extremely fast connection to the Internet.

> ➤ **Adjust the video quality settings to fine-tune your video image** In CU-SeeMe, you have to strike a balance between the quality of the video you send and how smooth the video motion is on the receiving end. When you make the image fuzzier, the video will appear smoother; when you sharpen the image, the video appears jerkier. Test moving the **Faster Video/Better Quality** slider to find the best medium for your particular computer and Internet connection.

Notice the small stoplight next to the video image. That light will let you know whether you've adjusted your settings properly for your connection speed or whether you might run into trouble with them. A green light means you've set them fine; yellow means that although your settings will work, they're not ideal; and a red means...well, you can take a guess. They're not right. Re-adjust them until you've gotten the green light.

How to Make Videoconferencing Calls with CU-SeeMe

Whew! You're finally there. The program is all set up and ready to go. And so are you. Here's how you'll make videoconferencing calls with CU-SeeMe.

There are several different ways you'll make video connections with others with CU-SeeMe. You can connect from the Conferencing Champion or from a directory, you can connect directly to someone, and you can go to a Web site to find a directory and connect from there. Here's how to do each.

Using the Conferencing Champion

Your main communications center in CU-SeeMe is the Conferencing Champion. It's from here that you'll make the vast majority of your videoconferencing connections. You can see the Conferencing Champion in Figure 16.4. When you're in the Conferencing Champion, make sure to click the **Addresses** icon on the left part of the screen—that brings you to the Addresses screen you see here.

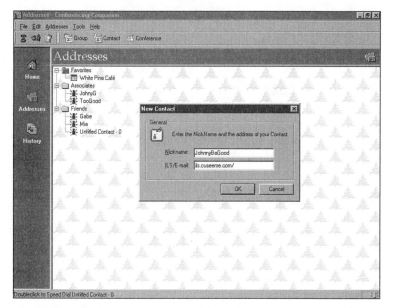

Figure 16.4

Communications central: CU-SeeMe's Conferencing Champion is where you'll make most of your video-conferencing connections. Here, you can see a new connection being added.

In the center of the screen you'll see a group of folders. This is where you'll organize all your addresses of people and conferences to which you want to connect. You'll be adding servers and people to this list. To do that, right-click the folder where you want the new contact added, and fill in the form that you see in Figure 16.4.

After you have a contact or server put into the Conferencing Champion, all you'll need to do is double-click the contact or server, and you'll make the video connection.

When you contact a server, you'll see a list of available conferences (many videoconferences are held simultaneously on a single server). Choose any and you'll jump right into it. If you're connecting to an individual, you'll instead make a one-to-one immediate connection.

Connecting via a Directory

Another way to connect for a videoconference is to go in through a directory. When you launch CU-SeeMe, you automatically log on to a videoconferencing directory. You'll be visible on that directory, along with hundreds of other people. There are many directories like this on the Internet. You can use directories to find videoconferencing partners. To do that, from the Conferencing Champion, click the directory icon on the toolbar. When you do that, a directory listing will pop up of all the people currently logged on to a directory, as you can see in Figure 16.5.

Figure 16.5

A very long list...here's how you'll connect to other people via a video-conferencing directory.

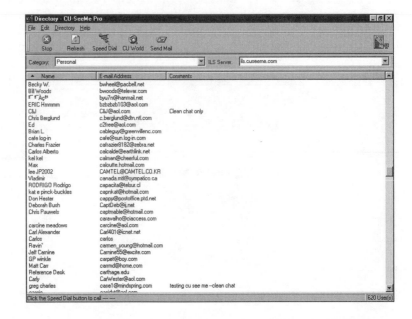

To connect to someone on the directory list, just double-click his name, or click the **Speed Dial** icon.

To check out who's on a different server, click the drop-down box next to **ILS Server** and choose it. If you know the address of another server, you can type it there as well.

Connecting Directly to an Individual

If you want to videoconference, you don't have to use a server or a directory. You can instead go the direct route and connect straight to people. In fact, if you're looking to set up a videoconference ahead of time, this is a much more efficient way of working—you won't have to deal with connecting to servers or directories.

Making a direct connection is quite easy. From the Conferencing Champion, click **Manual Dial**, and fill in the IP address of the person to whom you want to connect.

Connecting from CU-SeeMe World

There's a way to find people to videoconference with, without having to first run CU-SeeMe—you can visit a Web page, find people to videoconference with, and connect from there.

Head to http://www.cuseemeworld.com and register (don't worry—you've already spent $70 for the software and you won't have to spend any more; registration is free). When

Mayday

Many Directories Are Adult-Oriented

When connecting to someone else via a directory, keep in mind that many directories are adult-oriented, so be careful about which directory you log on to. Make sure to read people's comments about themselves before making or accepting a call.

you log on, you'll find many different ways to videoconference. You can look at directories straight from the Web, see who's online from the Web, and similar features. I find the best thing to do is click the **MeetingPoint** directory—a comprehensive listing of rooms where videoconferences are going on that you can join. Browse through the directory, and when you see a place you want to join, click it. You'll be shown a group of videoconferences going on, as you can see shown in Figure 16.6. Choose the videoconference you want to join, and you'll be in the middle of things.

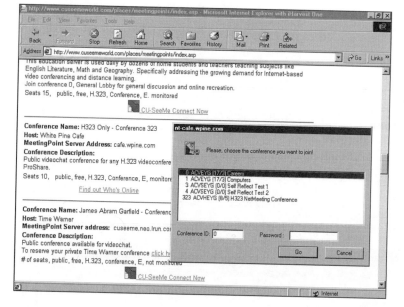

Figure 16.6

Often the best way to find a videoconference is on CU-SeeMeWorld. Here you can see me about to join a public videoconference.

Yes, I Can See You: Using the Conference Room

When you connect to a videoconference, you'll be in what's called the Conference Room. You can see it in action in Figure 16.7.

Figure 16.7

Where the action is: When you connect to a videoconference or to an individual, you'll be in the Conference Room, pictured here.

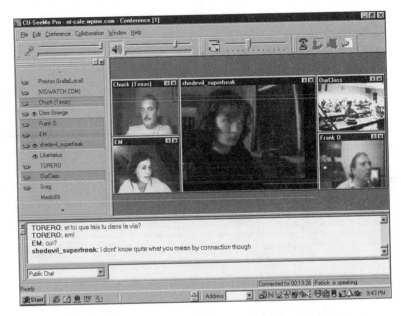

Audio Quality Is Often Bad, So Many People Do Text Chat in Videoconferences

When many people are in the same videoconference, the audio quality tends to be garbled. Because of that, many people choose not to speak at all, and instead chat via their keyboards.

Down the left side of the screen you can see everyone in the videoconference. The main part of the screen is made up of videofeeds of other people in the conference, each in its own window. At the bottom of the screen you can see text chat if people are chatting via their keyboards. In many conference rooms, there are more people connected than you can see on your screen. To view anyone in the videoconference, click their name on the left side, and you'll see their videofeed.

You can move windows around, you can close them, you can make the windows go full screen, and in fact, you can rearrange the room pretty much anyway that you want.

You'll notice that in the listing of people in the videoconference on the left side, there are icons next to most people. Here's what they mean:

➤ **An icon of a camera means that someone is connected to the confer-ence with a Netcam**   You can join videoconferences even if you don't have a Netcam—you can see other people, but they can't see you. Anyone with a camera icon next to them is sending a video feed, though.

➤ **An icon of an eye means that person is currently looking at you**   A little creepy, I know, but still, it's nice to know who can see you on their screen right now.

There are a lot of buttons, icons, and menus to fool around with in the Conference Room, so have fun testing it out.

Other Cool Things You Can Do with CU-SeeMe

CU-SeeMe goes beyond allowing you to videoconference. You can do a lot of other cool things as well. Here's a brief rundown on what they are and how to do them.

Share and Share Alike: Using Application Sharing

As we've all been taught since childhood, it's good to share. So it's time to do a good deed: You can "share" applications with other people in CU-SeeMe. When you share applications, you show what's on your computer screen to all the other participants in a videoconference, and they can see what you do as you make changes to a file—for example, working on a Word document. And you can even let them work inside the same document.

To share applications, everyone in a conference has to enable what CU-SeeMe calls "application services." To do that, run the Conferencing Companion, click the **Preferences** button, and then from the Preferences Editor that appears, choose **Collaboration** and then click the **Enable collaboration services** box.

After you do that, you'll be able to share and share alike. To do that, run the program you want to share, open the document you want to share, and then select **Share Application** from the **Collaboration** menu in the Conference Room. You'll see a list of programs running on your computer. Choose the pro-gram you want to share and you're ready to go.

Using the Whiteboard

CU-SeeMe's whiteboard lets you share ideas with others by drawing on a virtual white-board that everyone in the videoconference can see. And everyone in the videoconference can mark up the whiteboard as well. Figure 16.8 shows the whiteboard in action.

Mayday

You Can Only Use the Whiteboard if NetMeeting Is Installed

You'll only be able to use a white-board in CU-SeeMe if you have NetMeeting installed. In fact, CU-SeeMe's whiteboard program is NetMeeting. To install NetMeeting, turn to Chapter 15.

185

Figure 16.8

Here's an example of a virtual whiteboard being used in CU-SeeMe.

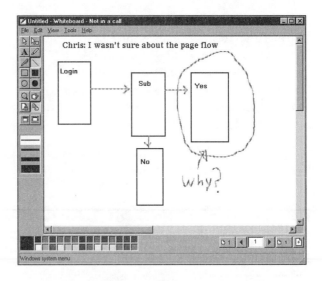

Make Sure to Virus-Check All Files that Are Sent to You

Never open a file sent to you unless you first virus-check it with a good virus-checker like Norton Utilities. Anyone can have viruses in files they send to you, and you don't want to damage your files or computer. Viruses can even be in Word and Excel documents, so check those as well.

To use the whiteboard, you'll have to enable collaboration services, as I just explained. Then, either click the **Whiteboard** button, or choose **Whiteboard** from the **Collaboration** menu of the Conference Room.

Special Delivery: Transferring Files

With CU-SeeMe you can send files to anyone in a videoconference. To do that, collaboration services have to be enabled, as I explained earlier in the chapter. Then, to send a file, choose **File transfer** from the **Collaboration** menu and follow the instructions.

Troubleshooting CU-SeeMe

Running videoconferencing software like CU-SeeMe can be a sometimes-frustrating experience because of troubles you might run into. Here are some common things to keep in mind when you run into trouble when using CU-SeeMe:

➤ **Your Windows colors should be set to 16-bit color or higher** The quality of video at 256 colors is extremely poor. So when using CU-SeeMe, always set your colors to 16-bit colors or greater. To set your Windows colors, right-click the desktop, choose **Properties**, click **Settings**, and then choose 16-bit color or better from the Color Palette area.

➤ **If you can't connect to an IP address, check the number again**
Because IP addresses such as 150.34.221.23 contain many numbers, it's easy to copy one down incorrectly. If you can't connect to a given IP address, make sure you copied it down right.

Cool Tips

Use ICQ to Connect to Others with CU-SeeMe

A good way to connect to your friends and co-workers with CU-SeeMe is to use ICQ. ICQ, a popular instant messenger program, will alert you when friends and co-workers are online. It also includes a feature that allows you to connect to them via CU-SeeMe. Turn to Chapter 14 for details on how to do it.

➤ **If you're having audio or video problems, download the latest drivers from hardware manufacturers**   Often hardware problems with microphones or Netcams can be solved by downloading and installing the latest drivers from the manufacturers' Web sites. Make it a habit to keep your drivers up to date.

The Least You Need to Know

➤ CU-SeeMe costs $70, but does many things that the free NetMeeting can't do, such as true group videoconferences.

➤ To use CU-SeeMe, you'll have to type your name and email address. You can, however, choose to hide that information when you log on to a server.

➤ Fine-tune your CU-SeeMe video by choosing the smallest video size if you have a slow Internet connection, and the medium video size if you have a fast one. Only choose the largest image if you have a very fast computer and a very fast connection.

➤ The easiest way to connect to videoconferences is with the Conferencing Champion, which organizes all your calls, servers, and contacts in a single place.

➤ Your Windows colors should be set to 16-bit color or higher if you want to have a reasonable video quality during the videoconference.

Part 6

Using a Personal Web Page to Communicate with the World

Here it is, your chance to tell the world about yourself. Let everyone know the names of your pet ferrets, that you're a license plate collector, and that you put cold cream on your face every night before going to bed.

Well, maybe you don't want them to know about the cold cream.

But you can use the Web to communicate with others in ways you never before imagined. You can create free Web pages—that's right, I used the word F-R-E-E—and use them to tell the world about yourself. And you can use your Web pages to get people to contact you as well.

More amazing still, you can use your Netcam video camera to show live pictures of video of whatever you want—the view outside your living room, your new baby boy, heck, even show them your pet ferrets running around their cages. Just don't show them your face at night with the cold cream on it. It's not a pretty sight.

Broadcast Your Interests to the World: Creating Your Own Web Page to Communicate with Others

In This Chapter

➤ All the reasons a Web page will help you communicate with others

➤ What you'll need to build a Web page

➤ How to use Netscape Composer to build a Web page

➤ How to build a Web page using Composer's wizard

➤ How to build a Web page using templates

➤ How to publicize your Web page after you've built it

One of the best ways to tell others about yourself, and to make new friends, is to build a Web page. With a Web page, you can tell the world about your fascination with collecting drainpipes or studying the mating habits of feral raccoons. And you can talk to others with similar interests. In this chapter, I'll show you all the ways that building a Web page can help you communicate with others, and I'll teach you how to build a Web page from scratch in minutes.

Why Create a Web Page to Communicate with Others?

When you think about the World Wide Web, you probably think about shopping sites such as www.amazon.com, news and entertainment sites such as www.cnn.com, computer sites such as www.zdnet.com, or big all-in-one sites such as www.yahoo.com, www.msn.com, and www.aol.com.

What you probably don't think about is you. Simple, plain old (or young) you. After all, you don't have millions of dollars to build and promote a site. (If you do, though, can you spare a few bucks? My kids are hungry and my mortgage is overdue.)

The truth is, you don't have to have a whole lot of money to build a Web site—in fact, you probably won't have to spend an extra penny over what you're now spending on Internet access. And you don't need a great amount of expertise as well—as I'll show you in this chapter, anyone can build a Web site pretty easily.

But just because you *can* build a Web site doesn't mean that you necessarily *should*. If your interest is in communicating with others, what's the point of building one?

In fact, there are a lot of ways you can use a Web site to communicate with others. Here's the rundown on the top ways you can use a Web site to communicate with others:

➤ **You can tell people about your interests and hobbies**   Are you a big fan of LEGOS and the amazing things you can construct with them? Let the world know about it or any other hobby by publishing information about it on a Web page. You'll find that you're not alone in your hobby—there will be others who share it and will appreciate your information. (Those with a serious LEGO obsession will find LUGNET, the unofficial LEGO Users Group Network, to be an invaluable resource for building, sharing, and announcing the publication of their own creations. Check it out at www.lugnet.com.)

➤ **You can share personal information about yourself, such as the birth of a child or other personal information**   Birth announcements sent by mail are so *passe*. And they're pretty dull as well—just some words and maybe a picture. Instead, you can build a Web page with all the vital information about the birth, including pictures, videos, a guest book, and more. (Please, though, no videos of the birth itself—some things are best left completely private.) You can build a Web page about any other personal information such as a wedding, a new job, or more. Pictured here in Figure 17.1 you can see a Web page built by Gregory Harris, a Macmillan editor (busy people, aren't they?), announcing the birth of his daughter Cecelia. She's a sweetie, isn't she? For more information about the Web and video, turn to Chapter 19, "Adding a Webcam to Your Web Site."

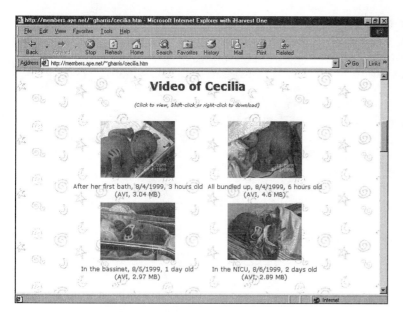

Figure 17.1

Share your news with the world: Here's a Web page built by proud Papa Gregory Harris to announce the birth of his daughter Cecelia. Mazel tov!

➤ **You can promote a business or service, or post your resumé** Do you sell widgets, doodads, and whoozamajiggies? Let the world know that you have the most winsome widgets, the most darling doodads, and the wackiest whoozamajiggies. You can use a Web page to promote any business or service, and you also can post your resumé online if you're looking for a job.

Publish Your IP Address on the Web so Other People Can Reach You

Whenever you're on the Internet, you have what's called an IP address—a set of four numbers, separated by dots, like this: 192.168.0.1. One way that people can connect to you for videoconferencing and Internet telephone calls is by connecting to you by using your IP address. Usually, though, every time you go onto the Internet, your IP address changes. However, you can automatically have a Web page published that will tell the world what your current IP address is. Do it by downloading and using the free program UFindMe. You can get the program at many download sites on the Internet, including www.zddownloads.com.

➤ **You can post information about a community, civic, or other kind of organization you're involved in**   Church groups, PTAs, neighborhood groups, wild-and-crazy accountant associations—the Web is a great way to keep everyone in a group in touch with the latest news and information. The neighborhood group of which I'm a member, the Porter Square Neighbors Association (PSNA, to those in the know), uses a Web site this way, and it's a great way to keep everyone in the group up to date on what's new.

➤ **You can do a live Webcam broadcast to show the world the view outside your window, or a view of your room or office**   Have exhibitionist tendencies? Want the world to see the beautiful view outside your window? You can use a Webcam to broadcast live pictures or video, and in essence build your own little broadcast studio. Turn to Chapter 19 for information on how to do that.

➤ **You can make new friends and email buddies**   Web pages are a great way to make new friends and to meet people with similar interests. As I'll show you later in this chapter, you can build email links on your Web page so that people only need to click a link to send you email.

Getting Down to Brass Tacks: What You'll Need to Create a Web Page

So by now you're probably convinced you should build a Web page. But what will you need to build one? Do you need to be a super-techie wearing a propeller beanie and pocket protector, and will you have to fork out mega-bucks to designers and Internet services?

No, not at all. You'll be able to build a Web page from scratch, probably without spending an extra penny, and without even having to wear a propeller beanie (pocket protectors are optional, though).

Here are the basics of what you'll need to build a Web page:

➤ **Software for creating a Web page**   Web pages are built using a language called HTML (Hypertext Markup Language). To create a Web page, you'll need a program that can create HTML. These are often called HTML editors. There are many different kinds of HTML editors. For Web novices, the best idea is to use one that simply lets you place elements on a page, without having to know the underlying HTML. The best of these kinds of editors are often free, such as FrontPage Express, which comes free with Internet Explorer, and Netscape Composer, which comes free with Netscape Communicator. Shown in Figure 17.2 is Netscape Composer. I'll show you how to build a Web page using these programs later in the chapter.

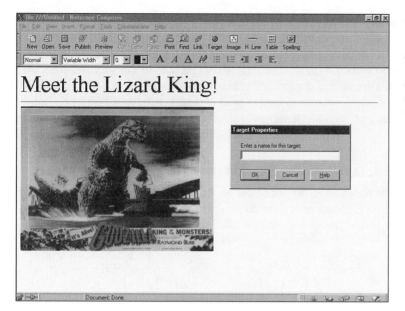

Figure 17.2
You don't need to be an HTML jockey to create Web pages when you use a simple-to-use HTML editor such as Netscape Composer.

➤ **A place to host your Web page** Your Web page has to live somewhere on the Internet. So you'll need a place that will "host" your Web page. Most Internet service providers (ISPs) provide free Web hosting, so check with yours to find out how to get them to host your Web page. America Online offers free hosting services as well (as well as Web-page building tools). To get there, use the keywords **home pages**. And there are many sites on the Internet that will host Web pages for free—and these are often an excellent place to go to get your Web page hosted. For information about these kinds of sites, and how to build Web pages on them, turn to Chapter 18, "Broadcast for Free: How to Get and Use Free Web Pages."

Walkie the Talkie

What Exactly Is an HTML Page?

An *HTML page* is really nothing more than a plain text page that contains a series of codes or tags that a Web browser interprets and displays in a certain way. The codes tell the browser which font and size of font to display, for example, and tells the browser where to find graphics to display, and similar information. Because it's a plain text page, some highly skilled HTML jockeys don't even use a special HTML editor to create HTML pages—they simply use Notepad. Real men (and women), it seems, don't use HTML editors.

➤ **Pictures and other elements to jazz up your page**   To make your page interesting, you'll need to use graphics. And especially if you plan to show pictures of yourself, your family, or similar cool stuff (assuming that you and your family are cool, of course), you'll need to have some way to get pictures into your computer. Scanners and digital cameras are ideal for this. For information on how to set up and use scanners and digital cameras, turn to Chapter 6, "How to Set Up Scanners and Digital Cameras."

The Quick-and-Easy Way to Build Web Pages

If you've never built a Web page before, the best way to build your first is to use a program such as Netscape Composer or Microsoft FrontPage Express. Both are free, easy-to-use Web page editors that let you create Web pages without having to know a lick of HTML.

In this chapter, I'll show you how to create a page with Netscape Composer, so if you're going to create one with FrontPage Express, what you do will look a bit different. But the same general concepts and ideas hold true.

Cool Tips

Where Can I Get FrontPage Express and Netscape Composer?

FrontPage Express and Netscape Composer are free programs that you can download from the Internet and use without ever having to pay for them. For FrontPage Express, go to `http://www.microsoft.com/downloads/search.asp?` and click **ProductName**. Then scroll down to find it. To get Netscape Composer, go to `http://www.netscape.com` and find the download page for Netscape Communicator. Composer is part of Communicator—but just to make sure, check that you're downloading Composer when you download Communicator before you download it.

To teach you how to create a Web page, first I'll show you how to use Composer, and then I'll show you super-fast ways to create Web pages using templates and wizards. Armed with that knowledge, you'll be able to whip up your first Web page faster than you can blink an eye.

The Basics of Using Composer

Fire up Composer and you'll see what's shown in Figure 17.3—a blank screen with toolbars, icons, and menus across the top.

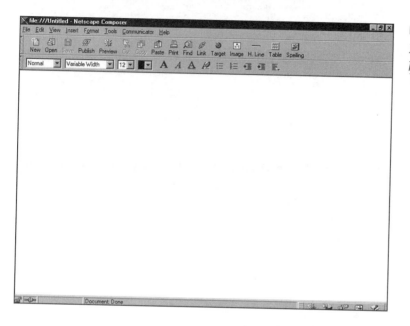

Figure 17.3

Netscape Composer—the first step to creating a Web page of your own.

As you can see, there are two sets of toolbars—a top one that lets you do things such as insert graphics, create hyperlinks, and similar features, and one below it that lets you format text.

You use Composer much like you use a word processing or similar program. To format text, use the text-formatting toolbar—you'll be able to change the font and size of the text; make it bold, italic, or underlined; align it however you want; and create lists.

For doing things such as inserting graphics, links, lines, and other components of the page, use the toolbar above the text formatting toolbar. Typically, when you click one of the icons, you'll fill out a form that will describe how you want the object to look or act on a page. For example, pictured in Figure 17.4, you can see the form you'll use to insert a graphic, and in Figure 17.5 you'll see the page after you insert the graphic.

What's great about Composer is that, as you build the page, you'll be able to see what it looks like. That's not the case with many other HTML editors, in which you can see what the page looks like only after you preview it or publish it.

You create your Web page in this way, by creating and formatting text, and adding graphics, links, and similar features to your page.

Figure 17.4

Here's how you'll insert a graphic in Composer...

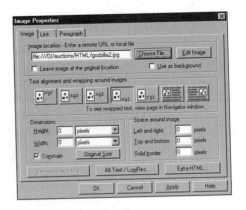

Figure 17.5

...and here's what the graphic looks like when it's been put on the Web page. With Composer, you'll see what it looks like as you build the page.

There's one important thing that people often neglect when building a page—that's to make sure the page is titled. The title is what will show up in the title bar of a menu page when people come to it on the Web. To title your page, choose **Page Colors and Properties** from the **Format** menu. You'll see the screen pictured in Figure 17.6. Fill in the title and other information. Other tabs will let you change the colors and background of the page, and adjust other features.

Figure 17.6

Make sure to title your page, using this screen in Composer.

Play around a bit with Composer, clicking the buttons, seeing what they can do, to familiarize yourself with it. After you do that, you're ready to go on to the next step. I'll show you how to build quick-and-easy Web pages first using a wizard (No, Harry Potter fans, you won't have to attend the wizard's school at Hogwarts to use this wizard). Then I'll show you how to build a page using instead a template. The difference between a wizard and a template is that a wizard takes you on a step-by-step process through creating a Web page, whereas with a template, you have a pre-designed page that you then alter according to what you want to put on the page. Note that you don't *have* to use a wizard or a template to build a Web page—you can just build a page from scratch. But for getting started, I suggest using wizards and templates. So let's move on and I'll show you how to do it.

Walkie the Talkie

What Are Meta Tags?

There's a tab you'll notice on the Page Properties screen entitled META Tags. What are these things? They're tags—codes—that are put into the HTML page, but that aren't displayed when someone visits the Web page. There are many purposes for meta tags, such as providing information about who created the page or how often the page is updated. Commonly, meta tags also include keywords that describe the content of the page. These meta tags are used by search engines such as www.altavista.com to index the site. This helps people find Web sites that match their searches when visiting AltaVista and other search engines. So if your site is about Beanie Babies, make sure to put a meta tag with the words Beanie Babies in it—that way it'll be more likely that people will find your page.

Time for Wizardry: How to Build a Web Page Using a Wizard

Put on your necromancer's hat. It's time to be a wizard. I'm about to show you how to build your first Web page using Composer and a page-building wizard.

To build a page using a wizard, you need to be connected to the Internet. So get online. Next, launch Composer. After you do that, here's how to build a page using a wizard:

1. Choose **New** from the **File** menu, and then choose **Page From Wizard**. When you do that, Netscape Navigator opens in a new window and heads you onto a special Internet site that will build your page for you. In the topmost right frame of that page, scroll down and click the **Start** button. That will get you started on the wizard, that you can see pictured here in Figure 17.7. Note that for the whole first part of this wizardry process, you'll be working in this window in Navigator. Later on you'll use Composer to finish everything up.

Figure 17.7

Put on your sorcerer's hat: Here's how to get started building a Web page with a wizard.

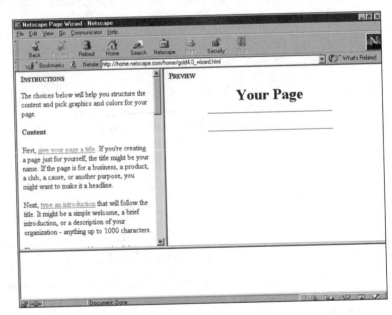

2. You'll now fill in a series of forms that will build your Web page. Click **give your page a title**, and when that's done, click the **Apply** button. You'll see a preview of your page, with the title in it, as you can see in Figure 17.8.

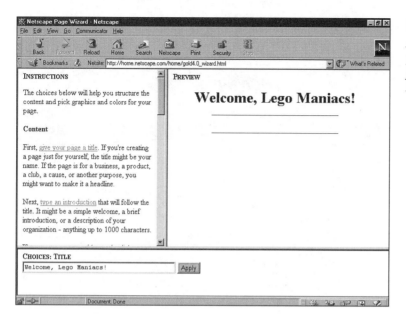

Figure 17.8

As you fill in the form, you'll see a preview of the page as it's being built. Here, I've added the title.

3. Continue to fill in the forms. You'll add an introduction, links to other Web pages, a conclusion, and choose color combinations, horizontal rules, and more. Just follow the directions on the wizard—it's quite easy to do.

4. When you're happy with the page, click the **Build** button. When you do that, the page will be built, and it will open in Navigator. You'll see exactly how it will look when published on the Internet. You can see such a page pictured here in Figure 17.9.

5. You can further edit your page, using Composer. And even if you don't edit it, you'll need to open it in Composer to publish it. To do that, choose **Edit Page** from the **File** menu. You can now edit the page, add links and pictures, and do anything else you want to do to the page, using Composer.

What's An Email Link?

When you put an *email link* on a Web page, it does more than just let people know your email address. Whenever someone clicks the email link, it will automatically open his email program, and address an email to you. All he'll have to do is write the message and send it. Email links are great for people who want others to contact them via email.

Figure 17.9

Almost there…here's what your page will look like when published on the Web.

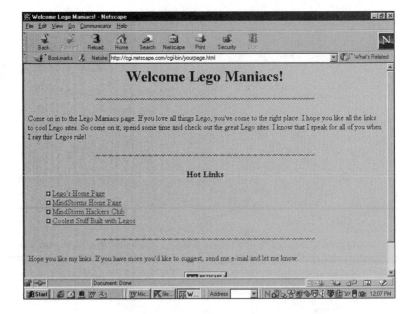

The Wizard Only Lets You Put Four Links on Your Site

For reasons known only to Netscape, its page-building wizard only lets you include four links on a page. However, when you open the page in Composer, you can add links, by clicking the **Link** button.

6. After you're done editing the page, save it to your hard disk. Choose **Save** or **Save As** from the **File** menu, and pick a location on your hard disk where you want to save the page. Make sure that your file is saved with an .html or .htm extension, or a browser won't be able to view it .

7. Now you can publish your page to the Web. Check with your ISP for details to find out to which server and directory you should publish to, a username and password if you need one, and similar information. After you know all that, click the **Publish** button, fill in the form that you see pictured in Figure 17.10, and you're done. Congratulations! You've just published a Web page.

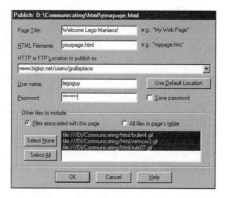

Figure 17.10

It's getting very near the end...here's how you'll publish your page to the Web.

How to Build a Web Page Using a Template

After you build a page or two using Composer's wizard, you'll probably find it a bit confining. The pages you can build are functional and useful, but they lack a certain style and pizzazz.

But what if you're the kind of guy or gal who likes style and pizzazz, but you don't know how to build a Web page that sizzles, sings, or otherwise sparkles?

You do it by using templates. Templates are pre-built pages that include a design and layout, and that include boilerplate text and pictures that you can replace with words and pictures of your own. To use a template, you load it into Composer, edit it, save it, and then publish it.

The best place to get templates is directly from Netscape's site. To build a page using a template from Netscape's site, you need to be connected to the Internet. So get online. Next, launch Composer. After you do that, here's how to build a page using a template:

1. Choose **New** from the **File** menu, and then choose **Page From Template**. A box will appear, like the one pictured in Figure 17.11. Click the **Netscape Templates** button.

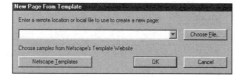

Figure 17.11

Here's how to get started building a Web page from a template in Composer.

2. Netscape Navigator will open in a new window. You'll be on a page where you can choose templates from a list. Click on the template you want to use.

3. The template will open in Navigator. You need to edit it in Composer. To open the page in Composer, choose **Edit Page** from the **File** menu in the Navigator window. Figure 17.12 shows a template ready to be edited in Composer.

Figure 17.12

On your mark, get set, edit! Here's a template in Composer, ready to be edited.

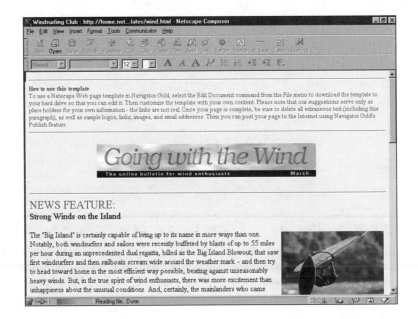

4. Edit the page using all of Composer's tools. To delete a graphic, click it and hit the **Delete** button. To delete text, highlight it and hit the **Delete** button.

Cool Tips

You Can Use Templates from Other Sources

The templates provided by Netscape aren't the only templates you can use—there are others you can use as well. Templates provided at the WebDiner site are particularly good. Get them at http://www.webdiner.com/templates/index.htm. In fact, you can use any Web page as a template. When you're on a page that you'd like to use as a template in Navigator, choose **Edit Page** from the **File** menu, and follow the directions outlined in this chapter for creating a page from a template.

5. When you're done with the page, save it to your hard disk and then publish it as I outlined earlier in "Time for Wizardry: How to Build a Web Page Using a Wizard." Congratulations! You've just created a page from a template.

If You Build It, Will They Come?

You've finally done it. You've built a Web page, and on it, you've told the world about your world-famous hubcap collection. Now you're waiting for the visitors to pile in, to send you email, and to give you a chance to make new friends. But you've given a party and no one's shown up. You've built it—and no one came.

That's because building a Web page isn't enough. You also have to let the world know about it. There are ways that you can easily publicize the site on your own. Here's how to do it:

➤ **Submit your site to search engines**   Many people go to search engines such as http://www.yahoo.com, http://www.excite.com, http://www.lycos.com, http://www.altavista.com, and http://www.hotbot.com to search the Web for information they're interested in. If you make sure that those search engines know about your site, people will be able to find you. For each search engine, there's a different way of submitting your site, so check each engine for details.

➤ **Use an automated site submission service**   In addition to the major search engines, there are literally hundreds of other search sites on the Internet, many of them specialized. You can spend your whole life trying to submit your site to them. Instead, you can pay a service to do it for you. Sites such as http://www.submit-it.com, http://www.site-see.com, and http://www.websitepromote.com will submit your site for a fee. Depending on what you want done, the fee can range from $10 to hundreds of dollars.

➤ **Use software to submit your site to search engines**   Instead of paying a site submission service, you can use software that will do a similar job for you. There are many different pieces of software that do this, including Web Submit Pro, Submit It, Major Submit , and many others. Typically, you can use this software for free for a certain amount of time, or you can use a portion of it for free, before deciding whether to buy. You'll pay something in the $20 price range for them. Get them at download sites on the Internet such as http://www.zddownloads.com.

➤ **Publicize your site in your email "signature"**   When you send out email, you can include a "signature" at the bottom of your email that includes any kind of information you want, such as your Web site. Put your Web site in your email signature as a way of drawing visitors. To learn how to create signatures, turn to Chapter 7, "Tons of Fancy Email Tricks."

The Least You Need to Know

➤ A Web page will put you in touch with other people who share your interests, will help you communicate with your community or civics group, and will let you share personal things about yourself, such as the birth of a child.

➤ To create a Web page, you'll need an HTML editor. Netscape Composer and Microsoft FrontPage Express are both excellent free editors especially suited for beginners.

➤ You'll also need a place to host your site when you create a Web page. Most ISPs, including America Online, include free hosting services as part of your fee.

➤ To build a Web page using a wizard in Composer, choose **New** from the **File** menu, and then choose **Page From Wizard**. To build a Web page using a template, instead choose **Page from Template**.

➤ You'll need to get information from your ISP, such as the location of your Web page, your username, and password, to publish your page.

➤ Publicize your page by submitting it to search engines, using special services that submit your page to the engines for you, and including your page in your email signature.

Chapter 18

Broadcast for Free: How to Get and Use Free Web Pages

In This Chapter

➤ Why you can build your own Web page for free

➤ Why you should build a Web page at a free site instead of your ISP

➤ How to use design and publishing tools to build your Web page

➤ How you can make money from your free Web page

➤ The best free Web page building sites on the Internet

Here's one of the great all-time deals on the Internet—you get to create your own Web page for free. No, there's no catch. It's free as in you-don't-pay-any-money-at-all-ever-no-matter-what-happens. Free. And there's no catch.

In this chapter, I'll show you how to get free Web pages, how to build them, how to use them to communicate with others—and even how to get *paid* to build them. Yes you heard right. So read on for the details.

What? They'll Give Me Web Pages for Free? What's the Catch?

Yet another way the Internet turns normal economics on its head: You can get free Web pages. There are many sites on the Internet that let you build your own Web pages for free, and provide you with all kinds of resources to do it.

These sites are among the most popular sites on the Internet. How can they stay in business if they don't charge you any money? Simple. The sites generally require that you put ads on your Web page, and the sites charge advertisers money for those ads. So every time someone visits your Web page, the site is taking in money. That's how they can afford to give you your Web page for free.

As you've seen elsewhere in this section of the book, a Web page is a great way to communicate with others. So all the rules about design and tips and tricks on how to use those pages to get your message out to the world, apply to free Web pages in the same way that they do to the Web pages that you get from your ISP or that you have to pay for. To be clued in on all that, turn to Chapter 17, "Broadcast Your Interests to the World: Creating Your Own Web Page to Communicate with Others."

Free Web pages offer some extras that you won't get if you build a Web page with your normal ISP. For details, read on.

Why Get Free Web Pages Instead of the Ones from Your ISP?

Almost any ISP you sign up with offers free Web pages. So why bother getting a free Web page from an Internet site that offers them if you already can have a Web page on your ISP? (Aside from the fact that free is free after all, and who can turn down a free offer?)

In fact, there are many good reasons. The first, of course, is that your ISP might not offer you the ability to build Web pages, or if it does, it might ask that you pay extra for it. But even if your ISP offers Web pages for free, there are reasons you'll also want to use a free Web page from a Web site:

➤ **They offer free page-building tools**   Most sites offer you very good tools for building your own Web pages. You won't have to know how to use HTML, the language you need to learn to create Web pages from scratch. The tools offered by Web sites usually include pre-built templates, fill-in-the-blank forms, and more. It's so easy to do that you'll be able to build your first Web page in a half hour or less.

➤ **They offer a built-in community of people likely to visit your page**   The whole point of building your page is to communicate with people. If you build a Web page on your own ISP, will visitors come? Probably not. But if you build a Web page on a free Web page site, they will. That's because these sites are all about community, and people spend a good deal of time browsing other Web pages. So you'll start off with a built-in audience.

➤ **They offer free art**   One of the hardest things about building Web pages is to find art to put on it—things like buttons, arrows, backgrounds, and other pictures. Many Web page–building sites include a free library of things to include on your site. In Figure 18.1, you can see an example of art you can add on the GeoCities Web page–building site at http://www.geocities.com.

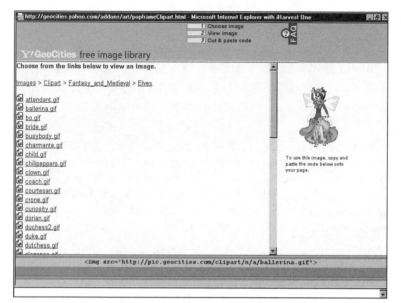

Figure 18.1
You'll find free art for the taking at Web page–building sites such as GeoCities. Here's a ballerina...or is it a fairy...well, whatever it is, it's free and you can put it on your GeoCities Web site.

➤ **They offer cool gizmos, interactivity, and other cool stuff you can put on your Web pages** Sites like GeoCities offer many kinds of cool stuff you can put on your Web site for free: trivia games, stock tickers, animated logos, guestbooks, and more. And as I'll show you later in this chapter, it's amazingly easy to put that cool stuff on your pages.

➤ **You can make money from the pages** Yes, you heard me right. At some of these places, not only do you get a Web page for free, but you're given an opportunity to *make* money. To do that, you can put links on your site that allow visitors to buy books, movies, toys, and more. Then when people buy something from that link, you get a cut of the selling price. What a country! What an economy!

Cool Tips

America Online Also Offers Free Web Pages

If you're an America Online user, you'll be pleased to know that the service offers you the ability to build Web pages for free. To get to the area where you can build Web pages, use the keywords **Web Pages**.

How You'll Get Pages at Free Web Page Sites

To build your own free Web pages, all you'll need to do is sign up at a site. (For a list of free Web sites, check the end of this chapter.) It doesn't take much more than visiting a site, filling out a form, saying you'll agree to the terms, and away you go.

There are a few things you should know about the agreements. At many of the sites, you're not allowed to use your Web pages for commercial purposes. So if you run a business selling T-shirts, and you want to sell them online, one of these sites is not the way to go. If it's found out you're selling them, you'll be banned from the site.

Generally, part of the agreement will be that ads will run on your page. After all, that's one of the primary ways that the sites make money and can afford to give you free pages.

When you sign up at one of the sites, you'll have to fill out some kind of registration form. You might be asked a lot of questions about your age, your interests, and similar information. There's a reason those questions are being asked: They might be used as a way to target email offers at you. In other words, when you fill out the form, you might get more spam in your email inbox. (*Spam*, by the way is the generally used term for unsolicited email—in other words, the junk mail of the Internet.)

If you want to cut down on the junk mail you get, or if you're worried about your privacy, examine the registration form carefully. On many forms, there will be certain required fields, such as your name and address, and there will be other fields you don't have to fill out, such as your annual income. Don't fill out the fields you're not required to fill out, and the site won't have personal information about you that you'd prefer to remain secret. Oh, yes, one more tip: Feel free to be creative in your response to questions you think are too personal. Required to provide your occupation to a site, but you'd rather not reveal the information? Just tell them you're a spider fashion consultant. Let them find an advertiser who wants to send junk mail to one of *those!*

Cool Tips

There Are Many Other Ways to Protect Your Privacy and Stop Spam

Worried that your privacy might be invaded on the Internet? Want to stop spam in its tracks? Then look for a copy of my book *The Complete Idiot's Guide to Protecting Yourself Online.* It'll teach you all that and more.

Also look for any boxes or questions that ask if you want to receive special offers from advertisers. Then just say no. Otherwise, you might well be deluged by spam.

How to Build Web Pages at Free Sites

So you've signed up and you're ready to build a Web page. Congratulations! It won't be long now before you're ready to build one of your own. Pretty much every site you go to that offers free Web pages also offers quick-and-easy publishing tools for building your own Web page—and if you're experienced at building Web pages, they'll also let you create HTML pages any way you like and upload them to the site. A full rundown on how to build HTML pages is beyond the scope of this book, so here I'll cover how you'll build a home page with the built-in tools of the sites.

How you'll build a page differs from site to site. So I'll go with the big guy—I'll cover how you'll build a page at GeoCities, the most popular page-building site on the Internet (see Figure 18.2). If you build your own Web page at another site, you'll build it slightly differently from what you do here, but the basic idea is the same.

After you register at GeoCities, you'll have to choose which "neighborhood" you want to build your page in. These range from the artistic and romantic of Paris and Soho in the Arts and Literature neighborhood, to the tech-heavy Silicon Valley in Computers, Science, and Tech.

After you choose your neighborhood, you'll have to fill out a brief form, describing your page, such as the one you see pictured in Figure 18.3. After you do that, you're ready to roll—you'll be given the location of your home page. Welcome to the neighborhood, and make sure to mow the grass!

Cool Tips

It's Easy to Learn HTML and Build Your Own Home Page

It's not hard at all to learn HTML and build your own home page without having to use the tools provided by free Web sites. To learn how to build your own page with HTML or by using a simple Web page editor, go out and grab a copy of *The Complete Idiot's Guide to Creating a Web Page, Fourth Edition,* by Paul McFedries.

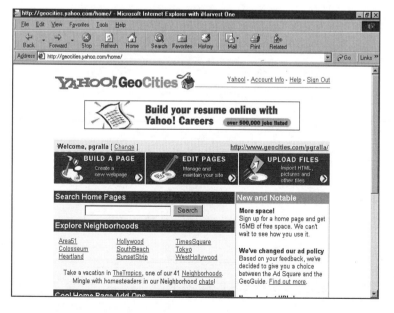

Figure 18.2

Yahoo! GeoCities offers an easy-to-navigate site to help you make your own Web page.

Figure 18.3

Nosy, aren't they? Here's the form you'll have to fill out at GeoCities before you can start building your Web page.

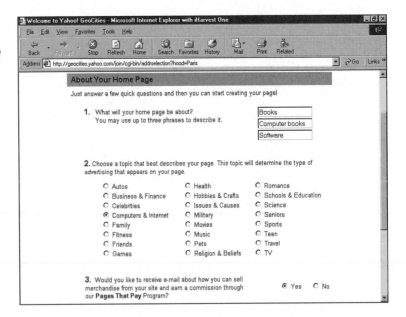

Click **Build Your Page Now**, and you'll be sent to the main GeoCities page that I showed you back in Figure 18.2. To get started, click **Build a Page**. When you do, you'll see the screen shown in Figure 18.4.

Figure 18.4

On your mark, get set...Here's how you'll start to build a Web page with the tools provided by GeoCities.

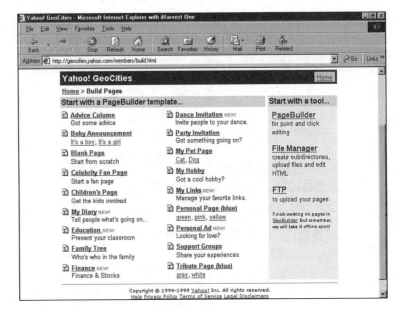

As you can see, you can either choose a template on the left side of the screen or PageBuilder on the right. When you choose a template,; you start with a certain look and feel; when you start with PageBuilder, you start using the PageBuilder tool right away. But the truth is, it doesn't matter much which of the methods you use—if you start with a template, you'll end up building it with PageBuilder, and if you start with PageBuilder, you can end up choosing a template! As they say here in Massachusetts, "Same difference."

In our example, we'll choose to start from a template. If this is the first home page you've built, you'll find it much easier to choose a template than start from scratch. So we'll choose a template. I want to share one of my favorite hobbies with the world, so we'll choose the **My Hobby** template. Figure 18.5 shows you PageBuilder, opened with a template, ready for us to build our home page.

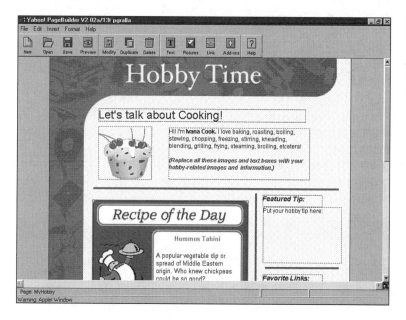

Figure 18.5

Time to build the home page: When you choose a template, here's what you'll see.

As you can see, the page comes already laid out and filled in with pictures, text, and assorted colors and doodads. What you're going to do is change those text, pictures, colors, and assorted doodads with your own—and you'll be able to choose pictures, doodads, and other stuff right from GeoCities.

To change text, highlight it, type what you want it to say, and then apply colors, formatting, and anything else you want to it using the toolbars at the top of PageBuilder. In Figure 18.6, I've started to replace the existing text with some of my own.

Figure 18.6

Take the first step: Replace the text on your page with text of your own. No, it's not a recipe for baked Godzilla.

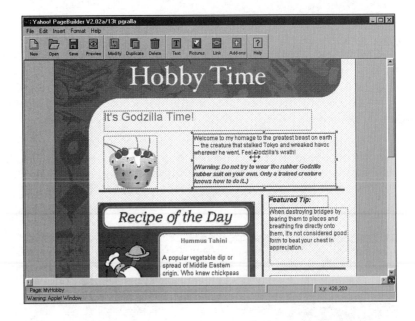

You can move text blocks and pictures around the page easily. Click whatever you want to move, and you'll see double-sided criss-crossing arrows appear, as you can see in Figure 18.6. When that arrow appears, you can move the text block or picture. Change the text how you want, move the blocks around, and you're on your way to creating your home page.

Adding Pictures to Your Home Page

A home page without pictures is like Abbot without Costello. When you choose a template, it will already have pictures chosen for you. But what fun is that? You want to add pictures of your own. It's easy to do with PageBuilder. Click the **Pictures** link and you'll be able to browse through a large clip art library and preview your pictures before adding them. If you instead have pictures of your own you want to use, you'll need to first upload them to the site. To do that, click on the **Upload** button, browse on your computer to the picture you want to upload, and follow the instructions. When the picture is uploaded, it will appear in the Imported Pictures collection. In Figure 18.7, you can see me choosing a picture of a Godzilla poster I'm going to add to my Godzilla page—a picture that I uploaded to the site.

After the picture is on your page, you can move it in the same way you move any other kind of block. You can resize it as well: Click it and drag any of the sides to make it larger or smaller.

Figure 18.7
Worth a thousand words: Here's how to choose to put a picture on your page in PageBuilder.

Adding Links to Your Home Page

Any home page worth its salt has links to other sites and resources on it. It's easy to add links to your page. To do that, highlight any text that you want to be a link, click the **Link** icon in the toolbar, and then type the location where you want the text to link to. That's all there is to it. No muss, no fuss—easy links.

Adding Gizmos and Other Cool Things

GeoCities makes it easy to put all kinds of cool things on your Web page—things like page counters, animated pictures, interactive forms, games, links to discussion groups, and much more. To do that, click **Add-Ons** on the toolbar, choose whatever you want to put on, and then move it to where you want it to go.

Now It's Time to Publish Your Page

After everything's ready it's time to take the leap—time to publish your page. You'll probably want to preview the page before publishing it, so that you can clean up any errors before the world sees your creation. So click **Preview**, and you'll see the page exactly as the world will see it.

Walkie the Talkie

What's a Page Counter?

It's nice to know how many people have visited your home page—and often visitors want to know as well. A *page counter* is something you can put on your home page that will count every time someone visits the page, and display the results.

Include a Message Board on Your Site

One of the best way to communicate with other people is with a message board—a discussion area where anyone who wants to can participate in a free-ranging discussion. GeoCities makes it easy to create a message board and to put it on your page. Just click the **Add-Ons** button and choose **Message Board** from the **Interactive** drop-down menu. Then place the graphic that appears on your page. You've just created a message board—when people click it, they'll go to your own personal message board.

After you have the page exactly as you want it, click **Save**. You can either save it as the existing index page, or else choose another name for it. Save your first page as an *index* page. The index page is the page that people will automatically be sent to when they come to your site. If you want to build more pages later, you can, and you can then link them all together. But keep the first page you build as your index.

After you save the page, you're done. You now have your official home page, complete with bells and whistles and other neat things. Shown in Figures 18.8 and 18.9 are the final two steps of the page-building process: First how to save your page, and then how it looks on the site.

Figure 18.8

Get ready to publish. First you save your page in PageBuilder...

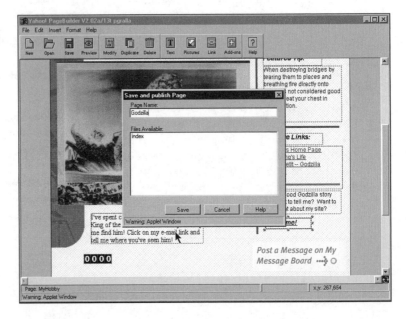

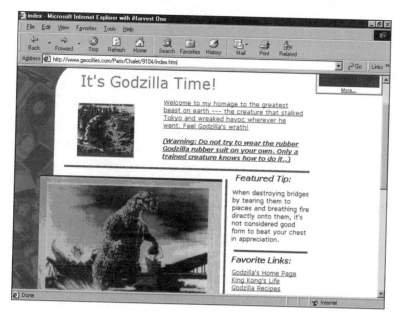

Figure 18.9
...and then it's ready for the world to see. Go Godzilla, go!

Yes, It's True. You Can Make Money with Your Web Site

Earlier in the chapter, I told you that you could actually make money on some of these free Web page–building sites. GeoCities is a perfect example of how you can do it.

To make money with your Web pages, you link to products on your site that people can buy—books, movies, toys, games, software, and more. Although the rules are different from site to site, and even from merchant to merchant, generally you'll get a percentage of what people buy when they click the link. For example, at GeoCities, you'll get seven percent of the sales of all books sold from your site.

To make money this way, you have to register with the "Pages that Pay" plan. Then you put links to products. Then sit back and collect the checks—that is, if anyone buys anything. For details on all this on GeoCities, click the **Pages that Pay** link. The AngelFire site detailed later in this chapter, as well as other free Web page–building sites, have similar programs.

Best Sites for Getting Free Web Pages

If you're looking to get free Web pages, you're in luck—there are many sites on the Internet that offer them. Here are the best.

217

GeoCities

`http://www.geocities.com`

Here's the big magilla of free Web page sites. It's huge, filled with many "neighbor-hoods" of sites built by people like you. There are great page-building tools, ways to make money through an affiliates program, ways to add gizmos, and message boards. In short, I think it's the best place online for building Web pages.

AngelFire

`http://www.angelfire.com`

Here's another good page-building site with a big complement of services: good page-building tools, the ability to make money through an affiliates program, and more. I particularly like the way it highlights favorite pages so that you can see the best of what other people have built.

Tripod

`http://www.tripod.com`

Just like the other good page-building sites, you'll get page-building tools, an affiliates program, and good community here. There's another plus—you can sign up for your own domain, so that instead of a very long and confusing URL for people to remember, they can type in a very short one. So if your last name were Rumpelstiltskin, and no one else owned that domain, you could buy it, and when people typed it, they'd visit your Web site here. Click **Your-Name.com** on the site for details.

Walkie the Talkie

What Does URL Stand For?

URL stands for *Uniform Resource Locator.* A URL is the precise location of any spot on the Internet—generally, though, it's used to refer to a specific Web page.

Xoom

`http://www.xoom.com`

You'll find all kinds of services at this site beyond free Web page building—greeting cards, a fax service, auctions, and more. I find the site a bit garish and at times confusing, but it's quite popular, so it might be for you.

FortuneCity

http://www.fortunecity.com

This site isn't quite as feature-packed as the other best page-building sites, but it's still worth a visit. One of the reasons I like it is that I think it's one of the cooler-looking page-building sites. It's pictured in Figure 18.10.

Figure 18.10

FortuneCity: One of the cooler-looking free page-building sites on the Internet.

theglobe.com

http://www.theglobe.com

In addition to the usual features you'd expect on a free page-building site, this one has some nice extras. My favorite: the ability to create an email mailing list of your own. It's a way to publish your thoughts to the world via email. For more information about these kinds of services and how to use them, turn to Chapter 22, "Tell It to the World: How to Broadcast Newsletters via Email."

The Least You Need to Know

➤ Free Web page–building sites let you build pages for free because they put advertising on all pages, and make money from advertisers.

➤ Free page-building sites offer better design and publishing tools than an ISP, let you incorporate many cool gizmos on your site, and offer a built-in community of people who will visit you.

➤ To build a free Web page, you'll have to register at a site and provide information about yourself.

➤ If you know how to build a Web page, you don't have to use the site's design and publishing tools—you can use your own.

➤ In addition to the clip art provided by the site, you can use your own pictures by uploading them and then incorporating them into your page.

➤ Many sites have an affiliates program that lets you make money by linking to products such as books and CDs. You'll get paid every time someone buys a product from your link.

Chapter 19

Adding a Webcam to Your Site

In This Chapter

➤ What a Webcam is

➤ What the difference is between a Webcam and a Netcam

➤ All the things you'll need to build a Webcam page

➤ How to code an HTML page to display the Webcam

➤ How to use SpyCam software to take pictures and upload them to the Webcam

➤ How to build and post your Webcam page

Are you hungry for fame? Have you always wanted to be on camera? Do you think the world is a poorer place because it can't see your breathtaking face every waking second of the day? Do you want everyone on the planet to see just how beautiful the view is outside your window? (After you clear away the rusted pickup truck on cinder blocks, and hide the chickens pecking at the red dirt in your yard, or course.)

It's time to unleash your hidden exhibitionist. It's time to set up your own Webcam. In this chapter, I'll show you how to set up a Webcam for all the world to see.

What Exactly Is a Webcam?

So what exactly is a Webcam? It's a video camera that's attached to your computer that takes still photos at regular intervals, and then uploads those photos to a Web

You Can Send Live Video with Webcams

It's possible to have a Webcam send live video, not just snapshots. But to do that, you need an extremely high-speed connection to the Internet, as well as experience with very complicated programming things such as CGI scripts and JavaScript. So for the purposes of this book, we'll stick to normal snapshots done with a Webcam.

site, where anyone in the world can see them. Don't confuse the terms "Netcam" and "Webcam." A Netcam is a term just for the video camera you attach to your computer that takes the pictures. A Webcam is a term that describes not just the Netcam, but also the Web page on the Internet that shows the world the picture your Netcam takes.

There are Webcams set up all over the Internet, showing you things like the view from Pike's Peak, Hong Kong street scenes, the inside of dormitory rooms, and more. There's even a view of Boston's Charles River and Beacon Hill as seen from Cambridge—and that Webcam lives right near my office at the ZDNet Web site, so I can look at the real-life view itself and then log on to the Internet and see the same view on the Web. Talk about post-modern experiences! Pictured here in Figure 19.1 you can see the view from the top of Colorado's Pike's Peak.

Figure 19.1

I can see for miles...Here's a view from the top of Pike's Peak, brought to you by a Webcam.

You might think that creating your own Webcam takes super-human programming resources, powerful computers, and high-end video equipment. Nothing can be further from the truth. As I'll show you in this chapter, it's extremely easy to set up your own Webcam. You'll just need some basic equipment and software and a bit of know-how. So read on for details.

Pike Never Made It to the Top of His Peak

Little-known fact: Pike's Peak is named after Zebulon Montgomery Pike, who was actually unable to climb the mountain later named after him. To add insult to injury, Pike traveled 2,000 miles by boat and foot to find the source of the Mississippi River—and he incorrectly identified the source as Leech Lake.

What You'll Need to Build a Webcam

You've decided that yes, you do want the world to see your living room, or your backyard, or you sitting glassy-eyed in front of your computer. It won't take much to do it. Here's what you'll need to build your window onto the world:

➤ **A Netcam** You'll need a video camera attached to your PC. For advice on what to buy and how to set it up, turn to Chapter 4, "How to Choose a Web Video Camera," and Chapter 5, "How to Set Up and Use a Web Video Camera."

➤ **An Internet connection** Faster is better. Even more important is that you need a connection that can stay on all the time, or at least as long as you want your Webcam to be live. A cable modem connection is ideal. If you're not connected to the Internet, your Webcam can't send live pictures.

➤ **A site to host your Webcam page** Your Webcam will live on a Web page that you build, so you'll need a site that will host your Webcam page. Many Internet service providers (ISPs), including America Online, offer free Web page–hosting services. And there are many sites, such as GeoCities at www.geocities.com, that offer free Web sites as well. For more information about where to get free Web pages, turn to Chapter 18, "Broadcast for Free: How to Get and Use Free Web Pages."

Publish a Schedule of When You're Live

Because you might not have an Internet connection that stays live 24 hours a day—and in any event, you might not want to have a camera pointed at you all the time—you can publish on your Web site when the Webcam will be live. On the Web page, note when the Webcam will be on, and tell people that at all other times, the Webcam image they see will be an old one.

➤ **Software and know-how for building your Web page**   To build a Web page, you'll need software and know-how. I teach you how to build Web pages in Chapter 17, "Broadcast Your Interests to the World: Creating Your Own Web Page to Communicate with Others," and Chapter 18.

➤ **Webcam software**   You'll need special software that will use your Webcam to take snapshots, and then upload those snapshots to your Web site automatically. Many Netcams that you buy include this software with them. But my favorite is SpyCam, because of how remarkably easy it is to use. It's included on the CD in the back of this book. In the rest of this chapter, I'll show you how to build a Webcam page using SpyCam.

The Steps You'll Take for Creating a Webcam

Now that you've got everything in place, it's time to start building your Webcam. Creating a Webcam page is a three-step process:

1. Build a Web page for your Webcam, and upload it to the site where it will live.

2. Launch and customize SpyCam so that it works the way you want it to.

3. Run SpyCam so that it takes photos and sends them to your Web site.

Let's get started with the first step—building a Web page for your Webcam and uploading it to the site where it lives.

Walkie the Talkie

What's a Pixel?

A *pixel* is a single dot on your computer screen, and is a term used to measure the size of graphics on your screen and on the Web.

First, Build a Web Page

Building a Web page for your Webcam is really no different from building any other Web page. The same rules apply. So check back to Chapter 17 and Chapter 18 on how to do it.

The main thing you need to know about building a Webcam page is that you need to include a link to a graphic, and you also have to specify the width and height of the graphic in pixels. That space where you specify the graphic is where your Netcam picture will go.

The graphic should be in the JPEG format, and it can be named anything you want to name it. Later, when you use SpyCam, you'll need to remember the name of this graphic. The size that you specify for the graphic is very important—it's the size that your Webcam will show on the site.

I recommend one of two different sizes for your Webcam—either 160 pixels wide by 120 pixels high, or else 320 pixels wide by 240 pixels high. When you use the smaller size, the photo will load faster when someone visits your site, but it will be less detailed. The larger size offers a more detailed picture, but will load more slowly. Figures 19.2 and 19.3 show the same Webcam photo, at the two different sizes.

Figure 19.2

Let's get small. Here's what a Webcam looks like at 160 by 120 pixels...

Figure 19.3

...and here's what it looks like at the larger 320 pixels by 240 pixels.

When determining the size of the picture you want, keep in mind what else you want on the page. At the smaller size, you'll be able to fit other things on the page. At the larger size, little else will be able to fit. Of course, if you have an ego the size of Donald Trump's, you don't *want* anything else on the page.

Here's the Secret Code

With all that in mind, let's take an example. Say you were going to have a Webcam, you decided that the filename for the graphic would be "me.jpg," and you want to have the graphic display at 320 by 240 pixels. Here's the HTML code that you'd use, assuming that the graphic will be in the same directory as your HTML document:

```
<img src="me.jpg" width="320" height="240">
```

Put that in the place on you Web page where you want your Webcam picture to be and you'll be ready to roll. Here's an example of HTML code for an extremely stripped-down Web page that will only have a title in the title bar, a headline for the page, and a Webcam picture:

```
<html>
<head>
<title>Here I Am!</title>
</head>
<body>
<center>
<h1>Welcome to my World!</h1>
<br>
<img src="me.jpg" width="320" height="240">
</body>
</html>
```

You of course can make your page as fancy or as plain as you'd like. Again, check the chapters I mentioned before for more information on how to build Web pages.

After you've built your page, upload it to whoever will be hosting your Web page. Now you're ready to move on and use SpyCam.

Next, Set Up SpyCam to Create Your Webcam

After you upload the page, your Webcam won't yet be live. If anyone visits the page right now (heaven forbid), they'll see a broken link where a graphic is supposed to be. That's because there's no picture there yet. That's what SpyCam will do for you—take the picture and then automatically upload it for you.

After you install SpyCam and you run it, it runs as a small icon in your system tray. To access its features, right click the icon, and you'll see the menu pictured here, in Figure 19.4.

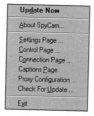

Figure 19.4

What's on the menu? Here's how you'll use SpyCam—choose any of the items on the menu.

You'll use these menu items set up in SpyCam to create your Webcam. Here's how to do it.

Cool Tips

You Should Pay $5 to the SpyCam Author if You Like the Program

SpyCam is free to try and use, but the author of the program asks that you pay for it if you decide you like it and keep using it. The fee is nominal—only $5—so it's a good idea to pay for it if you continue to use it. To register, you can mail a check to Bill Oatman, 12 Hawks View, Honeoye Falls, NY 14472. You can also head to `http://www.netacc.net/~waterbry/SpyCam/register.htm` to register or register by calling (800) 427-2770.

Start Off on the Settings Page

For SpyCam to upload a picture to your Web site, it needs to know where to upload the picture, and it needs password information and other details. It'll need your password because Web sites require you to have a password to upload files.

You put all this information into the Settings page, shown in Figure 19.5.

You'll need to get the name of your remote machine from the site that will host your Webcam page. By the way, *remote machine* is just a techie-sounding word for the name of the Web server where you upload your Web page. You'll also need to know the directory where you upload your page as well. And you'll need to fill in your password, also.

What might be the most important part of this page is the filename. Remember back when I told you to give a filename to a graphic on the Webcam page? Make sure the filename you give here is the same one that you specified on the Webcam page. If it's not, the picture won't be displayed and your Webcam won't work. And make sure that the graphic is uploaded to the same directory in which you put the Web page.

227

Figure 19.5

Here's where you'll tell SpyCam where to upload your picture, and where you give it super-secret information, such as your password.

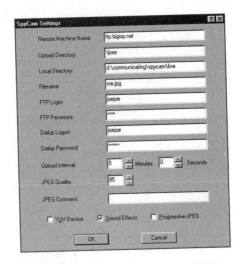

You Might Not Need to Put in an Upload Directory

Some sites that let you host Web pages don't require that you detail your upload directory when you send them files. These sites check your password, and based on your password, they automatically route the files to the proper directory. In fact, if you detail an upload directory on these sites, you might not be able to upload your files properly. Check with the site itself for details.

There are two other important parts of this screen to pay attention to:

➤ **Upload interval** This tells SpyCam how frequently to take your picture and send it to the Web site so the world can see it. The default time is five minutes, but if you want pictures taken more often or less often, just change the interval.

➤ **JPEG quality** This determines how crisp the picture will be, and also how large the JPEG file will be. If you make the picture too crisp, the file will be very large, and so will take a long time to load. So balance the crispness and file size. The default of 85% seems to work fine.

Now Move to the Control Page

After you've saved the settings, it's time to move to the page that controls your taking of pictures—the Control page. Choose **Control Page** from the menu, and you'll see a screen like the one shown in Figure 19.6.

Figure 19.6

Take control: Here's how to control your Webcam's picture taking. Who is that weird-looking guy? Oh, that's me. Gotta remember to shave more often.

You'll notice one thing odd: An off-kilter picture taking up most of the screen. I don't mean it's off-kilter because *I'm* in it (although that might be part of the cause)—I mean it's off-kilter because it doesn't match the actual picture that the Netcam is looking at right now. So my advice to you is just ignore that part, and don't worry about the various preview buttons and options.

The most important thing about this page is the little box next to the word **Active**. If that box is unchecked, your Webcam isn't yet working. To have it start taking pictures, check that box. When you do that, your Netcam will spring into action, taking pictures and uploading them to the directory you specified on the Settings page. And after that happens, the world will be able to see wherever your Netcam is pointed.

On this page, you also can manually force the Netcam to take a picture and upload it—click the **Update Now** button.

By the way, whenever your Netcam takes a picture, you'll hear sounds like a shutter moving and then a camera taking a picture. Just a little bit of audio confirmation that the thing is working.

Cool Tips

You Can Manually Take Pictures Without Using the Control Page

Want to quickly have your Netcam snap a picture and upload it to your Webcam page? It's a snap to do. Just double-click the **SpyCam** icon in your system tray.

Putting a Caption on Your Webcam with the Captions Page

If you'd like, you can put a caption across your Webcam. It can be any message you want: "Kilroy Was Here," "Will Work for Food," "Buddy Can You Spare a Dime?" And you can put a time and date stamp on it as well—in other words, show the exact date and time that the Webcam picture was taken.

To put on a caption, choose the **Captions Page**, shown in Figure 19.7. You can put a caption at the top and one at the bottom. To do it, check the **Enable** boxes and type your message. To change the font, click the **Font** button and choose the font and size you want.

Figure 19.7

Send your message to the world by putting a caption across your Webcam picture, by using this page. This picture shows how you can change the font and size of the caption.

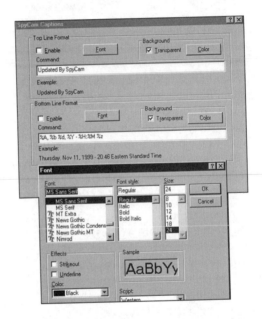

Notice that the caption at the bottom has all kinds of weird symbols. I'd suggest not messing with it. It's a kind of language that tells the program what date and time stamp to put on the Webcam picture. So if you want a time and date stamp, leave it as it is.

When you put a caption, it will appear over the picture itself. So, be careful not to make the caption so large that the picture can't be seen, or so small that the caption can't be read.

Oh, Yeah—There Are Some Other Techie Things You Can Do as Well

There are a few other screens in SpyCam that you probably won't ever need, but I'm feeling in a voluble mood (big word—can you tell I was an English major?) so I'll tell you about them.

➤ **The Proxy Configuration page**   For those people who have to use something called a proxy server to upload files. Most people should simply ignore this page. If for some reason you use a proxy server, then fill in the information on that page.

Check for SpyCam Upgrades

The author of SpyCam regularly releases updates to the program. You'll want to keep your program as up-to-date as possible. To check for updates, right-click the **SpyCam** icon, and then choose **Check for Update**. If you're connected to the Internet, the program will go out and see if there's an update available. If one is, it will tell you and will let you know how to get the update. If one isn't available, it'll tell you the program is the most recent one available.

➤ **The Connection page**   To let you say how you're connected to the Internet—via a dial-up connection, for example, or a connection that's on all the time, such as a cable modem. If you tell the program you're on a dial-up connection, it can connect you to the Internet when it takes a picture and needs to upload it.

Now Your Webcam Is Live

If you've gone through everything I've taught you in this chapter, your Webcam is now live. Just make sure that the **Active** box is checked on the Control page, that you're connected to the Internet, and that your Web page is live.

Shown in Figure 19.8 is the Webcam I've created to show the view outside my window in my home office.

Figure 19.8

Home, sweet home: Here's the view I see outside my home office in Cambridge, Massachusetts. I can look out the window at the same time I look at the precise same view on the Web. What's the point? Who knows, but it's fun to do.

The Least You Need to Know

➤ A Webcam works by taking still photographs of a scene at regular intervals, and uploading those photos to the Web, where anyone can see them.

➤ To run a Webcam, you'll need to build a Web page and upload it to a site that will host Web pages for you.

➤ When you build your Web page for a Webcam, you include a command to include a picture, with an HTML command such as this: `<img src="me.jpg" width="320" height="240">`.

➤ When you use a smaller image size for the Webcam, the page will load faster for visitors, but the image will be harder to see. A larger image size will load more slowly, but will show more detail.

➤ An excellent piece of software for building a Webcam is SpyCam, included on the CD at the back of this book.

➤ Make sure that the filename you specify in SpyCam matches the one you put on your HTML page.

Part 7

But Wait, There's More. Other Cool Ways to Communicate Online

Can we chat? Can we do group surfing without getting wet? Can we create our own customized newsletter and send it for free to anyone in the world who wants it?

Yes, yes, and yes. And there's more as well. In this section of the book, I'll show you all the cool ways to chat with programs like ICQ (pronounced "I Seek You").

Chapter 20

"IM Me": How to Use Chat and Instant Messenger Programs

In This Chapter

➤ Learning what chat and instant messenger programs are

➤ Understanding the different kinds of chat programs

➤ How you'll use chat programs

➤ Learning how to use chat programs

➤ Figuring out which chat program is best for you

Get ready to join the chattering classes. You're about to find out about chat and messenger programs—software that lets you talk in "real time" to people down the street, across the globe, and anywhere and everywhere in the world that people can use the Internet.

Every day millions of people chatter away. Kids chatting about school, soccer, Pokémon cards, ballet, and Ricky Martin. Adults chatting about work, opera, the singles scene, parenting, and *The X Files*. People from the United States, Sweden, the United Kingdom, Russia, Taiwan, Uganda, and any far outposts of the world. If anyone in Antarctica right now has a computer with a cellular Internet connection, they're probably chatting to someone in equatorial South America, warming themselves on the daily weather report.

Get ready to join them. In this chapter, you'll learn how to chat and use instant messenger programs—with an emphasis on the instant messenger programs, because they're hot, hot, hot these days on the Internet.

What Are Chat and Messenger Programs?

The Web gets all the publicity and visibility, but chat and messenger programs in the long run might have nearly as big an impact on how we interact with the world as does the Web. Because they make it easy to communicate with anyone, anywhere—and make the world a smaller, friendlier place.

Whew! Enough with the philosophy, already. Let's get down to what these programs do and how they work.

First the easy stuff. When you use chat and messenger programs, you type messages on your keyboard. Those messages are then instantly displayed to the people you're chatting or communicating with. And when they send you messages, you see them instantly as well.

Cool Tips

Kids Are the Ultimate Chatterers

Chat and messenger programs first caught on with kids and teens, and they're still among the biggest users of these programs. For teens in particular, life is about making and keeping in touch with friends, and gossiping. And as anyone with a teen or adolescent can tell you, chat is not enough. My daughter Mia (hi, Mia!), for example, chats online at the same time she talks on the phone to her friends (often to the same friends!). Talk about a wired generation!

People often use the terms "chat" and "messenger programs" (usually referred to as "instant messengers") to mean the same thing, but in fact, they're somewhat different. Although these days, the line between the two is blurring, because they're becoming increasingly similar to each other, still there are differences. Here are the differences between chat and instant messenger programs:

➤ **When you chat, you communicate with a lot of people at the same time**   So there might be 10, 20, or even more people chatting together at the same time in the same chat "room" or chat area. Everyone can see everything that every other person types—with some exceptions, as I'll explain later. Because of that, chatting for the first time can be a disorienting experience—

you're trying to keep track of many conversations simultaneously. Things can get pretty wild. Shown in Figure 20.1 is a chat room on America Online. It's a wild and crazy place!

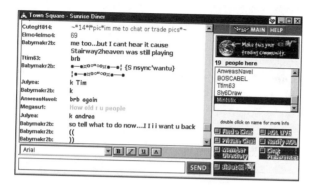

Figure 20.1

Get wild! Here's a typical free-for-all...er, I mean chat room on America Online.

➤ **When you use an instant messenger program, you communicate one-on-one with someone else** It's a one-to-one conversation, like a phone call. These programs also include "buddy lists"—they'll alert you when your "buddies" are online, so that you can immediately start a conversation.

Those are the basics. Some instant messenger programs also let you chat, and chat rooms often let you have one-on-one private conversations with others. Still, a chat program or site is one where the main purpose is to participate in group talk, whereas an instant messenger program's main purpose is to talk one-on-one. Pictured in Figure 20.2 is America Online's Internet Instant Messenger.

Figure 20.2

America Online's Instant Messenger is one of the most popular instant messenger programs on the Internet. Here, it's being used to communicate with someone on America Online.

So what kind of features do each of these programs have? Read on and find out.

Walkie the Talkie

What Does "IM me" Mean?

Spend time in an America Online chat room, and you might well have someone send you a message saying "IM me." What in the world does that mean? It means that someone is asking you to use instant messenger capability to have a private, side conversation, apart from the rest of the chat room. In some instances, you'll use an "IM" feature built directly into the chat room, whereas in other instances, you'll use a separate "IM" feature. In any event, it means someone wants to hold a one-on-one conversation.

What You Need to Know About Chat

Before the Web, there was chat. Chatting on the Internet has long been one of its most popular uses. And America Online, to a great degree, was built on the popularity of its chat rooms—and its success continues to be built on chat, chat, and more chat.

With most chat programs, to chat, you'll have to go to a certain area (such as a chat room on America Online) or log on to a certain location (such as into what's called an Internet Relay Chat [IRC] channel). After you're there, your computer will display all the messages that everyone in the room types into their computer—and everyone will be able to see what you type. You'll also see a list of all the people in the chat room. Generally, you'll be able to find out information about each of the people by clicking their names—although that information will be available only if the person wants to make it available. And most chat rooms and software let you hold private one-on-one conversations with people in the room.

This being the Internet, nothing is simple, even when it comes to chat, and there are many different ways you'll be able to chat when you head online. Here are the main ways, and what you need to know about each:

➤ **Chat on American Online** Here's the Big Daddy (or is it Big Mamma?) of chat. Approximately one zillion people chat per day on this service. To chat, you'll need to be an America Online member and log on. There are scores of places to chat, most of them specialized according to your interests. Use the keyword **CHAT** to go to a central place where you can find many different chat rooms.

➤ **Chat on a Web site**   Many Web sites now let you chat directly on them—all you'll have to do is head to the chat area and start jabbering away. You won't have to download any special software, pay any special fee, or do anything else special. Just show up and start jabbering away. You'll find many specialized chat areas as well as more general chats. Popular places to chat on Web sites are `http://www.excite.com`, `http://www.yahoo.com`, `http://www.talkcity.com`, `http://www.lycos.com`, and `http://www.thepalace.com`. When you head there, look for the chat link and click. Then get ready to yack and yammer. Figure 20.3 shows the computers and Internet chat area on Yahoo!.

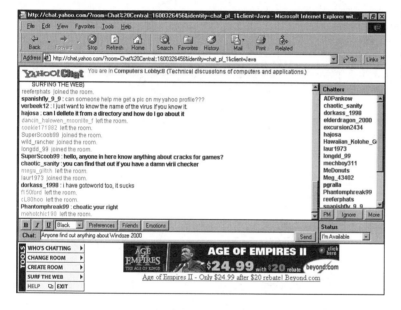

Figure 20.3

Yahoo for Yahoo! chat. Here's the computers and Internet chat area on Yahoo!.

➤ **Chat using IRC (Internet Relay Chat)**   For quite a while, the only way to chat on the Internet was to use something called IRC. IRC isn't a piece of software. Instead, it's a kind of way that computers can communicate with each other. To use IRC, you'll need special IRC software. There are many different kinds, and you can get many for free, or at least try them out for free at Internet download sites such as `http://www.zddownloads.com`. The best, from my point of view, is one called mIRC, which you can download for free from the `http://www.mirc.com` page. You can use it for free for 30 days; if you use it after that, you're expected to pay $20 for it. When you chat on IRC, you use software to enter *chat channels*. A chat channel is much like a chat room—it can be general conversation, or conversation about a very specific topic.

What's an Avatar?

On some sites and with some software when you chat, an *avatar* represents you online. An avatar is a picture that represents you, so that others can look at your representation when they chat with you. An avatar can be a full three-dimensional picture, or can be as simple as a line drawing. Performing a Web search on the keyword **avatar** should turn up dozens of collections to choose from.

➤ **Chat using special software** The final way to chat is to use special software. With this kind of software, you'll be able to chat only with others who use the same software, although in some instances, you also can use the software to chat with IRC as well. And in some instances, chat software doubles as instant messenger software. The free program LOL Chat is an example of special chat software—get it at Internet download sites or at http://www.lolchat.com. And the popular program PowWow lets you chat or send and receive instant messages, among many other features. Find it at Internet download sites or at http://www.powwow.com.

Chat While You Surf with Others

Here's chat with a twist: You can chat with other people while you surf from Web page to Web page. The newest generation of chat software lets you visit Web pages, and see who else is visiting that page, and then chat with them. Some of this software even lets you "group-surf" together and chat while you surf. One piece of popular software of this type is Gooey, available at many Internet download sites as well as at http://www.gooey.com. And the world's most popular instant messenger program and chat program, ICQ, has a companion program called ICQ Surf that lets you chat with other ICQ users when you're on a Web site. Get it at http://www.mirabilis.com. For more information about these kinds of programs, turn to Chapter 23, "Other Cool Communications Tools: Group Surfing and Web Graffiti."

Better than the Pony Express: What You Need to Know About Instant Messengers

Instant messenger programs let you talk one-on-one to other people. To use them, you download a piece of software, install it on your computer, and you're ready to start talking away. Sounds simple. Generally it is. But there are a few rules of the road you should know—and a bit of confusion about some of these programs. But without confusion, what would the Internet be? Here's what to know about the programs before you go, and advice on how to best use them:

➤ **You generally can't send and receive instant messages with someone else if you're using different instant messenger programs** So if you use Yahoo! Messenger and your friend uses MSN Messenger, you're out of luck. There's been a big controversy about this, because some companies want all instant messenger programs to communicate with one another, whereas others don't. I'll leave out the details, but suffice it to say that the companies involved have been acting with all the grace and dignity of three-year-olds fighting in a sandbox. And they show no signs of growing up. The point, though, is that if you want to communicate with your friends and family, make sure you all use the same instant messenger program. The exception is PowWow, a messenger program I cover later in this chapter. It lets you communicate with PowWow users as well as those who use AOL Instant Messenger, America Online, and MSN Messenger.

Cool Tips

MSN Messenger Users Can Communicate with AOL Instant Messenger and AOL Members...Sometimes

America Online has long had instant messenger programs, both on the America Online service itself as well as on the Internet. When Microsoft launched its MSN Messenger service, it wanted to do something somewhat revolutionary—allow users of its Messenger to send and receive instant messages with users of AOL Instant Messenger, and with those who use instant messaging on America Online itself. In fact, Microsoft figured out a way to do it and immediately turned on that feature. America Online, however, responded with some technical wizardry that shut MSN Messenger users out. The two companies went back and forth in this high-tech showdown, and continue to do so. So some days, people who use the two instant messaging programs can talk with one another, and some days they can't. There's a chance that by the time you read this, Microsoft and America Online will have come to some kind of agreement about how to handle the issue...but don't count on it!

➤ **The best way to use instant messenger programs is to use their buddy lists** When you set up a buddy list or similar feature, you'll be told whenever one of your friends is online. That way, you can start chatting away as soon as he logs on. In Figure 20.4, you can see how to add a buddy in Yahoo! Messenger.

Figure 20.4

How's it going, buddy? Here's how to add a buddy to your list in Yahoo! Messenger.

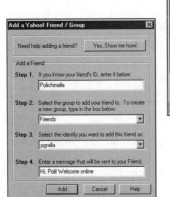

➤ **Don't give out your credit card number, passwords, or any other sensitive materials in an instant message conversation** When your message goes out over the Internet, it can be snooped on by hackers. So don't ever say or send anything that you don't want others to see.

➤ **When deciding which instant messenger to use, look for their extra features** These programs are getting increasingly sophisticated, and many have added all kinds of extra bells and whistles and all-around cool stuff and gizmos. Yahoo! Instant Messenger, for example, lets you track your stock portfolio and be delivered news and weather. And it lets you have voice chats with your buddies—you don't need to type your keyboard, you can talk into a microphone. America Online's Instant Messenger includes a stock ticker and a news ticker.

The most popular instant messenger program of all, ICQ (pronounced I Seek You) has more features than you can shake a stick at. In fact, it has so many cool features that I've devoted an entire chapter to it, and so won't cover it in this chapter. For how to use ICQ, and all kinds of insider tips and hints, turn to Chapter 21, "I Seek You: How to Use ICQ, the World's Most Popular Chat Program."

Although there are many instant messenger programs out there, four of the most popular (aside from ICQ) are America Online Instant Messenger, Yahoo! Messenger, MSN Messenger, and PowWow. In the rest of this chapter, I'll clue you in on what to know about each.

What You Should Know About America Online and AOL Instant Messenger

To a great extent, America Online started the chat craze, with its Instant Message feature. The feature has been most often used in chat rooms. Often, when people participate in a chat, they want one-on-one private conversations with another person on the room. When they do that, they use America Online's instant message program.

Mayday

How to Avoid Spam You Get After Visiting Chat Rooms on America Online

Spam—unsolicited email—floods America Online mailboxes. One reason it does is that spammers have programs that go into chat rooms and automatically "harvest" the names of people there—they add names from chat rooms to a spam list, and then send spam to everyone on that list. So the more you visit America Online chat rooms, the more spam you'll get. There's a way to avoid it. Create a separate screen name that you use only for visiting chat rooms. That way, the spam will be sent to that screen name, not the one you use regularly.

The program on America Online also allows you to set up buddy lists, to be told whenever one of your friends is online.

So far, pretty simple. So let's make it a little confusing. America Online also has a piece of software for instant messaging on the Internet—you don't have to be an America Online subscriber to use it, and you can use it whenever you're on the Internet. It's called AOL Instant Messenger, and it looks and works very much like the version on America Online. When you use AOL Instant Messenger, you can have conversations with people who are on America Online, and you can also have conversations with people who are other AOL Instant Messenger users. You can see it in action in Figure 20.5.

Figure 20.5

AOL Instant Messenger, for use on the Internet, lets you talk to people on America Online. Mia, go to bed! It's late!

Never Give Out Your Password to Someone Claiming He Works for America Online

One of the most popular scams on America Online is someone posing as an America Online employee and sending instant messages asking you to send your password to him. Don't send a password to someone who requests it—America Online employees will never ask for your password. And never send any information in a chat program that you wouldn't want to be publicly known.

AOL Instant Messenger is a simple, straightforward program. It tells you when your buddies are online—either on the Internet or America Online—and then lets you chat. It doesn't have a whole lot of fancy features beyond that. So why use it? Because what's *really* cool about an instant messenger program is the number of people you can talk to. And because America Online has over 10 million users, and millions of other people use AOL Instant Messenger, it means there are a whole lot of people you can talk with. Oh, and there's one other reason to use it: It's incredibly easy to use. Because there are not a whole lot of fancy features, everything you need is right there, in front of your face, as clear as can be.

In short, if you're looking for the widest possible number of people to talk with, and don't care about extra features, this is the way to go.

Get AOL Instant Messenger at download sites on the Internet, such as http://www.zddownloads.com, or at the http://www.aol.com Web site.

What You Should Know About Yahoo! Messenger

Let me be straight about this: Yahoo! Messenger is my favorite of the instant messenger programs. It's simple to use, and yet packed with all kinds of cool features. It integrates into the Yahoo! site, so anyone who uses Yahoo! for any reason will appreciate it. There's only one drawback: It's not as popular as AOL Instant Messenger, so there aren't as many people to talk with.

Cool Tips

Use "Bozo Filters" to Ignore Certain People

Most instant messenger programs include a feature that lets you ignore messages from certain people who you don't want to talk to. On Yahoo! Messenger, it's called an *ignore list*. But some people, including myself, call it a bozo filter, for an obvious reason—it lets you filter out messages from the bozos. If only my telephone had the same capability!

But if you're looking for an instant messenger program that does all kinds of cool stuff, this one's the way to go. Here are some of its highlights:

➤ **You can track your stock portfolio with it**   Type the stocks you want to track, and even the amount you're holding and the price at which you bought it, and it goes out regularly, gets the latest stock prices for you, and calculates your portfolio. Now if I only had a portfolio to track! Figure 20.6 shows the stock portfolio in action. If only I *really* had that amount of stock.

Figure 20.6

Here's how Yahoo! Messenger can track stocks for you. If only I really had this amount of *stock!*

➤ **It will give you reports and updates on the news, sports, and weather**   Want to find out how the Red Sox did last night? (Unless Pedro Martinez was pitching, you probably don't really want to know.) Want to see the weather forecast, or find out the latest national news? It goes out and grabs all that for you. Just click the appropriate tabs and follow the instructions.

➤ **It lets you chat, not just send instant messages**   If you want to invite a group of people to a chat, it's easy to do. When you're on the main screen, choose **Start a Conference** from the **Messenger** menu, and then type the IDs of the people you want to join you in a chat.

➤ **You can have voice chats** If you've got a microphone and a sound card, you don't have to type on your keyboard to communicate with your buddies. You can talk to them as well—do voice chat. To do that, right-click the person's name in the main window, and choose **Start a Voice Chat**.

➤ **You can send and receive files** Do you have a picture you want a friend to see? Does he have a music file he wants to send to you? It's easy to send files. Right-click the person's name in the main window, and choose **Send a File/Attachment**.

Mayday

Only Accept Files from People You Know—and Always Virus-Check Them.

If someone you don't know tries to send you a file, don't accept it—it might contain a virus or a Trojan Horse program he can use to take control of your computer. And even if a friend sends you a file, make sure to immediately virus-check it to make sure it doesn't accidentally contain a virus.

➤ **It integrates with many other Yahoo! services** If you use Yahoo! mail, it'll tell you when you have mail, for example. It'll open your Yahoo! calendar, let you search Yahoo!, and more as well.

Get Yahoo! Messenger at download sites on the Internet, such as http://www.zddownloads.com, or at the http://www.yahoo.com Web site.

What You Should Know About MSN Messenger

Poor MSN Instant Messenger. It's caught in the netherworld between AOL Instant Messenger and Yahoo! Messenger. (Can't any of these programs come up with a name other than Messenger by the way?) It doesn't have all the cool features that Yahoo! Messenger has—it's much like AOL Instant Messenger in how simple and straightforward it is. But it doesn't have the benefit of America Online's huge audience—so you won't have the largest number of other people to chat with. You can see MSN Messenger pictured in Figure 20.7.

To get around the problem, Microsoft engineers cooked up a way to allow MSN Messenger users to communicate with users of AOL Instant Messenger. As I explained earlier in this chapter, sometimes it works, and sometimes it doesn't.

There's one nice extra feature that the program has—if you have a free Hotmail email account, it will automatically check if you have mail, alert you if you do, and then log you on to your inbox if you'd like. (For more information about how to get free email accounts, turn to Chapter 10, "Getting and Using Free Email, Voice Mail, Faxes, and Other Services.")

Figure 20.7

Neither here nor there: It's as easy to use MSN Messenger as it is AOL Instant Messenger, but there aren't as many people to send messages to.

Cool Tips

Use MSN Messenger to Start NetMeetings with Buddies

MSN Messenger lets you not just send instant messages—it will also let you start NetMeeting video meetings with people as well. To invite someone to a NetMeeting, choose **Send an Invitation** from the **Tools** menu, and then choose **To Start NetMeeting**. For more information about NetMeeting, turn to Chapter 15, "Using NetMeeting for Internet Video."

Get MSN Messenger at download sites on the Internet, such as http://www.zddownloads.com, or at the http://www.microsoft.com Web site.

What You Need to Know About PowWow

It's a breath mint. No, it's a candy mint. It tastes great. No, it's less filling.

Use PowWow once and you'll be just as confused about what it is as well. Is it an instant messenger program? A chat program?

It's actually both, and more. You can use it to be only a simple messenger program, or you can use it as a full-blown chat program. It's by far the most complicated program of the bunch, and has a slew of features that aren't always easy to get to, because there's so much there.

Still, it's quite popular and has a huge audience, so it's easy to find people to chat with and to send and receive instant messages to and from. From my point of view, one of its best features is its capability to communicate with users of AOL Instant Messenger, America Online, and MNS Messenger. You can see it in action in Figure 20.8.

Figure 20.8

Universal communicator: PowWow can communicate with AOL users as well as those who use MSN Messenger. Here, you can see sending and receiving instant messages with someone on America Online.

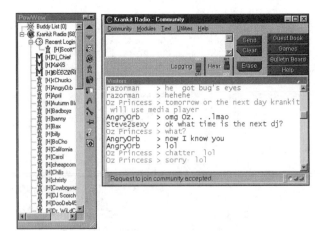

There's no way to enumerate (big word, that!) all the features of the program, but here are some of the highlights:

➤ **You can create your own chat room and host your own community** Have friends that want to get together and chat in a certain place? Want to have a family chat room so that family members all over the world can chat privately with each other? PowWow lets you host your own chat communities. To do that, though, you'll have to pay. How much you'll pay depends on the size of the community you want to host. It starts at $49.95 for 10 people for a year, and goes up from there on a graduated basis to $199.95 for 100 users.

➤ **You can do voice chat** You're not confined to the keyboard. If you have a microphone and sound card, you can talk away.

➤ **You can use a "whiteboard"** You and someone else can draw together on a whiteboard. Both of you can see what both of you draw.

➤ **You can play games** The program includes games you can play against others online. And you can taunt each other via chat and instant messages when you play—what fun!

➤ **You can have a weird computer voice read chat messages to you** One of the odder features of the program is its capability to have a computer voice read to you the messages in a chat room. There's an oddball kind of weird charm to a synthesized voice saying things like, "I am 2 sexy!" or "Hello, shee-niepooh." You might want to try this program only for this reason.

➤ **You can send and receive files with it** As with other instant messenger programs, you can send files to other people, and receive them as well, using PowWow.

Get PowWow at download sites on the Internet, such as `http://www.zddownloads.com`, or at the `http://www.powwow.com` Web site.

The Least You Need to Know

➤ Chat programs let you talk with many people simultaneously, whereas instant messenger programs let you talk to one person at a time.

➤ Popular places to chat are America Online and `http://www.excite.com`, `http://www.yahoo.com`, `http://www.talkcity.com`, `http://www.lycos.com`, and `http://www.thepalace.com`.

➤ Generally, if you want to send instant messages to someone, you and he will have to use the same instant messenger program.

➤ Never give out your credit card number, passwords, or any other sensitive materials in instant messages—it can be snooped on by hackers.

➤ Popular instant messenger programs are AOL Instant Messenger, Yahoo! Messenger, MSN Messenger, and PowWow. Download them from popular Internet download sites such as `http://www.zddownloads.com`.

Chapter 21

I Seek You: How to Use ICQ, the World's Most Popular Chat Program

---

In This Chapter

➤ What ICQ is and what all the fuss is about it

➤ How to download and install ICQ and get started

➤ Adding your friends as buddies in ICQ

➤ How to find other people with similar interests, using ICQ

➤ How to use ICQ to create your own personal communications center and ICQ home page

---

Get ready for one of the coolest ways to communicate online. Get ready for ICQ.

ICQ is an instant messenger program and buddy list that lets you communicate in more ways than you can imagine. Want to know if your Internet pal is currently online? ICQ tells you. Want to check your email without launching your email software? It does it. How about finding other people who have the same interests as you? It does it. Want to page people from the Web, or create your own personal communications center on the Web so people can get in touch with you easily? It does all that and more.

In this chapter, I'll introduce you to ICQ, and show you how to use it and install it. But it has so many features that the only way to truly appreciate it is to hop online, download it, and start chatting and talking. So get ready to go.

Why Should I Seek You? What Is ICQ?

If you're looking for an all-in-one instant messenger and personal communications program for your computer, look no further than ICQ (pronounced "I Seek You"). It's the most comprehensive program of its type you'll find—in fact, it's almost mind-boggling in how much it can do, so much so that probably very few people on the planet know how to use all its features.

It's also a great program because millions of people have downloaded and used it. That means there are millions of potential friends out there for you and me.

Because it has so many features, it can be difficult to explain exactly what it does. Here's a rundown on the program's main features:

➤ **It's an instant messenger and buddy list program**   It will alert you when friends come online. After they're online, you can send messages to them and receive messages from them.

➤ **It can check your email to see if you have messages, and will work with your email program to send emails**   Even when your email program isn't running, it can check your mail for you, and let you preview it. And in concert with your email program, it'll let you send email.

Walkie the Talkie

Why Is ICQ Called "Beta" Software?

Before a piece of software is released to the public, it goes through a testing phase called *beta test*. When software is in this testing phase, it's called *beta software*. You might notice that when you download ICQ, it's called beta software. There's no real reason why it's called that—it's been widely available to the public for several years and is being used by millions of people.

➤ **It will let you publish information about yourself so others with similar interests can contact you**   Via its White Pages and other directories, you can let people know your interests, occupation, and similar information, so they can get in touch with you. And you can look for people in a similar way. You don't have to supply this information if you don't want to.

➤ **It will let you create a personal communications center on the Web**   The program can create a personal Web page for you with all your contact information so that others can get in touch with you.

➤ **It enables anyone to "page" you from the Web** Anyone with an email program or the Web can "page" you—send you an instant message—whether or not they use ICQ.

➤ **It does a whole lot more as well** There's a lot more this program will do for you as well. You can create to-do lists, notes, and reminders. It lets you join groups of people with similar interests. It lets you chat via the Internet's IRC channels. Heck, at some point it will probably do the dishes, the laundry, and take out the garbage.

Getting Started with ICQ

Before you can use ICQ, you'll have to download it and install it. To get a copy, head to www.icq.com and click the download area. Then download the file and install it according to the instructions you find on the ICQ site.

You Might Not Be Able to Use ICQ at Work

ICQ has problems connecting through something called a *firewall*—a device that protects a corporate network from being attacked from someone on the Internet. If you install ICQ at work, and can't connect, choose **Preferences and Security** from ICQ's menu, click the **Connection** tab, then click the button that says you're behind a firewall and follow the instructions. Depending on the firewall you're behind, it might work, or it might not. But it's worth a try.

You won't be able to use ICQ until you've installed it and then registered yourself with the site. The registration is simple and straightforward. As you're registering, decide how much personal information you want to provide about yourself. Keep in mind that the more information you provide, the more likely you are to make new friends—but also keep in mind that whatever information you put in, the world can see.

When you register, you're given an ICQ ID—it's kind of like ICQ's version of a Social Security number. It's what identifies you as uniquely you when you use ICQ.

When you run ICQ, it runs as a small floating window as you can see in Figure 21.1. Think of this as ICQ's command central.

Figure 21.1

Here's how ICQ runs on your desktop—it starts off as a floating window.

The main part of the ICQ screen shows you all the contacts that you want to be notified about when they come online. You'll be shown whether they're online or offline.

Down toward the bottom of the screen is a set of buttons that lets you access many of the ICQ features. Click any of them and a menu will pop up, letting you choose which to use—shown in Figure 21.2.

Figure 21.2

To access ICQ's many features, click a button, and a menu will pop up. Then choose the feature you want to use from the menu.

I'd like to tell you that I find some grand scheme or underlying logic to the buttons and what features they let you get at. But I don't—there doesn't seem to be a whole lot of rhyme or reason to them. Generally, the Services button seems to let you get at features like reminders and to-do lists. And the ICQ button seems to let you do things like change the system preferences. But why can you get at the message archive—the history of messages you've sent and received—from both menus? Why is there a link to the ICQ White Pages on the Services menu (they let you search for users), and a link to find new users from the ICQ button? Who knows. My recommendation for finding your way around ICQ—don't look for logic. Click around and enjoy it.

How to Add Buddies with ICQ

To get the most out of ICQ, you'll add buddies to it—people with whom you regularly communicate. When you add a buddy, you'll be alerted whenever he's online. To add a user to your list, click the **Add Users** button. When you do that, you'll see the screen shown in Figure 21.3. You can only add someone to your list who is a registered ICQ member—non-members need not apply.

As you can see, there are several ways to look for buddies. You can search by email address, by name, and by ICQ number. Search that way when you're searching for a specific person—for a friend, for example. If the person you're looking for is registered with ICQ, you'll see the picture shown in Figure 21.4. Double-click the name to add it to your buddy list.

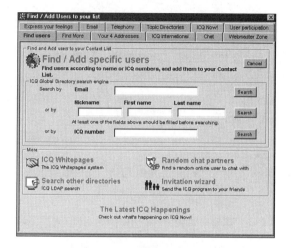

Figure 21.3

Where are my buddies? Here's how to look for a user to add to your buddy list in ICQ...

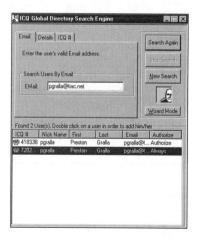

Figure 21.4

...and when you find him, you'll double-click his name here to add him to your buddy list.

Adding Users Based on Their Interests

A big reason to use ICQ is not just to talk with people you already know—it's to make new friends as well. To do that, you'll search the ICQ White Pages. From the screen shown in Figure 21.3, click **ICQ Whitepages**, and you'll come to a screen that lets you search for someone based on their interests, location, business, age, gender, language, and more. Do the search from this page, as you can see in Figure 21.5, and you'll see a list of them, as shown in Figure 21.6. Double-click their names, and they're added to your buddy list.

Figure 21.5

Here's how you'll search for users based on things like their age, gender, interests, and location...

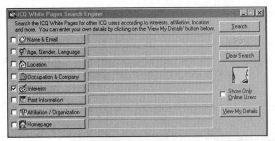

Figure 21.6

...and here's the list you'll see after you search. Double-click a name and you've added her to your buddy list.

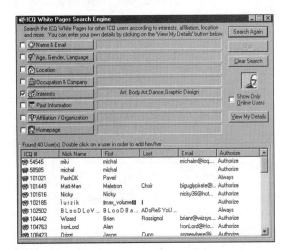

Now That You've Got Buddies, What Do You Do?

When you add buddies, they'll show up in your buddy list. When one of them comes online by using ICQ, you'll be notified. And even when they're offline, you can still send them messages and notification—when they log on to ICQ, they'll be sent your message.

After someone is in your buddy list, there are all kinds of ways you can communicate with him. To communicate with someone, whether he's online or offline, click his name and a menu pops up. (Menus seem to pop up all the time with ICQ.) Just choose the way you want to communicate with someone from the list. You can see that menu here in Figure 21.7, along with a message box, waiting to be filled in.

As you can see on the menu, there are many ways to communicate with a buddy. Here are the main ways, and what to know about each. In all these cases, you'll be able to communicate instantly if your buddy is currently using ICQ. If he isn't, the messages will be delivered as soon as he logs on. Here are the ways you can communicate using this menu:

Cool Tips

You Can Use Many of ICQ's Features Directly from the System Tray

When ICQ isn't running directly on your desktop, it sits as an icon in your system tray. To get at many of its features, you don't maximize it to your desktop. Instead, you can right-click it and a menu will pop up. You can then choose what you want to do directly from the menu.

➤ **Message**   Lets you send a brief, email-like message.

➤ **File**   Lets you transfer a file. A dialog box opens that lets you identify the file you want to send; you also can drag a file's icon onto someone's ID in the ICQ dialog box to begin the sending process.

Figure 21.7

Menus, menus, how many menus are there in this program? Here are all the ways you can communicate with a buddy on ICQ.

➤ **Web Page Address (URL)**   Lets you send the address of a Web page, along with a description of it. By default, the address of the Web page you're currently visiting is the address sent, and the description is taken directly from the page's title bar. By the way, many people often forward many Web pages to big lists of people indiscriminately. Don't do this: It's bad form, and needlessly annoys people.

➤ **Contacts**   Lets you send information about one of your ICQ contacts.

➤ **Voice Message (Online Only)**   Lets you record a voice message that will be sent and then listened to by your buddy. You can only send a voice message if the person is online—it can't be recorded and delivered later.

➤ **Greeting Card**   Enables you to send an online greeting card that includes colors, fonts, animated graphics, and a personalized message.

➤ **Email**   Lets you send an email to the person's email box. It won't be delivered via ICQ, but rather instead to their normal email account. It sends email by launching your normal email software and creating a message.

You Seek Me: How to Use ICQ to Let the World Know About You

The cool part about ICQ isn't just that you can talk to old friends and find new ones—it's that people can use it to easily contact you as well.

When you registered, you provided information about yourself—or perhaps you didn't. If you want others to be able to find you, the more information you provide, the more easily they'll find you. Again, you have to balance your desire for the world to know about you with your need for privacy.

The best way to let others know about you is to provide information about yourself in the program—and that information will be published in the ICQ White Pages so that people can find you that way. To publish information about yourself, click the **Services** button, choose **ICQ White Pages**, and then choose **Publicize in White Pages**. You'll have a whole set of screens that you can use to put in information about yourself. Figure 21.8 shows just one of those screens.

As you can see from all the tabs here, there's all kinds of information you can put about yourself, including hobbies, interests, your location, work information, a photograph, and much more.

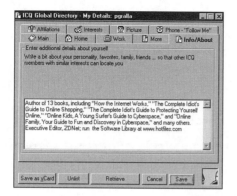

Figure 21.8

Tell it to the world: Here's how to publish information about yourself in the ICQ White Pages. When anyone looks at your ICQ information, they'll be able to see what you put on these screens.

If You Use an Internet Telephone, Put Information About It in ICQ

Internet telephones can save you big bucks when you use them to talk PC-to-PC. When you do that, you won't pay a penny when you talk to someone, even if they're located on the other side of the earth from you. If you put information about your Internet telephone in ICQ, it will be easy for others to call you. Put it in the **Phone—Follow Me** section of information about you in the ICQ White Pages. You also can choose **Phone—Follow Me** from the **Services** menu as a way to put in that information. Turn to Part 4, "Can We Talk? Using the Internet as Your Telephone," for information about Internet telephones.

Using Your ICQ-Created Web Page to Tell the World About You

No one ever accused ICQ of being a simple program to use. It's as full of twists and turns as a plate of linguini—and sometimes as slippery to get a handle on exactly what's going on.

That certainly holds true when it comes to ICQ-created Web pages. ICQ gives you the ability to have Web pages created about you. Here's the confusing part: There are two different kinds of pages it can create—a "Communication Center" and an ICQ home page. Here's what to know about each:

➤ **The Communication Center** This is automatically created when you register with ICQ. It includes information that you provided about yourself, but includes much more than that—it provides ways that anyone can contact you immediately. There's all your contact information, including your ICQ number,

259

email address, and personal home page. There's a link that people can click to send you an immediate "page"—message to you via ICQ. They also can send a page directly from this page. And there's other contact information, such as your Internet telephone number if you have one. The address for your Communication Center is `wwp.icq.com/YourICQnumber`. So if your ICQ number is 7202344, your Communication Center address would be `wwwp.icq.com/7202344`. Figure 21.9 shows my Communication Center page.

Figure 21.9

The universal communicator: Here's my ICQ Communication Center page.

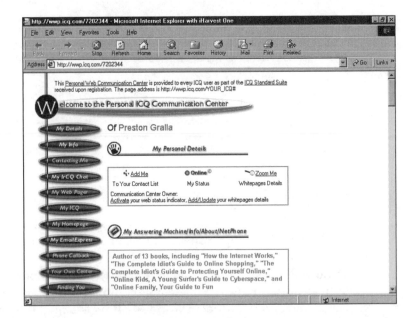

Cool Tips

Chat While You Surf with ICQ Surf

An add-in for ICQ called ICQ Surf lets you chat with other ICQ'ers while you surf the Web. You can head to a Web page, and if there are other users of ICQ Surf there, you can chat to your heart's content. For information about ICQ Surf, turn to Chapter 23, "Other Cool Communications Tools: Group Surfing and Web Graffiti."

➤ **The ICQ Homepage** This is a Web page that you create that includes information about yourself, but also things such as your favorite Web sites, the ability to chat directly with you, and more. Unlike the Communications Center, it isn't created automatically for you. To build it, choose **My ICQ Page** from the **Services** menu and then **Make My ICQ Home Page**. You'll be able to create a Web page with a home page creator—essentially you fill out a form, although you can also put in HTML if you want. You can see the home page creator here in Figure 21.10.

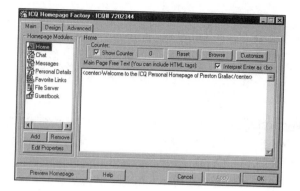

Figure 21.10

Home, sweet home: Here's how to create a Web page with the home page creator.

Mayday

When You Create an ICQ Home Page, You Might Give People Access to Your Computer

When you create an ICQ Home Page, you also might give people access to the files on your computer. There's a "file server" section where you can put files in a folder that enables people anywhere to look at and download. You can password protect the folder, and not put any files in there if you don't want. Still, if you're made queasy about the idea of people being able to look at even a single empty folder on your computer (which I am), don't use the ICQ Home Page. The Communications Center doesn't give people this kind of access, so you don't need to worry about that.

There's Tons of Other Cool Stuff, Too

As I said earlier in the chapter, there's an amazing amount of things ICQ can do for you, and more are being added every day. There's no way I can cover them all in this chapter.

The best way to find out about all of them is to head to www.icq.com and install the program. Give it a whirl—you'll find it's one of the most amazing ways yet invented to communicate online.

The Least You Need to Know

➤ ICQ is an instant messenger program that has many extra features, including the capability to check your email, to let you build Web pages about yourself on the ICQ, and much more.

➤ After you download and install ICQ, you'll have to register to start using the program. The more personal information you include about yourself, the easier it will be for people to find you, but you'll also give up your privacy.

➤ You can add buddies to your ICQ list by searching for people you already know, or else by using the White Pages to find people with similar interests.

➤ There are many ways to communicate with people on your ICQ list, including chatting, sending short email-like messages, sending voice messages, and more.

➤ When you register with ICQ, a Communication Center page is automatically created for you on the Web that includes all your contact information and that lets people send you messages straight from the Web.

➤ You can use ICQ to create a personal home page with information about yourself. But be careful when you do this, because it also might give people access to files on your computer.

Chapter 22

Tell It to the World: How to Broadcast Newsletters via Email

In This Chapter

➤ Understanding what email broadcasts and newsletters are

➤ Why you would want to create an email broadcast and newsletter

➤ The different kinds of ways you can create email broadcasts and newsletters

➤ Tips for creating the most effective email broadcasts and newsletters

➤ How to publicize your email broadcasts and newsletters

➤ Where to find email broadcasts, newsletters, and mailing lists you want to subscribe to

There's a saying that goes something like, "Freedom of the press goes only to those who can afford to buy a printing press."

Whoever said that never heard of the Internet (or a photocopier, for that matter). The Internet can be your own personal virtual printing press. With it, you'll be able to broadcast your words and wisdom to the world for free. You'll be able to send out broadcasts to friends and family, to members of groups such as the PTA or neighborhood groups, and to customers, if you run a business.

In this chapter, you'll find out everything you need to know about how to create your own email broadcasts. As you'll see, it's easy to do, it's fast, and it's fun.

What Are Email Broadcasts?

Got a story you want to tell to the world? Want to create a newsletter telling the world about your pet mongoose? Or one that you send out to your PTA after your meetings every month? Maybe you have a small business you run, and want to keep in better touch with your customers.

It's easy to do all that, and more. You can use email broadcasts to create your own personal newsletter, and send it out for free to anyone who requests it. You won't have to pay a penny for doing it—and it's one of the most effective ways for telling your story to the world.

Before doing that, though, you need the answer to one simple question: Just what the heck is an email broadcast?

Put simply, an *email broadcast* is an email that is sent to many people simultaneously from a person or business. An email broadcast can be as small as just a few people, or can be sent to millions of people. There are all kinds of email broadcasts going out every day, most of them from large and small businesses, and from Web sites and news organizations. Think of any kind of topic you're interested in, and the odds are there's an email broadcast going out about it.

These broadcasts can be plain-old text email, or they can include pictures, colors, fonts, and links, and use HTML commands—in other words, they can essentially be a Web site sent via email. Pictured in Figure 22.1 is the HTML email broadcast sent out by the ZDNet News and Investing Alert, and in Figure 22.2 is a plain-text broadcast sent out by Internet journalist Dylan Tweney.

Figure 22.1

Get rich, quick? Maybe you can, when you subscribe to the ZDNet News and Investing Alert, one of the thousands of email broadcasts available over the Internet. It's in HTML, so it includes pictures, colors, fonts, and more.

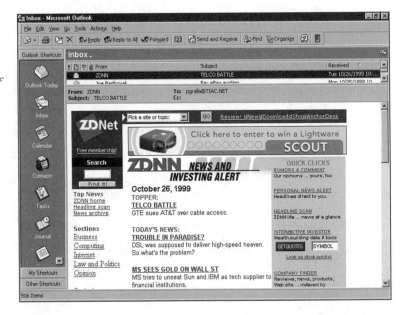

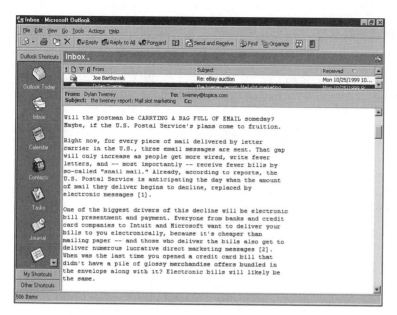

Figure 22.2

An email broadcast doesn't have to be in HTML to be effective. Here's a text-based broadcast sent out by Internet journalist Dylan Tweney.

In recent years, individuals have gotten into the act, and are sending out email broadcasts as well. As I'll show you later in this chapter, it's easy to do, and you can do it for free.

To be successful, an email broadcast also should enable people to subscribe to it and unsubscribe to it easily—by doing something as simple as sending an email to a certain mailbox with a simple instruction such as "subscribe" and "unsubscribe."

Walkie the Talkie

What's a Listserv and in What Army Does Majordomo Serve?

Email broadcasts are the latest variation on a kind of technology that's been around the Internet for a long time. There are ways that people can hold discussions via what are called *mailing lists*. In a mailing list, people send messages to a list, and everyone on the list gets the message as an email, and can see and respond to the messages. These kinds of mailing lists are commonly managed through two similar kinds of software, called *listserv* and *majordomo*. Listserv is so common, in fact, that many people generically refer to any kind of mailing list or email broadcast as a listserv. Later on in this chapter, I'll show you how to subscribe to mailing lists using listserv and majordomo. And by the way, you can set up your own mailing list so that not only can you broadcast your email to everyone on the list, but everyone on the list can respond to you and each other as well.

Why Would I Want to Create an Email Broadcast?

So, now you know what an email broadcast is. And so here's the second big question of this chapter: Why go to the bother of creating an email broadcast in the first place?

There are a whole lot of reasons you might want to create one of these. Here are the big ones:

➤ **You have a group of friends and family with whom you want to keep in touch** Let's say you have a far-flung family, and far-flung friends (say all that five times fast, please) spread out all over the globe. You'd like to keep them in touch with your doings—your new baby, your new house, your giving up of all your worldly goods (such as they are) to live in a Tibetan monastery. Create an email broadcast and send them the latest news every month. (Although because most Tibetan monasteries don't have Internet connections, you might be out of luck when you move there.)

➤ **You're a member of a civic, community, or similar group and you want to keep all the members up-to-date on news and meetings** Anyone who's been a member of any of these groups knows how difficult it is to keep everyone informed about news, meetings, and similar information. There's a simple solution: Create an email broadcast that you send out. It's the simplest way to keep in touch. I'm a member of a neighborhood organization and my wife is a member of a neighborhood arts groups, and both these groups keep everyone up-to-date with email broadcasts. So I can tell you from personal experience that it works.

➤ **You run a small business or home-based business and want to promote yourself and keep in touch with your customers** There's no easier way to promote your services or products and keep in touch with customers and potential customers than by using email broadcasts. It's free, and it's amazingly effective if done right.

➤ **You have a hobby or some kind of expertise and you'd like to share what you know with the world** Are you an expert on Depression-era pencil sharpeners? Do you know more about the physiology of the wombat than anyone else on earth? Are you a collector of trivia about Barry Manilow? Let the world know about it! (Although if I were you, I'd keep the Barry Manilow information private. Your reputation would never live it down.)

Cool Tips

You Can Subscribe to My Email Newsletter

Time to toot my own horn here: I know a whole lot about the Internet (I've written about a dozen books about it), and so I publish my own email newsletter offering free tips, tricks, hints, advice, and insider information, in Gralla's Internet Insider. You can subscribe to it for free. Just send an email with the words **SUBSCRIBE NETINSIDER** to preston@gralla.com.

Time to Toot Your Own Horn: How to Create Email Broadcasts

So you've decided that the world absolutely needs a weekly update about your research into the life and times of esoteric animals from Australia, among them wombats, platypuses, and Tasmanian Devils. Time to create your own email broadcast. Easier said than done, you no doubt think. But in fact, it's easy to do. There are two ways you can do it. You can use special group mail software that will let you create your email mailing list and send out broadcasts from your own computer. Or you can instead go to a Web site that will send out your broadcasts for you.

No matter which you use to create your email broadcast, there are several things that the software or site should be able to do for you:

➤ **It should let you easily set up a mailing list** When you send out an email broadcast, you'll be sending it to dozens, hundreds, or even more people. So you need some way to create a mailing list that contains all the email addresses you want to send the broadcast to.

➤ **It should automatically subscribe and unsubscribe people to your broadcast** It's a pain to manually go into a program or Web site and have to add or take away people from your list. So it should be able to do that for you automatically, so that when people send a subscribe or unsubscribe request, it's done automatically, without you having to do anything about it.

Mayday

Don't Become a "Spammer"

Spam refers to unsolicited email that's sent to people—in other words, junk email. Spam is rightly considered one of the scourges of the Internet. It wastes people's time and the resources of the Internet. People hate spammers. Be careful, when you create an email broadcast, that you don't become a spammer. That means that you should never send your email broadcast to strangers who haven't asked for it.

➤ **It should automatically send out a "thank-you" message when people subscribe or unsubscribe**   When people send a note to subscribe or unsubscribe to your broadcast, they want some kind of notification telling them that you've taken action on their request. So you want to have the ability to create "thank-yous" and introductions to the list that are automatically sent out when someone subscribes or unsubscribes.

➤ **It should let you easily create your broadcast and mail it out**   After you have the list set up, it'll be time to do the work—create you broadcast and send it out. So you should be able to easily create your broadcast, and have it easily and quickly broadcast to your list.

➤ **It should be able to handle email woes**   After you create one of these lists, there's all kinds of oddball woes that might pop up. People might subscribe, for example, but then delete their email address. You want to have a way to easily handle that kind of problem and others.

Decisions, Decisions: How to Choose Which Way to Create Your Email Broadcast

As I told you earlier, the two main ways to create email broadcasts are to use software on your own computer, or else go to a Web site that will let you create a broadcast. There are pros and cons to each approach, and a few "gotchas" along the way. Here's what to know about each, and how to decide when to use which:

➤ **Group mail software**   This software runs on your own computer. That means you have full control over your mailing list, you manage your mailing list yourself, and you're not dependent on a Web site—which can sometimes crash, or can even go out of business. And if you keep your list on a Web site, you can't be completely sure that they'll keep the names on your list confidential. Also, when you use a Web site, if you're getting the services for free, it might put advertising in your newsletter. The downside of running this software on your computer, though, is that that it might mean more work on your part; if your computer crashes, you could lose your whole list; and the software's use might interfere with your email software. In general, I recommend that for small mailing lists of under 100 people or so, you use group mail software. For larger lists, consider using a Web site. Figure 22.3 shows Aureate Group Mail in action.

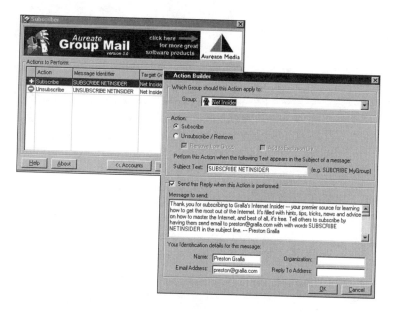

Figure 22.3

Aureate Group Mail runs on your own PC, and makes it easy to create and manage email broadcasts.

➤ **Web site broadcasts** What's appealing about using a Web site to create email broadcasts for you is that they have to deal with all the problems and hassles, and you don't. Especially if you have a large list, these sites are a godsend. However, many of these sites charge money—well over $100 a year at many of the sites if your list is large enough. There are sites that do it for free for you, but they'll typically put ads inside your newsletter. When you go with one of these sites, you're trusting that they won't misuse the names on your list. And if the site goes down, you're out of luck. Still, they're an easy way to get started. Figure 22.4 is the eGroups site that manages lists for you for free.

Figure 22.4

Here's how you'll send out an email broadcast using the free service offered by the www.egroups.com *site.*

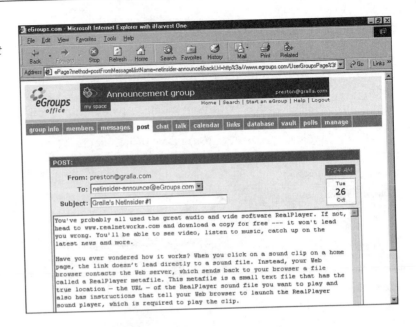

Cool Tips

Use Your Email Software to Create Email Broadcasts

If you're going to be sending email broadcasts to a small number of people, and won't be asking a lot of people to subscribe, you don't need special software or use a Web site to create email broadcasts. You can easily do it using your email software—just create a mailing list, and then send an email to the list when you want to broadcast a message. To do that in Outlook, choose **Address Book** from the **Tools** menu, and then click **New Group**. Type the name of the group, and click **Select members** to add names to the group from your Address Book. To add people to the group who aren't in your Address Book, click **New Contact**. After you have your list done, just send an email to the list, and it'll be sent to everyone on it—no muss, no fuss, no special software required.

Creating Email Broadcasts Using Group Mail Software

You've decided to create an email broadcast using software—but which software to use? There's a good deal of software available for doing this, and the prices you'll pay vary enormously—from about $25 up to hundreds of dollars.

How's this for a deal, though: What I consider the best software for doing email broadcasts is available for free. That's right, free, as in no money. The program is called Aureate Group Mail, and you can get it from www.group-mail.com.

It'll do everything you need in a broadcast program—it's easy to set up mailing lists, to send out broadcasts, and all the other things you need a broadcast program to do. You can even use it to create HTML broadcasts easily—just attach an HTML file, and your broadcast is sent out as HTML. In Figure 22.5, you can see how you create an email broadcast using the program.

Figure 22.5

Your own virtual printing press: It's easy to create email broadcasts using Aureate Group Mail.

The program is available for free, but there are a few drawbacks to it when you use it for free. All the email you send out with it will have a little tag line at the bottom, telling people that you created the broadcast with the program. And while you use the program, ads flash at you—a minor annoyance, but an annoyance nonetheless. And there are a few other minor things that the free version can't do. If you want, you can pay $49.95 for a version that has no ads, no tag line, and a few more bells-and-whistles thrown in. From my point of view, though, for most people the free version will do perfectly fine. And you can always try out the free version, and later on pay for the upgrade version if you want.

Cool Tips

You Can Try Out Group Mailers for Free

Many group mail programs are available for you to try out for free—you download them, use them, and only if you like them do you need to pay for them. Check Internet download sites for them, such as www.zddownloads.com. Search for **listserve, listserv, mass mail,** and **email**.

Creating Email Broadcasts from Web Sites

Did you decide you'd rather have a Web site help you create your email broadcasts? Here's some good news for you—several good sites will do it for you for free.

Three good ones are TopicA at www.topica.com, eGroups at www.egroups.com, and ListBot at www.listbot.com. They work fairly similarly. You register, describe your group, fill out some forms, and you're ready to go. I know it sounds like nothing can be that simple, but it's true—it's easy to create broadcasts at all three sites. After you've created a list, then you fill in more forms and send out your broadcast. Presto! You're a big-time publisher. The form you'll fill out on TopicA to create an email broadcast list is shown in Figure 22.6.

Figure 22.6

Become a big-time Net publisher: Here's how to set up an email broadcast list at www.topica.com.

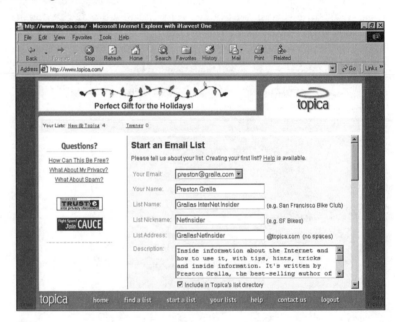

When you use these kinds of free services, there are a few drawbacks. First off, your broadcasts might be required to carry advertising messages. If the site goes down, you're sunk. And if you become extremely successful, and your email lists grow over a certain size, you'll have to pay the site.

These sites will generally sell you "premium" services that you can't get if you don't pay. You'll usually get better ways to manage your list, be able to send out advertiser-free email broadcasts, and be able to send out higher volumes of mail than if you don't pay.

Dos and Don'ts of Email Broadcasts

As you can see, it's easy to create your email broadcasts about wombats, platypi, and anything else you want. But that doesn't mean it's easy to create a *good* broadcast—one that people will ever want to read. And when creating a broadcast, you don't want to violate some very basic rules of etiquette. Here are the top dos and don'ts of creating email broadcasts:

➤ **Always include unsubscribe information**   You might think your words are golden, but at some point, people might want to unsubscribe to your newsletter. It's good form to include unsubscribe instructions at the bottom of every one of your broadcasts. If you don't include that information, you will no doubt find yourself on the end of some angry email.

Cool Tips

There Are Also For-Pay Group Mail Web Sites

TopicA, ListBot, and eGroups are free sites (unless you want to pay for premium services). But there are also high-end sites that you can pay to handle your email broadcasts. One of the most popular of the for-pay sites is www.messagemedia.com. Prices vary, so check the Web site for details.

Cool Tips

Include Unsubscribe Information in Your Signature

Email broadcast software and sites let you include a signature at the bottom of all your broadcasts—information about yourself that you want included in every broadcast. Your signature is automatically appended to the bottom of every broadcast, so you don't have to remember to put it in. It's a good idea to include unsubscribe information in your signature; that way it'll always be on every broadcast you send out, without fail.

➤ **Never sell your list to anyone**   There are many marketers on the Internet looking for email lists they can send their pitches to. Don't be tempted to sell your list to any of them. You'll do a bad deed, and earn the undying ill-will of everyone on your list.

➤ **Keep your information relevant**   If your broadcast is about the mating habits of wombats, don't write about the possibility of Ken Griffey, Jr., breaking Hank Aaron's home run record. People subscribe to your list for targeted information; don't turn them off by rambling about irrelevancies.

➤ **Don't be blatant about self-promotion**   Even if you're creating the email broadcast for the sole purpose of promoting yourself and your services and products, tone down your broadcast. If you're too blatant about your self-promotion, no one will listen.

➤ **Include links to related Web sites**   People love links. They love delving deeper into a subject for related information. So whenever possible, include links to related information on the Web. Don't worry that you're sending them away from your newsletter—if your newsletter keeps giving them sources of information, they'll keep coming back to it.

Cool Tips

Don't Charge for Your Broadcast

At some point in the life of your broadcast, you might think you're sitting on a gold mine. If people are interested enough in your newsletter, why not try charging for it? Don't bother—that's the quickest way to oblivion. Publishers have found that people aren't willing to pay money for Internet newsletters.

➤ **Keep the size of the broadcast small**   Especially if you're sending HTML email, the size of your email broadcast can get large. When you start including pictures and other kinds of content, it can get pretty heavy. So put your broadcast on a diet—keep it under 20–25KB or else people will become annoyed at how long it takes to download and read.

If You Broadcast, Will They Come?

Maybe you've created the greatest email broadcast on the face of the planet. But if you don't have an audience, that won't matter worth a darn. Without subscribers, you're nobody. If an email broadcast is sent into the wilds of the Internet and one reads it, does it really exist?

If you're creating a kind of list where you want to publicize yourself or your services, or for some reason want to gain a large number of subscribers, you'll have to do a little bit of marketing. Follow these tips for gaining subscribers to your email broadcasts:

➤ **Include subscribe information in every broadcast** The most effective way of getting subscribers is by word of mouth—people passing your newsletter around. You want to make it easy for people to let others know how to subscribe to it. So if you include a line in your newsletter, asking people to send it along to their friends, and including subscribe information, it's more likely that you'll get more subscribers.

➤ **Register information about your broadcast at Web sites and search engines** There are many sites on the Internet where people go to look for newsletters. Head to those sites and register your newsletter with them. Good places to go are www.liszt.com and www.topica.com. Also go to popular Internet search sites such as www.yahoo.com to register your newsletter.

➤ **If you have a Web site, include a way to subscribe to your newsletter from your site** If people enjoy your Web site, they'll probably also want to read you email broadcast.

➤ **Put subscribe information in your email signature** Think of all the emails you send out in a month. If every person you send your email to sees subscription information, you'll get new subscribers.

You Can Be a Reader, Too: How to Subscribe to Email Broadcasts and Lists

Maybe you're not an expert on wombats. But you'd like to read what the wombat experts have to say. Great news—you can probably find an email broadcast or mailing list to find out about broadcasts.

Walkie the Talkie

How Is a Mailing List Different from a Broadcast?

In an email broadcast, a person or company sends out an email to many people, who then read it. But they can't publicly respond to the broadcast. In mailing lists, in general, everyone can respond to messages that other people send out—it's a way to carry on public conversations via email. However, some mailing lists can be set up so that people can't respond to others.

There are tens of thousands of broadcasts and email lists to choose from. Although there are often different ways to subscribe to each, there are a few general things you should know about subscribing. You'll need to know the name of the list you want to subscribe to, and the email address where you should send your subscription.

Many mailing lists are created using software called either listserv or majordomo. Generally, you subscribe the same way to most mailing lists built with these pieces of software. Let's say you wanted to subscribe to the "wombats" mailing list, and the subscription address is `listserv@aussiestuff.com`. You'd send an email to `listserv@aussiestuff.com` with the text:

    Subscribe wombats

If the software was instead majordomo, and the address were `majordomo@aussiestuff.com`, you'd send an email to `majordomo@aussiestuff.com` with the same text:

    Subscribe wombats

To unsubscribe, send email to the same respective addresses, with the text:

    Unsubscribe wombats

Note that for both subscribing and unsubscribing, sometimes the `subscribe` or `unsubscribe` needs to be on the subject line and sometimes in the body of the email. If you're not sure, include it in both—the software will just ignore the line it doesn't need.

Cool Tips

There Are Other Commands for Listserv and Majordomo

There are other commands you can send to a listserv and majordomo apart from `subscribe` and `unsubscribe`. If you want to find out information about the wombat mailing list, send an email with the text `info wombat`, and you'll be sent an email that has information about the wombat mailing list. And to get information about other commands you can use, just send an email with the text `help`, and you'll be sent an email telling you what other commands you can issue.

When you subscribe to a mailing list—one with which you can respond to other people—you'll be given an address to send your responses to. It will be different from the subscription email address, so pay close attention to what it is.

One final note: If you're worried that your email inbox will be full of dozens of messages a day, you can ask to be sent a *digest* instead. The digest will be a single message that contains all the messages for a day, a week, or a month. Check the details of the mailing list to see how to do it.

How to Find Email Broadcasts and Mailing Lists

With so many broadcasts and lists out there, how to find the one you want? I find the best way is to go to one of the Web sites that specializes in these kinds of lists. These sites let you browse or search for broadcasts and lists. They'll give you descriptions of the lists, and information about how to subscribe and unsubscribe to them.

The three best places to go for this are www.topica.com, www.onelist.com, and www.liszt.com. Figure 22.7 shows the www.liszt.com site.

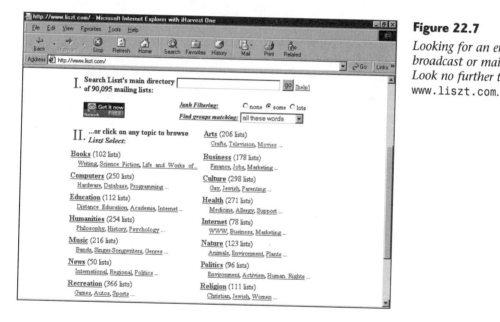

Figure 22.7

Looking for an email broadcast or mailing list? Look no further than www.liszt.com.

Many Web sites also have lists of free email newsletters and broadcasts put out by major publishers. For example, if you use the free email service www.hotmail.com, you can subscribe to many newsletters from major publishers. Check the Web sites of major publishers for their list of free newsletters.

The Least You Need to Know

➤ You can create email broadcasts with software on your PC, or you can instead go to Web sites that will let you create them.

➤ Aureate Group Mail is an excellent free program for creating broadcasts. The www.egroups.com, www.topica.com, and www.listbot.com Web sites are great sites for letting you create broadcasts for free.

➤ Email broadcasts are an excellent way to keep in touch with family and friends, maintain a relationship with customers, or keep together civic or neighborhood groups.

➤ For very large broadcast lists, you'll do best to rely on a Web site for creating the lists.

➤ Always include subscribe and unsubscribe information on the email broadcasts you send out.

➤ To find email broadcasts or mailing lists to subscribe to, go to www.topica.com, www.liszt.com, or www.onelist.com.

Chapter 23

Other Cool Communications Tools: Group Surfing and Web Graffiti

---

In This Chapter

➤ How chat-and-surf programs work

➤ Where to get the most popular chat-and-surf programs

➤ How to use ICQ Surf, one of the most popular chat-and-surf programs

➤ How to use Gooey, another popular chat-and-surf program

➤ What is Web graffiti software?

➤ How to use ThirdVoice, the most popular Web graffiti software

---

So we're finally at the end of the book. By now, you probably think you've read about all the cool ways possible to communicate on the Internet. Fat chance! There's always more.

In this chapter, I'll show you some of the more amazing, newer ways to communicate online. You'll learn how you can chat while you surf the Web, and how you can leave graffiti on Web pages for others to read, and read their graffiti. So come on in. More coolness to follow.

Surf's Up! How to Chat While You Surf the Internet

Here's a strange secret: When you surf the Internet, people are on many of those sites, chatting away, talking to each other, and you can't read a word they say or even know they're there.

That's because they're using special software that lets them chat with each other while they surf the Internet. And you can use it, too. It's one of the best ways to find and chat with people with similar interests.

Here's how it works. You load the surf-and-chat software, and then you surf the Web as you would normally with your browser. When you come to a site that has people on it using the same software, you'll be able to chat with them, as if the Web site was a chat room. You'll find all the chat functions you'd expect: You see a list of all the people on the site; you can send public and private messages; you can ask to see information about each other. In Figure 23.1 you can see one of the more popular pieces of this type of chat software, ICQ Surf, in action.

Figure 23.1

Surf's Up! Here's how to chat with others while you surf the Web, using ICQ Surf.

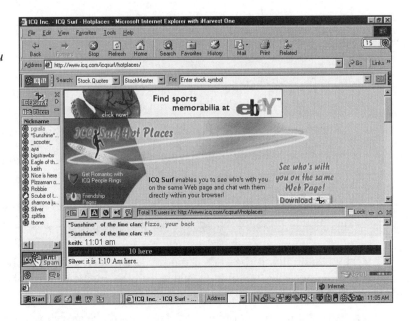

If no one using the software is at that particular site, nothing happens. Just surf the Web as you normally would, all by your lonesome.

Software of this kind usually has all kinds of other features as well. Some let you send files to each other, so you can do things like share MP3 music files. Some allow live news feeds. But the main reason you'll use it is to talk to other people visiting the same Web site as you are, and so who probably have similar interests.

There are many different kinds of software that allow you to chat while you surf the Web. But the two most popular are Gooey and ICQ Surf —and those are the ones I'll show you how to use in this chapter. Another one you might come across is called Virtual Places. You can get details on it at www.vplaces.net.

I Seek You While Surfing: Using ICQ Surf

ICQ is the most popular instant messenger program in the world. Millions and millions of people have downloaded and used it. (Turn to Chapter 21, "I Seek You: How to Use ICQ, the World's Most Popular Chat Program," for information on how to use it.) In fact, if you stacked all the ICQ users end to end, they'd reach from here to...well, I don't know exactly where, but it would be really, really far away.

Mayday

You Can Only Chat with Others Who Use the Same Software

When you use surf-and-chat software, you'll be able to chat only with others who use the same software as you do. So if you're using Gooey and you visit a page on which ICQ surfers are chatting, you won't see them or be able to chat with them. And they won't be able to see you or chat with you, either.

A companion program to ICQ, called ICQ Surf, lets you chat with other ICQ Surf users when you're on a Web site. One big reason for using this program: Because there are so many ICQ users, there's a huge potential group of chatters available for you to chatter away with. After all, if you stacked them end to end, they'd reach...well, you get the idea.

To install ICQ Surf, head to http://www.icq.com and install ICQ if you haven't already, and then install ICQ Surf. After you do that, you're ready to go. When you run the program, nothing will happen until you hop onto the Web, except that you'll see a little green icon in your system tray to tell you the program is running. After you go onto the Web, though, the program springs into action. It runs as a green flower icon in the upper-right side of your browser. When you visit a Web page, it checks to see if any other ICQ Surfers are present. If they are, the flower icon shows you the number of people present, the program makes a little "Whoa!"-like sound, and suddenly the Web page becomes a chat room—you can see a list of everyone in the room on the left side of the page, and a chat box opens at the bottom of the page. Turn back to Figure 23.1 to see what ICQ Surf looks like in action.

You can now chat away to your heart's content. It works like any other chat. You'll see the chat messages scroll by, and to send a message of your own, simply type it and press **Enter**. You can use different colors and fonts when you send messages, you can send sounds and annoy the heck out of anyone in the immediate vicinity, and you can even send hyperlinks so that people can click them and head to a Web page you want to send them to.

Cool Tips

You Can Turn Off the Bell Sounds that ICQ Surf Makes Whenever Anyone Sends a Message

There's one thing about ICQ Surf that drives me around the bend: Any time anyone sends a message, a metallic, bell-like noise sounds. So if you're in a chat room that's busy, the bells rings constantly, and can be immensely annoying. Luckily, it's easy to turn that sound off. Right-click the **ICQ Surf** icon in the upper-right of your screen, choose **Preferences**, and then click the **Sound** tab. You'll be able to turn off those sounds and any other sounds the program makes that might annoy you.

How to Find Places to Chat with ICQ Surf

The Web is a big place, and even though there are a lot of ICQ users out there, they're not always online. And at this point, most ICQ users still don't yet use ICQ Surf. So many times, when you get to a Web page, there will be few or no other ICQ surfers, so if you stacked them end to end they wouldn't even reach into the living room from where you sit.

But what if you're in the mood to chat with other surfers? It's easy to find where they are. Right-click the **ICQ Surf** icon in the upper-right part of your screen and choose **Hot Places**. You'll see the screen pictured in Figure 23.2. It'll show you every place on the Internet where ICQ Surfers are hanging out, starting with the most popular, and moving down. To head to any of those sites, double-click and you'll be sent there so you can chat to your heart's content.

Figure 23.2

Looking to find other ICQ Surfers to chat with? Here's how to find out where they are.

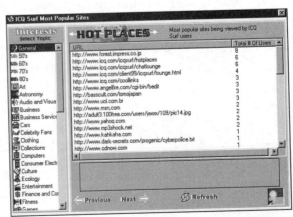

Finding Information About Other ICQ Surfers

If you're like me, you're an inquisitive sort. You're curious about everything and everyone. So you might want to know more about your fellow chatterers.

ICQ Surf lets you get information about them—although only information that they want the world to see. When you installed ICQ Surf, you were asked questions about your personal interests. Those answers create a profile of you that anyone who wants can view. To see someone's profile, right-click her name, and choose **ICQ Surf User Info**. You'll then see a screen, like the one you can see here in Figure 23.3, that has information that she's provided about herself. When you right-click, you're also given the option of seeing information she's provided about herself for ICQ itself, instead of ICQ Surf.

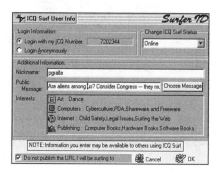

Figure 23.3

Are you curious about other chatters? Here's a sample of the kind of information they make public about themselves.

Surf, Get Gooey, and Make Friends

ICQ Surf is a great program. But there's another very popular program, much like it. It's called Gooey. Why it's called that, I have no clue. But who cares—it's a lot of fun to use and that's all that matters.

Gooey works a lot like ICQ Surf. To get Gooey (I love writing that—how many chances do you get to say something like that in print!) go to http://www.gooey.com. After you install it, you'll choose a username and you're ready to start chatting while you surf.

Gooey works a whole lot like ICQ Surf. Head to a Web page, and you'll see a list of everyone there, and you can start chatting using all the usual chat tools. Figure 23.4 shows the program in action.

As with ICQ Surf, you can see a list of the most popular places on the Web where people are being Gooey. Click the little bulls-eye on the screen and a page pops up listing all the places on the Web where people are running Gooey, with the most popular at the top.

Figure 23.4

Ready, set, chat...Here's how you'll chat on a Web page with Gooey.

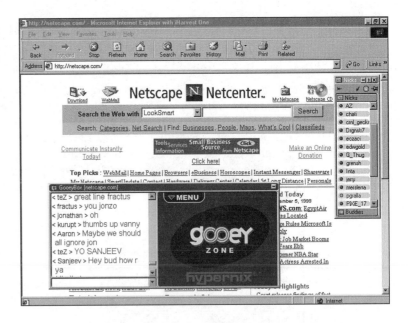

Chatting Can Get Raunchy

Be aware that when you use a chat-and-surf program like Gooey or ICQ Surf, the chats can sometimes get off-color and use language you might not think is suitable. That's the nature of the beast. The best thing to do is leave a Web page when chat on it becomes inappropriate for you.

Some Extra Gooey Features

Gooey works like ICQ Surf and other chat programs. But there are also a few neat extras it offers. Here are the coolest:

➤ **You can use it like an instant messenger program** With it, you'll be able to create buddy lists. Then, whenever one of your buddies launches Gooey, you'll be notified and you can exchange messages. You don't have to be on the same Web page to do it.

➤ **You can get multimedia news and entertainment feeds** To the right of Gooey's chat area is a box called the Gooey Zone. (Don't worry, you can click there and your mouse won't get stuck.) You can watch news and entertainment feeds from inside it—video clips, news, and more. To watch them, click the little **Menu** button and then choose the feed you want. It'll appear inside the screen.

➤ **You can send files to other people** Do you have an MP3 music file or a video file you want to share with someone? It's easy to send it to him using Gooey. Right-click his name, choose **Send File**, and you'll be able to send one to him instantly.

As you can see, surf-and-chat programs like ICQ Surf and Gooey are undoubtedly cool. But there are other similar cool ways you can communicate while surfing the Web. Read on to see how you can become a Web graffiti artist.

You, Too, Can Become a Web Graffiti Artist

How many times have you visited a Web page, and found something that intrigued you, or enraged you, or that you thought was super cool—so much so that you wanted to write a note to the world about it? Something that anyone coming to the site could see, and could then comment on.

If you're like me, it happens all the time. The Web is such a personal medium, that sometimes you just want to shout at something you read, or give it a big thumbs-up. And you'd also like to see what other people think of what they're finding on the site. And you'd like to engage them in some kind of spirited discussion.

Thanks to the mysterious technology of the Internet, all this is possible. And it's being done every day. People all over the Internet are marking up Web pages with their comments, notes, suggestions, criticisms and yes, sometimes with just plain blathering.

And now you can join in the fun as well.

To do it, you'll need to use a piece of software that lets you see other people's comments, and that lets you make comments of your own. This software is different from the chat tools I covered earlier in the chapter. With those, you chat with others who are on the same Web site. You chat about anything you want, not necessarily about the content of the site you're visiting. And with those, you have to be on the page at the same time as other people to see the comments and make the comments—in other words, it's a real-time chat. You can't make a comment that permanently stays on the page so that anyone coming to visit sees it.

Mayday

Only People Who Use the Same Graffiti Program Can See the Graffiti

When you use a piece of software to make comments on a Web page, only other people who use that software can see your comments. If they don't use the software, they won't see the comments. And if they use a different kind of software for making comments, they won't be able to see it, either. And you, of course, can only see comments made by people who use the same software that you're using.

With graffiti-type software, when you visit a page, you leave a note about it—and you can leave the note right on the information you're commenting on. So if you're visiting a page that mentions the Congress, and would like the world to know in what low esteem you hold them, just post that note right on the site. And anyone else will be able to see it, and respond to you as well—including Senators, if they're so inclined!

Okay, You've Sold Me—How Do I Do It?

To do all this cool stuff, you'll need to get a piece of software. The best one is called ThirdVoice, and you can get it at http://www.thirdvoice.com. Start using it, and the Web will never seem the same again—you'll feel free to comment on anything and everything. To see an example of ThirdVoice in action, look at Figure 23.5.

Figure 23.5

Anyone and anything can be commented on— including the President— when you use ThirdVoice.

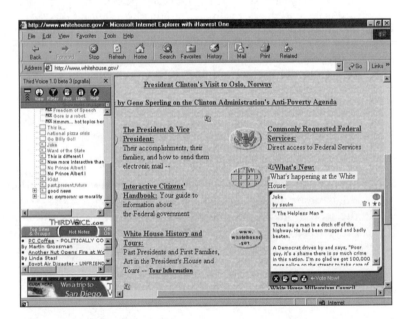

When you run ThirdVoice and visit a Web page, the page itself at first looks no different from any other Web page—although your browser looks different, because ThirdVoice runs down the left side of it, as you can see in Figure 23.5. To see the notes posted on a page, click the small button next to **Show notes on page** at the top of the ThirdVoice window. When you do that, two things happen—a series of notes appear in the ThirdVoice window, and on the page itself, you'll see small red arrows inside small yellow boxes. Wherever you see one of those arrows, there are notes.

To view a note on the page, click the arrow, and the note will appear. If there is more than one note, a box will pop up, with a list of all the notes attached to that place on the page. To read an individual note, highlight it and click it. Figures 23.6 and 23.7 show this in action.

You also can navigate through the notes by highlighting them in the ThirdVoice window on the left side of the screen.

If you're like me, you don't want to just *read* things—you want your voice heard as well. You want to write a note. It's easy to do. Highlight the text on the page you want to comment on, and then click the **Post** button in ThirdVoice. You'll then be able to post a note, as you can see in Figure 23.8.

If you'd like, you can instead comment on a note that someone posted, instead of making a comment on the page itself. To do that, when you're reading a note, click the little icon of a memo pad on the bottom of the note. That'll let you create a response.

Cool Tips

ThirdVoice Looks Slightly Different When You Use Netscape Navigator

In this chapter, I show you how to use ThirdVoice with Microsoft Internet Explorer. There are some small variations with how the program works when you instead use Netscape Navigator, so if you use that program instead of Internet Explorer, it won't quite look and work the way you see pictured here. But in almost all ways, it's the same.

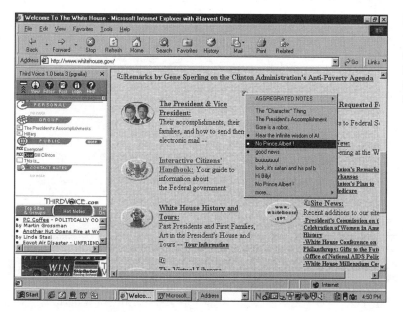

Figure 23.6

When there's more than one note at a location on the page, a pop-up list appears. Highlight the note on the list...

Figure 23.7

...and click it and you'll be able to read it.

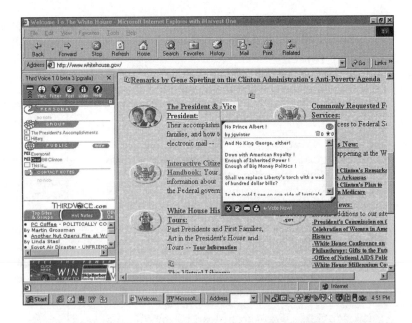

Figure 23.8

Make your voice heard! Here's how to post a comment on a Web site using ThirdVoice.

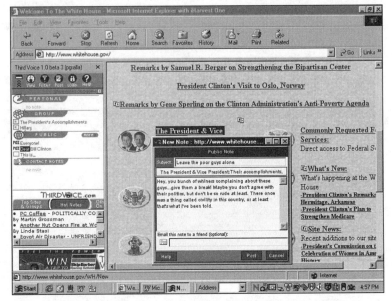

That's the basics of the program. But there's a whole lot more to this program than I can possibly cover here. Here are just a few of the highlights of the other things it can do:

➤ **You can create and read private notes, notes just addressed to a group, or just notes to yourself** So if you'd like, you can get together with a group of friends, and post notes that only each of you can see—no one else will be able to. You can even create notes to yourself that only you can see. And you can, of course, create notes that anyone under heaven can see as well.

➤ **You can "filter" notes so that you only see certain kinds of notes**
Want to see only your own personal notes? No problem. Only want to see notes you haven't yet read? Again, no problem. You can even filter out spam/junk notes that are things like solicitations for business, or that aren't about the topic of the page.

➤ **You can "vote" on notes that you read, saying whether the notes are good ones or bad ones** Here's your chance to turn a thumbs-up or thumbs-down on what other people say. Vote on whether the note is appropriate or not. Everyone sees the ratings, so it's a way to help other people decide whether to read certain notes.

➤ **You can email any note you read** See a note that you'd like someone else to read? Send it to them. Click the little icon of an envelope on the bottom of the page, fill in an email address, and off it goes.

There's even more to this unique program as well. So head to `http://www.thirdvoice.com` and give it a try.

The Least You Need to Know

➤ Surf-and-chat software lets you chat with others while you browse the Web. The two most popular programs are ICQ Surf at www.icq.com and Gooey at www.gooey.com.

➤ To use ICQ Surf, you'll have to first install the popular instant messenger program ICQ.

➤ ICQ Surf users can only chat with other users of ICQ Surf, and Gooey users can only chat with other users of Gooey.

➤ Several programs let you mark up Web pages by leaving notes about those pages for others to read. The most popular one is ThirdVoice at www.thirdvoice.com.

Speak Like a Geek: The Complete Archives

add-in card A card you install in your computer that gives it extra capabilities. Some devices, such as Netcams, can use an add-in card to connect to your computer.

AOL Instant Messenger (AIM) A popular instant messenger program that enables anyone on the Internet to chat with America Online users, and with other users of AOL Instant Messenger.

ASCII characters Plain-text characters that you usually get by pressing keys on your keyboard.

attachment A file added to an email message. It can be a picture, a video, or any other kind of file.

avatar A picture that represents you in picture-oriented chat rooms.

broadband connection A very fast Internet connection, such as via a cable modem, dual-channel ISDN-CF, or DSL. Informally known as a *big pipe*.

buddy list In instant messaging software, a list of friends you create so that you are alerted whenever one of your "buddies" comes online.

BuddyPhone A popular piece of software used for making PC-to-PC telephone calls.

cable modem A device used to connect a computer to the Internet at very high speeds over cable TV lines. The device isn't a true modem, though, and uses a network card to connect to the cable line.

chat A way that two or more people can communicate in real-time, by typing messages on their keyboards. *Voice chat* enables users to speak to each other via a microphone.

chat room   A location in cyberspace where people go to chat.

color depth   The total number of colors that a scanner can recognize and put into a computer. The greater the color depth, the better the scanner.

CU-SeeMe   A popular piece of videoconferencing software, made by White Pine Software.

digital camera   A camera that stores its images electronically in digital format. The images can be easily transferred to a computer.

digital video camera (DV camera)   A video camera that uses a hard disk rather than videotape to record video images.

driver   A piece of software required to make a piece of hardware work with an operating system.

DSL (Digital Subscriber Line)   A way of providing very high-speed access to the Internet using existing telephone lines.

email broadcast   An email message sent to many people simultaneously. Email broadcasts are often used as a way to send newsletters.

email reader   A piece of software used to send and receive email.

emoticons   See *smileys*.

Eudora   A popular email program.

frame rate   The number of frames per second of motion displayed by a video camera or Netcam.

full duplex   Allowing two-way communication. When people talk to each other using Internet telephone software and they are talking in full-duplex mode, both can talk at the same time.

Gooey   A popular program for allowing people to chat with others while they surf the Web.

H.323   A videoconferencing standard designed to allow people using different videoconferencing software to communicate with one another.

half duplex   Allowing one-way communication. When people talk to each other using Internet telephone software and they are talking in half-duplex mode, only one can talk at a time.

HTML (Hypertext Markup Language)   The computer language that forms the basis of the World Wide Web. Web browsers interpret HTML commands and display Web pages based on the HTML commands.

HTML editor   A piece of software that allows you to create Web pages using HTML.

ICQ (pronounced "I Seek You")   The most popular instant messenger software.

ICQ Surf   An add-in program for ICQ that allows people to chat with others while they surf the Web.

ils (Internet Locator Service) server   A server that allows you to find other people to videoconference with.

IM   Slang for instant message.

instant message   A chat-like message sent to another individual in a private, one-on-one conversation.

instant messaging software   Software that allows people to know when their friends are online, and lets them send person-to-person messages.

Internet service provider (ISP)   A company that provides dial-in or other kind of access to the Internet for a monthly fee.

Internet telephony   Using the Internet as a telephone. In Internet telephony, you can "call" another person sitting at a computer, or you can make a call to a real-life telephone.

IP address   An Internet address that is a series of four numbers separated by dots, like this—155.40.112.23. Every time you go onto the Internet, you use an IP address; without it you can't do things such as surf the Web.

IP telephony   See *Internet telephony*.

IRC (Internet Relay Chat)   A standard that allows people to chat with each other over the Internet. You'll need special IRC software to chat via IRC.

JamCam   A popular, inexpensive digital camera for kids.

listserv   A kind of software that manages sending and receiving email broadcasts and discussions. The term is often used generically to describe an email broadcast.

majordomo   A kind of software that manages sending and receiving email broadcasts and discussions.

MediaRing   A piece of software used to make telephone calls from a PC and PC-to-PC calls over the Internet.

megapixel camera   A digital camera capable of capturing and displaying an image with one million pixels in it.

meta tag An HTML tag put into a Web page that provides information about the page, such as describing the content of the page by using keywords. Meta tags are used by search engines to make it easier for people to find Web pages with content they're interested in.

Microsoft Outlook A popular email program.

MSN Messenger A popular instant messenger program made by Microsoft.

Net2Phone A popular piece of software used to make telephone calls from a PC, and PC-to-PC calls over the Internet.

Netcam A video camera that attaches to a computer, and is often used for Internet videoconferencing or videochat.

NetMeeting A popular piece of free videoconferencing software made by Microsoft.

nut driver A special kind of screwdriver used to open up a computer's case.

optical character recognition (OCR) The conversion of a page of text into a text document on your computer. OCR works in concert with scanners.

parallel port A port on the computer where you plug your printer. You also can plug certain digital cameras, scanners, and other devices into it.

pixel A single dot on a computer monitor; it's the basic measurement of screen resolution.

POP3 A communications protocol used by email servers to deliver email.

PowWow A popular instant messenger program that also lets you send and receive instant messages with users of AOL Instant Messenger and MSN Messenger.

printer port See *parallel port*.

RealPlayer A popular piece of software that plays video and audio files.

scanner A device that converts pictures into a digital format and transfers it to a computer so that the computer can use it.

signature Personalized text that identifies you added to the bottom of an email message.

smileys Small faces and pictures that are drawn with keyboard characters, and that are often used to express emotions in email, via instant messages, and in chat rooms. Also called *emoticons*.

SMTP (Simple Mail Transfer Protocol) A communications protocol used to send email.

sound card   An add-in card that allows your computer to play music, sounds, and to send and receive voice messages. Most computers come equipped with one.

spam   Junk email sent to people who haven't requested it. Most spam are commercial offers, and also can be fraudulent.

stationery   Colors, fonts, and pictures added to an email message to give it a personalized look.

ThirdVoice   A piece of software that allows you to leave and read messages on Web pages.

Universal Serial Bus (USB)   A technology that allows many devices to connect to a computer, such as Netcams, scanners, and digital cameras. The devices can be attached to one another in daisy-chain fashion, allowing many to be connected at once.

URL (Uniform Resource Locator)   The precise location of any spot on the Internet, such as www.mcp.com.

video capture board   An add-in board that lets your computer capture images from a video camera. It can be used in concert with a video camera to allow a video camera to be used as a Netcam.

video mail   Email that includes a video file.

videochat   A one-on-one conversation between two people in which they can talk to one another and see each other using video cameras over the Internet.

videoconference   A conference among several people in which they can talk to one another and see each other using video cameras over the Internet.

videoconference directory   A publicly available list of people on an Internet server that lists people who are available for a videoconference.

videophone call   See *videochat*.

voice chat   A way for people to talk to each other, using their voices, over the Internet.

Web page template   A preformatted design for a Web page that includes colors, fonts, layout, and other elements. Templates make it easy to create Web pages—you only have to put in your own words, pictures, and content.

Webcam   A video camera that sends live still or video images to a Web site.

whiteboard   In videoconferencing, an application that allows several people to work on the same screen simultaneously.

Windows Media Player   A popular piece of software from Microsoft that plays audio and video files.

Yahoo! Instant Messenger   A popular instant messenger program, available for users of the Yahoo! Internet site.

Best Sites for Information About Cool Ways to Communicate Online

Want to get free email and faxing, find out where to get free ASCII art, go to sites that let you set up your own free email broadcast, build your own Web pages, and chat with others? You've come to the right place. Here are the coolest places to go online for communicating and for information about communicating.

ASCII Art and Emoticons

You can dress up your email, chats, instant messaging, and signatures with ASCII art and emoticons. Here's where to get the best.

Joan Stark's ASCII Art Gallery

`http://www.ascii-art.com`

A great site with a big collection of ASCII art created by one person. The art is clever, elegant, and above all, useful. All the art is copyrighted on this site, so you're using it at the discretion of the site owner. She asks that you leave the initials on the art, that you don't accept money for using the art, and a few other requests as well. The site will explain the details.

The Signature Museum

`http://huizen.dds.nl/~mwpieter/sigs/`

Big collection of ASCII art of all types, suitable for using in your signature. From animals to humor to sports and more, you'll find all kinds of art. In addition to art, there are quotes you can use in your signatures as well.

Christopher Johnson's ASCII Art Collection

`http://chris.com/ascii/`

Huge collection of ASCII art. A lot of it is too large to put into a signature file, but if you hunt around, you'll find something.

Sig Software

http://www.sigsoftware.com

Site of Sig Software, which makes the Email Effects program that lets you draw using ASCII characters. You also can import simple drawings into it, and it will automatically convert the drawing into ASCII art.

Bronwen & Claire's Really Huge Emoticon Collection!

http://www.angelfire.com/hi/hahakiam/emoticon.html

As the title says, it's a huge collection of emoticons that you can use in your email, chats, and instant messaging.

Online Greeting Cards

You say you're still sending out *paper* greeting cards? How uncool. Check out these sites for sending out free electronic greeting cards over the Internet—and they're all free.

American Greetings

http://www.americangreetings.com

One of the big real-world greeting card companies comes to the Internet. In addition to free email greeting cards, there are those you can pay for as well. (Although why you would want to do that, I don't know.)

Blue Mountain Arts

http://www.bluemountain.com

Here it is—the greeting card motherlode. You'll find more cards here than you can count, complete with pictures, music, sound, and animations. There's a card for every occasion, purpose, and holiday that you can possibly imagine—and in multiple languages.

E-cards

http://www.e-cards.com

Here's a greeting card site with a twist—many of the cards offer environmental themes, and when you send cards, the company donates money to environmental groups, such as The Nature Conservancy.

Hallmark

http://www.hallmark.com

The greeting card giant whose name is synonymous with greeting cards comes to the Web. Big site, many multimedia cards. Free. Need I say more?

USA Greetings

http://www.usagreetings.com

This site features many cards, most of which feature photographs. There's no multimedia here, but you'll be able to send greetings in several languages.

Free Email

Let a thousand email boxes bloom! The Web is full of places that offer free email. Check these out and you won't go wrong.

Bigfoot

http://www.bigfoot.com

Whether you have big feet, small feet, or something in between, you can still get free email here. There are some nice, clever extra services here. You can, for example, have all your email sent to you from here automatically forwarded to any other email address of yours—and you can even have the mail forwarded to more than one account.

Excite Email

http://www.excite.com and click **Free Voicemail/Email**

Good mail service, and it offers free voice mail as well. Especially if you're a fan of Excite, check this one out.

Hotmail

http://www.hotmail.com

Now owned by Microsoft, this is probably the largest free email service you'll find. It's simple to use, offers good email management, and is all-around a top pick. One of the nice features here is that you also can check your regular POP3 email accounts from this site as well, so you can check all your email in one place.

MailCity

http://www.mailcity.com

Free email, along with 4MB of storage space for storing your messages. It's simple to use, and it's connected to the various services offered by the www.lycos.com Web portal.

Yahoo! Mail

http://www.yahoo.com and click **Yahoo! mail**

This one's my favorite free email service, and the one I use more than all the others. In addition to all the usual features you'd expect, it has one other very big benefit— you can configure it like your normal POP3 email, so you can check mail from it using your normal email program. And you also can check it the normal way, from the Web. There's a lot more here as well, such as the ability to check your other email accounts from this one spot, and the ability to send greeting cards.

ZDNet Mail

http://www.zdnetonebox.com and go to the mail area

The email on this well-known technology site is the same as that offered by OneBox (covered later in this appendix), and includes all the extras that OneBox provides, including voice mail and more.

Free Faxing Services

Who needs a fax machine? You won't, because you have the Internet. Check out the following free-fax sites. Most let you receive faxes for free, but you'll usually have to pay if you want to send them—except the Fax4Free site, which lets you send faxes for free, but not receive them. Go figure.

eFax

http://www.efax.com

I have accounts with at least five free fax services, but this is the one I use all the time. To view the faxes you're sent via email, you use a small program called a microviewer to see them. That's why I like this site—it has a great microviewer, and the fax attachments tend to be small.

FaxWave

http://www.faxwave.com

Here's another free faxing site. Just sign up and start receiving your faxes. It's that simple. As with eFax, you can't send faxes for free from this site. To do that, you'll have to pay extra.

Fax4Free

http://www.fax4free.com

You don't receive faxes from this site. Instead, you can send faxes from it for free. Unlike the other faxing sites, you don't have to register to get an account here. Just visit the site, and compose a fax. You can fax a document that's already on your computer, such as a Word or Excel document. Or you can instead use a form that uses word processor–like features and compose faxes to send.

Free All-in-One and Voice Mail Sites

Free voice mail, free email, faxing...many sites offer several of these, or all of them in combination. Here's where to go when that's what you want.

GetMessage

http://www.getmessage.com

This site combines email, faxing, and voice mail in one site. It's not as good as OneBox, which I cover later on, but it's free, and so worth checking out.

jfax

http://www.jfax.com

This started off as one of the first free faxing services, and has since added voice mail as well. I've been using this one for a long time, and I can vouch for it—it's a good, solid service.

MyTalk

http://www.mytalk.com

This one offers free email and voice email with a twist. You can call a phone number and have your email read to you, and can then record a message to respond to the email. And it also lets you place a free real-life telephone call—that's right, a free one—to anywhere in the U.S. for two minutes. The catch is that you have to listen to three ads first, and you can only talk for two minutes. Still, free is free.

OneBox

http://www.onebox.com

Here's a superb, all-in-one service. From one place, you'll be able to get free email, free voice mail, and free receiving of faxes. It's simple, easy, and free...what more is there to say?

ShoutMail

http://www.shoutmail.com

This site offers many different kinds of services, some of them a bit hard to believe or even understand. So let's start straight. It gives you free email. But it does far more as well. You'll be able to send voice emails with the service—and without using your computer. Just call a toll-free phone number, address your message using the telephone keypad, and record your message, and it'll get sent as voice email. You also can call a toll-free phone number and have your emails read to you over the telephone. And there's more, still—for example, it will notify you when other users of the popular ICQ chat program are online.

TeleBot

http://www.telebot.com

Like OneBox, this site offers free email, free receiving of faxes, and free voice mail. There are some limits, though—for example, voice mail is limited to 20 seconds per call. But it also has a service that will alert your pager when you receive a voice mail or fax message.

RocketTalk

http://www.rockettalk.com

With this one, you'll be able to send voice mail for free over the Internet. If you send to another RocketTalk user, he'll hear it right away. If not, a small utility is sent, and he can use that to hear your voice.

Best Sites for Getting Free Web Pages

If you're looking to get free Web pages, you're in luck—there are many sites on the Internet that offer them. Here are the best.

GeoCities

http://www.geocities.com

Here's the big magilla of free Web page sites, part of the Yahoo! network. It's huge, filled with many "neighborhoods" of sites built by people like you. There are great page-building tools, ways to make money through an affiliates program, and ways to add gizmos and message boards. In short, I think it's the best place online for building Web pages.

AngelFire

http://www.angelfire.com

Here's another good page-building site with a big complement of services: good page-building tools, the ability to make money through an affiliates program, and more. I particularly like the way it highlights favorite pages so that you can see the best of what other people have built.

Tripod

http://www.tripod.com

Just like the other good page-building sites, you'll get page-building tools, an affiliates program, and good community here. There's another plus—you can sign up for your own domain, so that instead of a very long and confusing URL, people can type in a short one. So if your last name were Rumpelstilsken, and no one else owned that domain, you could buy it, and when people typed it, they'd visit your Web site here. Click **Your-Name.com** on the site for details.

Xoom

http://www.xoom.com

You'll find all kinds of services at this site beyond free Web page building—greeting cards, a fax service, auctions, and more. I find the site a bit garish and at times confusing, but it's quite popular, so it might be for you.

FortuneCity

http://www.fortunecity.com

This site isn't quite as feature-packed as the other best Web-building sites, but it's still worth a visit. One of the reasons I like it is that I think it's one of the cooler-looking page-building sites.

theglobe.com

http://www.theglobe.com

In addition to the usual features you'd expect on a free page-building site, this one has some nice extras. My favorite: the ability to create an email mailing list of your own.

Places to Chat

There are about fifteen zillion places to chat on the Web, so I won't even begin to pretend to list them all or even list all the best ones. But here are some good general places to start.

Yahoo!

http://www.yahoo.com

The Web's most popular site has one of the Web's most popular chat areas. Are you surprised? Of course not. Go here and get ready to yammer about anything you can imagine.

Excite

http://www.excite.com

This is another popular "portal" site with a great chat area. Talk about whatever you want. Others will want to join in.

Lycos

http://www.lycos.com

Yet one more big portal site—and yes, you guessed it, it has a great chat area. Talk, talk, and talk some more.

thepalace.com

http://www.thepalace.com

Here's a chat site with a twist—it's a 3D visual chat where you enter virtual rooms and chat with other people, and you'll see avatars as you chat.

TalkCity

http://www.talkcity.com

City is right—this place is at least as big as a city, if not bigger. You'll find a huge number of chats, covering everything you can ever imagine.

Free Mailing Lists and Broadcast Emails

Want a little bit of fame? Then you've come to the right place. These sites will all let you create your own email broadcasts so you can set up your own free email newsletter.

TopicA

http://www.topica.com

Here's my favorite email broadcast site. It's easy to set up your own list, and it's free—you just have to put up with a little bit of advertising. It's also a great site for finding email lists to subscribe to.

eGroups

http://www.egroups.com

Here's another place where you can set up a free mailing list. It's a bit more confusing that TopicA, but after all, it's free and who can beat the price?

ListBot

http://www.listbot.com

Yet one more site for creating free email broadcasts. It's a good site—it's extremely easy to set up your own list.

Liszt

http://www.liszt.com

You won't be able to set up your own email broadcast here. But you *will* be able to find a mailing list to subscribe to on just about any topic you can name or imagine.

Cool Communicating Software Downloads

The Internet is chock-full of great sites that let you download cool communicating software for free. In some instances you're supposed to pay after you try out the software and decide you like it, but in other cases, it's free to use forever. Here's the rundown on the coolest sites for cool communicating downloads.

ZDNet Downloads

http://www.zddownloads.com

Here's the best place on the Internet to get cool communicating downloads—in fact, to get downloads of any kind. How do I know? I'm the executive producer of the site, that's how! Anything you want, we've got.

Net2Phone

http://www.net2phone.com

Want the great Internet telephone Net2Phone? Then head to this site. The software is also on the CD in the back of this book, but you might want to check here for new versions.

BuddyPhone

http://www.buddyphone.com

BuddyPhone is a very good piece of Internet telephone software. Head here and you'll be able to download it.

MediaRing

http://www.mediaring.com

Yet one more piece of good Internet telephone software—head here to download it.

Mirabilis

http://www.mirabilis.com

This is the home of the most popular instant messenger in the universe—ICQ. Head here to download it for free and find out all kinds of cool things about it.

Gooey

http://www.gooey.com

Chat with others while you surf the Net. You'll be able to download Gooey here, software that lets you chat with other Gooey users when you're on any Web page.

ThirdVoice

http://www.thirdvoice.com

Here's the place to go to download the very cool ThirdVoice software that in essence turns you into a Web graffiti artist. Read and leave notes for others on any Web site with it.

SpyCam

http://www.netacc.net/~waterbry/SpyCam/SpyCam.htm

If you want to set up a Webcam, you need special software—and SpyCam is my favorite. The software is on the CD in the back of this book, but if you want the latest information about it, head to this site.

Webcam32

http://surveyorcorp.com/webcam32/

Webcam32 is another very nice piece of software for setting up your own Webcam. Here's where to go to get it.

Aureate Group Mail

http://www.group-mail.com

If you want to set up your own mailing list, you don't have to use a Web site—you can use a piece of software and do it from your own computer for free. The best software is Aureate Group Mail—and here's the Web site to get it.

mIRC

http://www.mirc.com/

If you want to chat using the Internet's IRC chat channel, you need special software. mIRC is the best—and here's where to get it.

PictureWorks

http://www.pictureworks.com

Site of the company that makes the excellent PictureWorks video program, as well as the free MediaCenter program for use with Netcams.

Microsoft

http://www.microsoft.com

Whatever you think of Microsoft, they do have a lot of freebies for cool ways to communicate, most notably NetMeeting. Head here to get them all.

What's on the CD

As I've shown you throughout this book, there's a lot of software that will help you communicate in cool ways on the Internet. To make it even easier for you to do that, I've put together this special, free CD for you. It has a great collection of software on it—chat and instant messenger tools, software for videoconferencing and creating Webcams, all kinds of cool email tools for doing things such as creating video mail, Web browsers, and all kinds of other amazing things as well.

All of the software you'll find here is free to try out and use. Some of it is free forever, and some of it is *shareware*, which means that if you continue to use it for a certain amount of time, you're expected to pay for it. To find out the details on which software is shareware, and which you never have to pay for, just check the software after installing. It'll have all the details you need.

So come on along. Put that CD in your computer and get started. Here's the rundown on what you'll find on the CD. (By the way, all the software on the disk is for PCs, not Macintoshes.)

How to Run the CD

To install the software from the CD, you first have to run the CD. To do that, you need a 486-based PC or better; be running Windows 95, Windows 98, or Windows NT; have at least 24MB of RAM; and have at least 10MB of free memory. (You'll need more, depending on what software you plan on installing.) If you have all that, you're ready to go. If you have **AutoPlay** turned on, just put in the CD and it automatically runs by itself. If you don't have it turned on, or if the CD doesn't run, here's how you can run the CD:

1. Insert the CD-ROM in your CD-ROM drive.
2. From the Windows desktop, double-click the **My Computer** icon.
3. Double-click the icon representing your CD-ROM drive.
4. Double-click the icon titled **START** or **START.EXE** to begin.

That's it. You're ready to start installing very cool software.

And what software can you install? I'm glad you asked that. In the next sections I tell you what you'll find.

Chat and Instant Messengers

Chat and instant messenger programs are extremely cool ways for you to communicate online. So here are three great ones for you.

AT&T I M Here Service

This excellent program, based on the popular PowWow instant messenger, lets you exchange instant messages with your buddies, see when they're online, and more. It's unique in that it also lets you send instant messages with users of other instant messenger services.

mIRC

An extremely popular way to chat over the Internet is to use something called IRC (Internet Relay Chat). To chat this way, you need a special piece of software. And this program, mIRC, is the best Internet chat software you'll find. It lets you easily find chat partners and chat areas, and do all kinds of amazing chat things. If you want to chat using IRC on the Internet, it's the way to go.

Yahoo! Instant Messenger

This instant messenger program is my favorite and the one I use the most. It connects you to all the other fans of Yahoo! and it does a great job of it. It also lets you chat using your voice, and tracks stock quotes and complete portfolios, lets you check the latest news, and even alerts you when you have Yahoo! mail.

Email Tools

There are all kinds of cool ways you can communicate via email: You can send video mail, have your computer read your email to you, create special stationery and signatures, and more. Here's software that will do it all for you.

CloudEight

If you want stationery for Outlook and Outlook Express, but don't want to have to create it yourself, this is the file for you. It's a collection of ready-to-use stationery. Just install it and use it like any other stationery, and you'll be dressing up your email in cool ways in no time at all.

Objective Voice Email

Are you still sending email the old-fashioned way—just using text? Then try out this program. It lets you send voice email instead. Just address a message, click a button, record your message, and send it on its way.

Paper Maker

I showed you in the book that adding stationery to your email is a great way to dress up you online communications. This program makes it a breeze for making stationery. It lets you add backgrounds and graphics, use fonts, and even include a music file that plays when someone gets your email. It's high on the coolness factor.

Quotes

Here's a great all-in-one program for managing signature files, and using different quotes at the end of all your email correspondence. You can have it put in a random quote, or the ones you want. And this program makes it easy to pick different signature files whenever you send email.

Talking Email

Here's a newfangled way to get email. Don't read email; instead, have your computer read it to you. When you get mail, an animated figure pops up and reads your email to you. It's simple, fun, and a time-saver.

Videomail

A picture is worth a thousand words, especially when you're sending email. This great program lets you record a video and then send it via email. You record the video with this program and can either send the email with your normal email program, or with Videomail itself. If you don't have a Netcam, then you'll be able to use the program to record and send voice email.

Video Tools

If you've got a Netcam or video camera attached to your PC, there are all kinds of neat things you can do with it. You can make a Webcam so that the whole world can see pictures taken by your camera. And you can do videochats and videoconferences as well. Here's software that'll do all that for you.

ICUII

This is a great program for videochat and videoconferencing. Set up your camera, run this program, and then it's easy to find others to see and talk to. ICUII links you to a server that acts as a meeting place where you can easily find chat partners. You also can connect directly to other people, or use ICQ as a way to find others online to videochat with.

KABcam

Here's another easy-to-use program that lets you make your own Webcam. You can determine at what intervals you want a picture sent to your Webcam, and it's easy to configure the program to work with your video camera or Netcam. KABcam even includes a basic Webcam page that you can use as a starting point.

SpyCam

If you want to quickly create a Webcam on a Web page, here's the simplest and quickest way to do it. Just install this program and go. It'll take pictures from your Netcam and upload them to your Web site at any interval you want. You also can create a customized caption and put all kinds of time and date stamps on it. I go into great detail in the book about how to use this program. For details, turn to Chapter 19, "Adding a Webcam to Your Web Site."

Webcam32

Here's another very good program for creating your very own Webcam. It also lets you send live video images, not just still images to your Webcam. It's well worth checking out.

Web Browsers and Internet Access

To go anywhere on the Internet, you need to have a Web browser. So I've included the two best here for you. And you'll need to get access to the Internet via an Internet service provider. I've put one on the disk as well.

Microsoft Internet Explorer

This Web browser does everything you want. Fast, simple to use, with top-notch features—you won't go wrong with this browser.

Netscape Communicator

Like Microsoft Internet Explorer, this browser lets you go anywhere you want on the Web. Some people like this better than Explorer, others favor Explorer, so you might want to install both.

Total Access by Earthlink

If you need a way to get onto the Internet, check out Total Access by Earthlink—an Internet service provider. It's a great way to get onto the Internet.

Other Cool Tools

There are all kinds of other cool tools you can use for communicating online. Check these out; they won't lead you wrong.

Paint Shop Pro

Pictures are among the coolest ways you can communicate online. You can use them on your Web page, send them via email to others, and more. Here's the best program for dressing up pictures. You can use it to touch up photographs and pictures, you can add special effects, and you also can create graphics from scratch. This one's a must-have for anyone who uses pictures in any way on the Internet.

WinZip

When you download software from the Internet, often it's compressed—shrunk in size—using a format called ZIP. To use those files, you first have to uncompress them. This program is the best unzipper you'll find. It makes it easy to unzip any file. You also can use it to compress files on your hard disk to save space, or compress files that you're sending to others via email so that the files get sent more quickly.

WS_FTP

When you create Web pages, you have to have some way to send the files that make up the pages from your computer to the Internet. Here's the best way to do it: Use WS_FTP. It makes transferring files a breeze. WS_FTP also is great for downloading files from the Internet as well.

On many Web sites there are all kinds of cool and neat things you can read and view—but to view them and read them, you'll need this special software. It's free, it's easy to use, and it's cool. What more do you need to know?

Index

C

Q-R

X-Z